SHAPING THE
IMMIGRATION DEBATE

Contending Civil Societies
on the US-Mexico Border

Cari Lee Skogberg Eastman

FIRST**FORUM**PRESS

A DIVISION OF LYNNE RIENNER PUBLISHERS, INC. • BOULDER & LONDON

Published in the United States of America in 2012 by
FirstForumPress
A division of Lynne Rienner Publishers, Inc.
1800 30th Street, Boulder, Colorado 80301
www.firstforumpress.com

and in the United Kingdom by
FirstForumPress
A division of Lynne Rienner Publishers, Inc.
3 Henrietta Street, Covent Garden, London WC2E 8LU

Library of Congress Cataloging-in-Publication Data
Eastman, Cari Lee Skogberg, 1974–
  Shaping the immigration debate : contending civil societies on the
US-Mexico border / Cari Lee Skogberg Eastman.
  Includes bibliographical references and index.
  ISBN 978-1-935049-46-3 (hc: alk. paper)
  1. United States—Emigration and immigration—Government policy.
2. Illegal aliens—Government policy—United States. 3. Border security—
Government policy—United States. 4. Civil society—Arizona.
5. Immigration advocates—Arizona. 6. Immigration opponents—Arizona.
7. Mexican-American Border Region—Emigration and immigration. I. Title.
  JV6483.E37 2012
  325.73—dc23   2011046196

British Cataloguing in Publication Data
A Cataloguing in Publication record for this book
is available from the British Library.

This book was produced from digital files prepared
using the FirstForumComposer.

Printed and bound in the United States of America

∞ The paper used in this publication meets the requirements
   of the American National Standard for Permanence of
   Paper for Printed Library Materials Z39.48-1992.

5 4 3 2 1

*For those who have lost their lives crossing borders,
and for those who have dedicated their lives
to making a difference on this complex issue*

Contents

Illustrations

Figure

Photos

Acknowledgments

This work is the result of great faith and great hope. I wish to acknowledge and thank the many people who believed in the merits of the research and provided the wisdom and encouragement that helped me see it through to completion.

Tremendous thanks to the leaders and members of Humane Borders, the Minuteman Civil Defense Corps, and No More Deaths who willingly shared their stories and included me in their activities. I am eternally grateful for their kindness, trust, honesty, and most of all, their convictions to change a policy that currently results in such chaos and desperation. The dedication shown by these individuals is remarkable, and their actions are shaping a critical chapter in U.S. history. Most importantly, their efforts are saving lives. I am in awe of the amazing work they do on a daily basis under often difficult conditions.

My gratitude also goes out to the representatives of the U.S. Border Patrol who were so kind to share statistics, pictures, and information about their work, and who allowed me to accompany them on ridealongs, hikes, and tours of the detention and processing facilities. Their openness and clarity was critical to my understanding of the border.

This project would have been incomplete without the experience and insights of the media professionals who offered critical perspectives on how the story of immigration is told through mass media channels. Many thanks to Daniel González, Brady McCombs, Ernesto Portillo, Jr., Michel Marizco, Margaret Regan and Darla Jaye for their willingness to share time and thoughts with me. The knowledge and perspectives of these media professionals proved invaluable.

Special thanks to Dr. Shu-Ling Chen Berggreen, a constant source of support, who offered essential, constructive feedback throughout my doctoral studies. Her compassion and dedication are an inspiration to me. Thanks also for the insight and wisdom offered by Dr. Andrew Calabrese, Dr. Lynn Schofield Clark, Dr. Robert Ferry and Dr. Albert Ramirez. I am grateful for their expertise and confidence in the merits of this research.

I am blessed with an amazing family and extended family that have encouraged me to use the gifts of scholarship and writing to make a positive difference in the world. I am particularly grateful for my parents, who have always cheered me on and reminded me to stay focused on what matters most throughout this journey. Their love and support are unbounded; I could not have done this without them.

The insightful comments and suggestions made by reviewers have strengthened this work tremendously. I am grateful for their contributions. I also benefitted from the dedication of phenomenal proofreaders whose input further helped tighten and clarify the text. Enormous thanks to my incredible father, whose sharp eyes scoured the contents of chapters at all hours of the day and night. Thanks also to Uncle Dave, Ed, Dena, Linda and countless others for their great proofing and wise insights. I am grateful to Rachel for help with typing transcriptions, and to Grace, Charlotte, Barbara, John, Jerry, Harold, Ron, Elaine and many other friends and neighbors too numerous to mention, who have challenged the way I think about the border and who offered invaluable support.

Finally, deepest thanks to my husband, Scott, who constantly reminded me that a greater purpose guides this work. I am grateful for his love and faith in me and in this project.

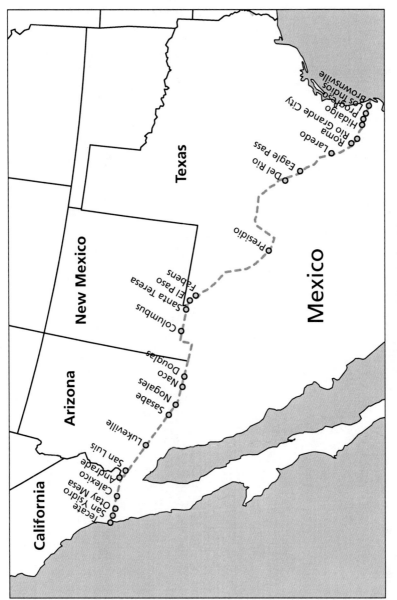

Southwestern U.S. Border Map
(showing major Ports of Entry)

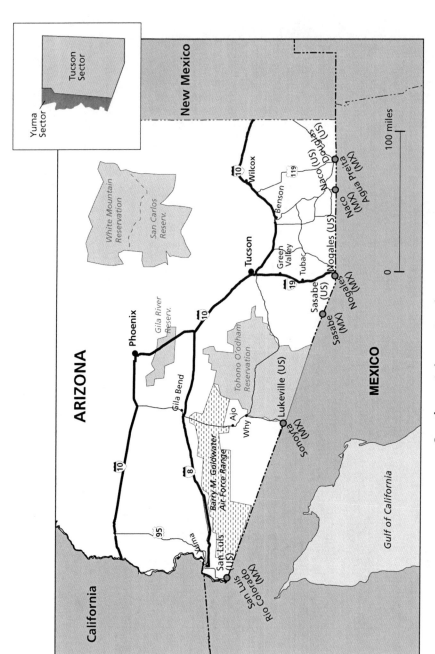

Southern Arizona Border Map
(with U.S. Border Patrol Yuma and Tucson Sectors inset)

1
Disorder on the Border

"Borders are scratched across the hearts of men, by strangers with a calm, judicial pen, and when the borders bleed we watch with dread the lines of ink along the map turn red."

Marya Mannes, American Author (1904-1990)

Memorial crosses along the San Diego/Tijuana border fence. January 2006 (Eastman photo)

What exactly is a border?

Is a border meant to block something out or keep something in? Does it separate or simply define parameters? Is it transparent or concrete? How does the creation of a border reflect upon its creators, or upon those separated by it? Questions like these and divergent views about the functionality of a border make it a difficult entity to describe. The meaning and importance of any border varies according to the role it plays in the lives of the people creating and defining it. Likewise, each border's particular history adds complexity to the way it is understood and the view of how it should function.

The borders of the United States are most commonly classified in terms of location, such as the northern U.S. border, southern U.S. border, or the U.S./Mexico border. However, such broad descriptive sweeps fail to recognize the complexity of the smaller regions comprising these borders that hold their own challenges, historical precedents, cross-border ties and interactions. It is difficult to fully understand such differences without living or spending time in the varied border regions. Residents of border regions will attest that the area separating San Diego from Tijuana is vastly different than the El Paso/Ciudad Juárez border and all those crossing points in-between. Each landscape, each pair of communities separated by a demarcation line confronts unique challenges related to physical and social environments, culture, and even language. In recent years, as borders have become a key component in the debate about U.S. immigration policy failures, those differences have too often been misunderstood.

I, too, misunderstood the complexity of the United States / Mexico border prior to spending time at various points along the line. During my doctoral studies, I thought I had cultivated a fairly broad understanding of the nature of our nation's boundaries. I had pored over a wide array of border-related articles and books and had taken a vested interest in border-related news stories in newspapers, magazines, and television reports. I read extensively about the problems and issues surrounding the increased numbers of migrants passing through Arizona's southern corridor and kept abreast of developments in border-related policies and social issues.

However, it was the experience of physically stepping across the invisible line that best helped me understand how varied the Southwest U.S. border really is. I crossed from El Paso, TX into Ciudad Juárez where I visited communities in the poorest border neighborhoods, and ventured from San Diego to Tijuana to hear the stories of migrants seeking help at a shelter there. These experiences enabled me to better understand the look and feel of critical crossing areas along the southwestern border. By incorporating these experiences with the knowledge I had gained from scholarly articles, photos and journalistic reports, I thought I knew what to expect in the Sonoran Desert as well.

However, when I began conducting research on media and civil society in the desert of southern Arizona, it quickly became apparent that my preconceived ideas about the geography, population, and appearance of the Arizona/Sonora border were far from accurate. In many parts of the rugged desert terrain, cow trails formed the only demarcation line separating the United States from Mexico. There was rarely any type of fence or other apparent barrier designating a physical boundary between two nations. More often than not, steep mountains or vast expanses of lonely shrubs and cacti hundreds of miles from the nearest town marked the separation. In many cases, even the rough, kidney-jolting secondary roads that connected farms or communities were located miles away from the border itself, leaving no vehicular access to any crossing point except the eight primary Tucson Sector stations already under the surveillance of the U.S. Border Patrol.

In other areas, the border crosses Tohono O'odham Reservation land – or more accurately, the reservation crosses the border and extends into northern Mexico. Tribal members flow freely back and forth across what the U.S. Government has defined as a dividing line, but what the tribe considers part of a united, sovereign territory. Migrants often cross here too, seeing the vast expanses and scattered roads as opportune remote entry points. Unfortunately, those same isolated expanses have also been sites of tremendous desperation and loss of life for individuals who lose their way or succumb to heat exhaustion or other desert dangers. In 2007 alone, sixty bodies of unauthorized border crossers were recovered on Tohono O'odham Nation lands, making illegal immigration one of the primary concerns of the tribe today (McCombs, 2007, August 19).

This was not the border I had read about in Texas, seen in San Diego, or pictured in my mind before coming to Arizona.

As my familiarity and knowledge of this place grew, what became most stunning to me was the sheer magnitude of critical issues arising from the seemingly stark Arizona desert. This is not just a location where a handful of migrants have lost their lives trying to enter the United States. This is the site of a major human tragedy unfolding on U.S. soil. Hundreds upon hundreds of individuals have died along the Arizona/Sonora border in the past decade – a staggering statistic considering there were only seven documented crossing-related deaths across the entire Arizona border in 1996 (Cornelius, 2001).

Typical migrant pick-up site. Bisbee, Arizona.
May 2007 (Eastman photo)

In addition to the tragedy of human deaths, environmental impact is also a primary concern along the U.S./Mexico border. Vehicles trying to elude or escape law enforcement often abandon major roads and attempt to maneuver through the cacti and brush, destroying primary habitat for desert wildlife and often damaging fences enclosing grazing lands. Those who are unsuccessful at steering their way through the spiny obstacle course leave wounded vehicles, or components of those vehicles, littering an otherwise untarnished landscape. When human smugglers from within the United States arrive in the desert to pick up their "loads," they require border crossers to abandon everything that might disclose their identities as unauthorized travelers who have just survived a trek through a hot, rugged desert. Thus, huge piles of backpacks, clothing, water bottles and other trash are left behind on migrant trails and in pick-up areas. The amount of waste is not incidental; tons of garbage are removed every year from federal, state and private lands, and tons remain strewn amid the spiny vegetation in washes and along dusty trails.

The economic impacts of the current phenomena are stunning on many levels, but perhaps most of all because illegal passage through the desert has brought great wealth to a powerful underground network of human smugglers. The costs of hiring a coyote (human smuggler) have more than tripled in recent years. The required payment is hardly a paltry sum; Mexicans pay between $500 - $5000 USD[1] per person, depending on the type and location of the attempted entry. Citizens of other countries pay much more. Fees for Chinese border-crossers, for example can range from $35,000 to $60,000 (Cornelius, 2006). The fees are often an entire life savings for an already poor family.

Finally, the demographics describing the border crossers themselves are stunning. The same desert trails that once led young, working men northward are now the routes for women, children, and elderly grandparents, all seeking work and/or a better life en "el norte"[2] (Alba, 2004; McCombs, 2007, August 3). Add to this mix a conglomeration of drug dealers and human traffickers who also transport their goods through the same corridors and it becomes frighteningly apparent what a strange mix of humanity – from those motivated by hopefulness and humility to those possessed with greed - can be found on the secluded routes leading north from the Mexican border.

Immigration is not a simple black and white issue, and its many complexities are revealed in the migration taking place along the southern border of the United States. For this reason, the southern border has become the line "scratched" into the sand which has motivated civil society groups to try to effect change in immigration policy, be it for benevolent concern or for reasons of national security. An honest and fair analysis of the motivations and implications of unauthorized border crossing and of the responses of active civil groups requires a dismissal of common stereotypes and a commitment to deeper exploration of the complex relationships and needs that inspire such movement.

As a scholar who intentionally acknowledges that any issue – political, economic, social, or otherwise – is driven by human decisions, I seek not only to uncover the details and consequences of the issue itself, but also to understand the motivations of the individuals who produced it. I feel it is critical to explore questions of "why" and "how," so as to better understand what it is that provokes human reactions to politically-charged issues such as immigration. Because I am convinced that exploration of any issue is incomplete without the stories of the individuals who shape it, my research is very deliberately poised around questions of human agency and human response to official policy.

I also wish to acknowledge my personal biases in this approach to the study of media and civil society along the Arizona/Sonora border. I have studied and traveled abroad extensively, spending time in 16 different countries, learning two languages other than English and earning my Master's degree in Spanish at a foreign university. Those rich experiences have given me a great appreciation of what it means to be a minority, an outsider, a foreigner and a guest in a country that is not my own. I am thankful for the way those experiences have shaped my perceptions of the world community. As a U.S. citizen in a foreign country, I have often been challenged to look critically at my country's relationship with other nations, particularly in terms of power and negotiation. I learned to see foreign policy from the perspectives of those directly affected by the decisions of my country's political leadership, and have wrestled with the ethical issues involved when actions taken by the United States have created animosity and distrust abroad. I have been forced to place myself in others' shoes when evaluating the effects of U.S. strategy, and I have come to value the insight gained through thought-provoking, often fiery discussions with those critical of my country's chosen role in world affairs. Engaging in thoughtful dialogue with people who see things differently has made me a more appreciative citizen, and has strengthened my conviction that public involvement and debate are critical to a healthy democracy.

Finally, prior to beginning my doctoral studies, I taught Spanish for seven years at middle school, high school and college levels. I led groups of students on study trips to four different Spanish-speaking countries. As a teacher and a mentor, I am very passionate about helping students develop critical thinking skills that enable them to view the world and its complex issues from multiple angles. The goal of my instruction has always been to help willing minds master not only a language, but also an appreciation of the histories, geographies, cultures, and people from whom that gift of language has come. It is my hope that by recognizing the value of diversity and cooperation within any society, we can all become more knowledgeable and productive citizens of an increasingly globalized world community.

Together, all of these life experiences have enriched my scholarship as well as my own development as a citizen and human being. I do wish to recognize that my experiences abroad and my teaching background shape the way I approach my research. I have visited impoverished villages in Mexico, Central and South America. I understand, at least to some degree, the poverty and desperation of many of our southern neighbors because I have seen and confronted it face to face. I have witnessed the despair of parents who cannot afford to send their children to school or provide nutritious meals for their families. Given adequate opportunities and resources, I cannot help but believe they would not only survive, but thrive.

At the same time, back on U.S. soil, I appreciate the challenges of a citizenry concerned about security – particularly in the wake of 9/11.[3] I was personally touched by the heartache caused by the domestic terrorist attacks, and was witness to the impassioned pleas of concerned citizens who feared that unsecured borders would invite subsequent acts of violence. I recognized frustration in the faces of ranchers living along the border who described livestock deaths caused by the consumption of plastic bags and other garbage discarded by border crossers. I documented stories of families unable to travel and celebrate holidays with relatives for fear of leaving their border properties unattended. I examined pools of blood dried into the dirt at a secluded desert site where a human smuggler had shot the hand off an escapee of his group. These, too, are valid concerns of human beings whose lives have all been affected by immigration policy.

Because I see the application of human rights and appreciation of divergent perspectives as critical to a healthy worldview, my study of this issue is driven by questions about the consequences of immigration for people on both sides of the border. I do not apologize for approaching my research from a perspective that places concern for the human at its center. As scholar Santa Ana explains, "Placing justice at the center of the research agenda creates socially engaged scholarship. In such an enterprise, at minimum, injustice can be addressed through a scientifically principled research agenda that leads to deeper understanding" (2002, p. 17). It is my hope that such an approach to immigration-related issues will encourage productive, reflective dialogue and cooperation among those best equipped to offer meaningful resolutions. We are, after all, neighbors in a global community. Learning to understand immigration from the point of view of the people most affected by it will enable us as a citizenry to appreciate the conditions and perspectives that inspire civil action along the border. I hope it will also inspire us to seek solutions that give priority to one another's well-being — no matter which side of the border we call home.

Notes

[1] United States dollars.

[2] "El norte" is the Spanish term for "the north" (the United States).

[3] 9/11 refers to the September 11, 2001 terrorist attacks on United States soil in which more than 2700 people were killed.

2
Researching Immigration in Arizona

"Remember, remember always, that all of us, you and I
especially, are descended from immigrants and revolutionists."

Franklin Delano Roosevelt

*In a speech before the Daughters of the
American Revolution (DAR) in 1939*

*Migrant "Amnesty Trail" – Sonoran Desert, Southern Arizona. November
2007 (Eastman photo)*

Enter the Sonoran Desert in Southwestern Arizona and you have entered
another world. This desert is like no other place on earth. It is an
environment of contrasts and extremes – a canvas of nature's stunning

beauty blended with equally dramatic harshness. Temperatures here can reach upwards of 120 degrees on a mid-summer day and plummet to near freezing during winter nights. The landscape is primarily arid and rugged, but monsoon season introduces violent thunderstorms that wash out roads and transform dusty creek beds into torrential rivers. Stately saguaro cacti – found only in the Sonoran Desert – are surrounded by an amazing array of brush, trees and cacti coated with protective spines to discourage predators – or humans – from approaching.

Even the animal life in the Sonoran Desert is extreme. At first glance the only movement seems to be that of jackrabbits and a plethora of colorful birds that nest in the saguaro and cholla cacti. Amid the placid scenery, however, venomous snakes, scorpions, spiders and Gila Monsters make their homes. A direct encounter with any one of these can be disabling, or even life-threatening in remote areas where medical attention is hours away.

It is both an unforgiving and enchanting land. Despite the prickly flora, venomous critters, extreme temperatures and scarcity of water, people have been drawn to this amazing place for centuries. Ranches covering thousands of acres dot the landscape that parallels the border separating Mexico from the United States. Tiny towns located on and near the Tohono O'odham Reservation interrupt the otherwise unbroken vistas. Organ Pipe Cactus National Monument and numerous state parks draw in avid hikers, photographers and outdoors enthusiasts. For those who are familiar with the terrain, this is a desert paradise. For those who arrive unaware of the dangers of the desert, the antithesis of such beauty is an unrelentingly harsh environment in which survival can become a nightmare.

Because the population of this area is so small and the conditions so harsh, the Arizona Sonoran Desert seems an unlikely location in which to encounter large numbers of people. However, enter this desert, and you have entered ground zero[1] – the most heavily trafficked illegal crossing area into the United States, and a primary meeting point for activists on all sides of the national immigration debate.

While all of Arizona has seen an increase in the number of migrants crossing its borders in the past decade, it is the U.S. Border Patrol's Tucson Sector – a 262 mile stretch of linear border that extends from the New Mexico/Arizona state line to the Yuma County, AZ line – that is considered the center of undocumented entry activity. The Tucson Sector leads the nation in every statistical category – including the number of crossers and number of migrant deaths.[2] Each day, an average of 1500 unauthorized border crossers from Mexico and other countries are apprehended by Border Patrol while trying to enter the

United States through the Tucson Sector.[3] It is unknown how many total people cross through this area daily *without* being apprehended, but one civil group estimates the figure at well over 2000 for this sector alone (Hoover, 2007). As the number of crossers has increased, so have the numbers of deaths. Between 2001 and 2007, the bodies of over 1500 unauthorized border crossers were recovered in Arizona; approximately 1100 of these were discovered in the Tucson Sector.[4] Roughly 650 more have been recovered in the Tucson Sector in the three fiscal years from 2008-2010 (McCombs, 2010, Oct. 5).

The activity in this area is not limited to migrants alone. Nearly 3000 Border Patrol agents are stationed in the Tucson Sector, patrolling 90,500 square miles beginning at the largely unmarked boundary between Arizona and Sonora, Mexico. Drivers of charter-size Wackenhut buses, under contract with the Department of Homeland Security, transport loads of apprehended migrants to nearby processing and detention facilities. Officials from the Bureau of Land Management, State Parks, and Game, Fish and Parks make regular trips through this desert corridor. In addition, on any given day, volunteers from dozens of active civil groups are spread out across the miles upon miles of private and public lands, trying their best to change what they see as a disastrous situation along Arizona's southern border. Some are there to protest the entry of undocumented persons into the United States. Others wish to ensure that no one – regardless of entry status – dies a gruesome death in the desert. All, regardless of their motivations, have come because they feel the current immigration system is broken and needs to be fixed.

Three such groups in particular have drawn massive awareness to the current Arizona/Sonora border debacle through savvy use of media and somewhat controversial on-the-ground activities that have captured the attention of media around the world. Humane Borders, No More Deaths, and the Minuteman Civil Defense Corps (MCDC) – though approaching the issue from very different ideological standpoints – have all played a crucial role in making the world aware of the current migration phenomenon playing out in southern Arizona. Humane Borders has vowed to take death out of the desert by providing life-saving water stations in remote areas of the Sonoran wilderness. The group also sponsors trash pick-ups, provides various public education programs, assists with searches for missing persons in the southern Arizona desert, and advocates for changes in immigration policy consistent with its mission of establishing a more humane borderland. No More Deaths volunteers reach out to border crossers in distress by offering food, water, and medical aid as they walk migrant trails, and by engaging in various advocacies for migrants who have been mistreated, abused or injured. In addition to their efforts to provide immediate assistance in the desert, members of this organization are also very active in the political arena, urging legislators to change the current state of immigration policy. The Minuteman Civil Defense Corps aims to discourage illegal crossings by sponsoring border watches, during which volunteers are stationed in watch areas and trained to detect unauthorized crossers who are then turned over to the Border Patrol. The group also engages heavily in lobbying, advocacy work, and political activity aimed at cracking down on illegal immigration and illegal status in the United States.

Each of these three groups has also made great efforts to educate the public about the nature of Arizona's southern periphery and the dangers arising from ineffective border management policies. Their activities and efforts to promote immigration reform have highlighted the failures of current U.S. policy and focused public attention on the need for alternative solutions to current border strategies and practice. Each of these groups has developed a different approach to and different relationship with mass media, but in the end all have found a voice on a national (and international) stage thanks to mass media coverage of their activities and of the situation along the border. The myriad of issues faced by border crossers, as well as those posing challenges to receiving communities, would not be so well recognized today were it not for the massive efforts of civil society groups who draw attention to the problems stemming from misguided policies and the various forms of media that give voice to their concerns.

Largely as a result of media coverage, public audiences have turned their attention toward a desolate, sparsely populated section of desert in southern Arizona that now serves as the venue for a fierce national immigration debate. As news reports have intensified and rhetoric has reached new heights, the discussion about immigration has captured the hearts and imaginations of citizens who have never even seen a desert or traveled to southern Arizona. Members of communities throughout the United States, even in states as far away as Washington or Maine, have developed strong opinions about what should be done in regard to the immigration issue. Their attitudes and feelings of involvement are remarkable for a number of reasons, not least of all because the question of "what to do about immigration" was, as recently as the 1990s, asked primarily and almost exclusively by federal agencies and residents who lived close to the border. The national public was not talking about borders or migration, and had little conception of the fact that growing numbers of individuals were crossing into the United States without legal status.

All of that changed by the year 2000. As official U.S. border strategies were drastically modified during the 1990s and huge numbers of border crossers began entering through remote stretches of desert rather than the typical urban crossing areas, someone was there to notice. In one case, an individual vacationing in Organ Pipe Cactus National Monument noticed that large numbers of migrants and drug smugglers were now frequent travelers on the quiet hiking trails he had once enjoyed. In another instance, a humanitarian became aware that the number of dehydration-related deaths in the desert was increasing by alarming levels year after year. A group of concerned residents of southern Arizona later took note that even after large drums of lifesaving water were placed in strategic desert locations, crossers were still perishing for lack of medical attention, food, and basic care. All were outraged, and as a result of their efforts to organize and make a difference, three of the most active civil groups on the Arizona border – the Minuteman Civil Defense Corps (MCDC), Humane Borders and No More Deaths – were born.

Yet it was not until media picked up on the efforts of these organizations that the events unfolding in the Arizona desert reached a wider public. Residents of Tucson, Nogales and other cities close to the border were aware of changes in crossing patterns, but few outside this region realized that a humanitarian and/or security crisis – depending on how the situation is viewed – was occurring along the Arizona/Sonora divide.

What made the difference? Local media had reported on immigration issues in the area for years, but border issues drew little attention outside of southern Arizona. What finally brought immigration-related concerns to the attention of an otherwise vaguely interested media? To a large degree, the activities that spurred public controversy stemmed from the frustration of civil society groups with what they deemed was irresponsible inaction on the part of the government. Leaders of these organizations determined that if anything were to change, citizens would need to take matters into their own hands. Suddenly, the issue of immigration and its consequences was framed in terms of ideas, statistics and moral arguments the public had never heard before. As memberships in the civil groups began to expand and volunteers arrived from across the United States to make their presence known in the desert, media outlets throughout the country took notice. The subject of immigration reform had found a national forum.

By the spring of 2010, the fervor surrounding immigration-related issues had reached a remarkable level. Reactions to the presence of unauthorized persons in the United States led to dramatic responses in various regions of the country. Most notable of these was Arizona's Senate Bill 1070, a controversial law granting the state greater power than ever before in enforcing immigration laws. Controversial aspects included the requirement of law enforcement officials, during a lawful stop, to determine immigration status of individuals they reasonably suspect to be illegal aliens. Critics charged that such aspects of the law would legalize racial profiling. Just one day before the law was to go into effect, a federal judge blocked many of its most controversial provisions (Preston, 2010, July 29). Approximately three months later, a three-judge panel of the Ninth U.S. Circuit Court of Appeals reinstated those provisions, although in a weaker form (Egelko, 2010). Protests of the bill were widespread across the United States, and numerous lawsuits challenging SB 1070 were brought forth by individuals as well as national governmental and non-governmental organizations (Foley, 2010; Preston, 2010, May 2). Additionally, travel and economic boy-cotts of Arizona were declared by a handful of officials in major U.S. cities, as well as by prominent musicians and entertainers (O'Dell, 2010; Rohter, 2010). However, the passage of SB 1070 was deemed a victory by supporters of tougher immigration enforcement, and many states have since proposed similar legislation (Romano, 2011; Seattle, 2010).

How were civil society organizations able to spark interest and action among the media and public alike? Different groups employed different strategies, but each very skillfully crafted a message about the border that resonated with the sympathies of wider audiences. From its inception, the intent of the Minutemen was to draw media attention to the issue of immigration and to embarrass the federal government into "doing the job it would not do" [enforcing the border] (Simcox, 2007). Humanitarian groups Humane Borders and No More Deaths instead focused on the message and mission of saving lives in the desert. However, leaders of both groups were keenly aware that to change the policies that were contributing to migrant deaths, they would need to deliver their stories to members of a wider public who could then pressure policy makers (Fife, 2007; Hoover, 2007).

Regardless of their original intent, since 2000 the actions of all three groups have provided headlines and lead stories for media across the nation – and even the world. Much of the general public's understanding about the border and the current immigration situation has stemmed from the actions, stories, and efforts of these civil society organizations to create "noise" on the border and thus inspire change.

It is the unique, sometimes delicate relationship between civil society and media in such a remote, desolate, and yet vibrant setting that motivates this research. The effect these civil groups have had on creating a national awareness about immigration is remarkable, and the continued effectiveness of such groups in influencing national sentiment with the help of media is nothing less than extraordinary. However, the role of media in "telling the story of the border" raises numerous questions about the types of stories being told and the degree to which the framing of the stories and agendas of these civil society organizations have shaped our national understanding of border-related issues. It also leads to questions about the nature of media consumption among the volunteers themselves, and the degree to which civil society effectively promotes specific agendas through media channels.

This book argues that three civil society organizations in particular along the Arizona/Sonora border have been successful in generating public debate about the status of the border and failed border policies.

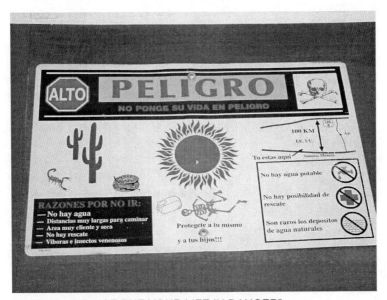

"DANGER – DO NOT PUT YOUR LIFE IN DANGER"

Warning sign placed along the Mexico side of the Sonora/Arizona border, explaining the dangers of crossing through the desert. May 2007 (Eastman photo)

Humane Borders, the Minuteman Civil Defense Corps and No More Deaths have done so not only through direct action and on-the-ground responses to what they see as failures of current immigration policy, but also and perhaps most importantly through strategic and creative framing of border and immigration issues to the mass media and thus the general population. As a result, these groups have directed the public's attention toward specific aspects of the immigration debate that they perceive as the most critical. In doing so, they have influenced the nature of popular discussion about immigration and have shaped public understanding of the border in general.

With questions about desert border crossings, the activities of civil society groups in the area, and the nature of the media messages about immigration swirling through my head, I packed my bags and headed for the dusty Arizona/Sonora divide. It was time to find out firsthand what things looked like from the line.

Description of Research

It is amidst the harsh terrain of the Sonora desert that the primary work of some of Arizona's most active citizens takes place each day. Humanitarian aid groups and border watch organizations gather in a wide setting of mesquite trees, cholla, and prickly pear to address problems created by current U.S. immigration policy and the consequences that have ensued.

The work of these activist groups in the desert does not go unnoticed. Stories of their desert presence have resonated with audiences both near and far from the southwestern United States. The issues of immigration, identity, security and human rights that such groups have helped to force into the public's consciousness, largely through media coverage of their efforts, have been closely followed in an international arena by leaders and citizens of countries dealing with similar immigration-related problems.

Welcome to the Arizona border. This is as much a site of ideological struggle as it is a place where physical struggles to define, maintain and secure the border have left citizens and non-citizens alike asking, "Now what?"

While history contains no shortage of examples of failed immigration policy on the southern United States border, there are certain characteristics that distinguish the atmosphere surrounding immigration-related politics in the first decade of the 21st century. First, increasing attention has been given to record numbers of migrant deaths along the southern Arizona border. As federal policies tightened security around traditional crossing points and would-be crossers were channeled into more remote, desolate areas, the numbers of dead and missing migrants increased dramatically and the media and public not only took note, but forced the issue into the spotlight. Second, economic conditions and policies have pushed workers out of Mexico and into the United States for jobs. This in itself is not a new phenomenon. However, in the past, such push-pull cycles were generally followed by federal efforts to toughen immigration policies, thus appeasing a restless public and creating a sense of control. Throughout the first decade of the new millennium, however, public dissatisfaction with federal handling of immigration-related issues grew so great that numerous civic groups formed to challenge federal policies and promote reform. Never before had such a strong civil presence fought to make its voice heard in regard to the immigration-related issues, and never before had new media technologies enabled the stories and ideals of those groups to be relayed so widely and easily to the general public.

The purpose of this study is to examine the ways in which Humane Borders, the Minuteman Civil Defense Corps and No More Deaths, among the most active civil society organizations along the Arizona/Sonora border, have effectively framed the issue of immigration and utilized savvy media strategies to generate wider public support for their goals and ideologies. The study examines the role and effectiveness of mass media in both telling the stories of an outraged civil society and communicating the calls for reform made by these organizations to a wider public. It also examines specific strategies and framing techniques used by these civil society organizations to define their causes as they seek to promote their ideas and ideologies among a larger audience.

Inspiration for the Research

It is the involvement of these nongovernmental civil society organizations and the stories they relay to the American public about immigration in southern Arizona that provide the foundation and inspiration for this study. Although I have read countless newspaper articles over the years that list statistics, describe governmental programs, and cite official responses to the immigration issue, it was stories depicting the personal involvement of these civil society organizations that first captured my attention and challenged me to think differently about the border. Whether protesting the porosity of the border by organizing groups that detect and report migrant crossers in the desert (Minuteman Civil Defense Corps), or challenging "funnel effect" policies by placing life-saving water stations in the desert (Humane Borders), volunteers for these varied groups spend enormous amounts of time, resources, and energy trying to deliver the message that the status quo is unacceptable; something has to change.

The sheer determination and dedication of volunteers, who through on-the-ground action make it their business to do the work they feel the government *will not* do, reflects a remarkable sense of resolve and civic empowerment. At the same time, it elicits an interesting set of questions about both the willingness and power of ordinary citizens to challenge the role of federal authority and, in the process, shape public opinion. What is it that motivates these individuals to dedicate so much time and energy to border-related concerns? Where did activists from distant states first read or hear about the border? How is it that some of the most passionate responses to the immigration issue come from organizations with such differing positions and viewpoints? How have lobbying efforts by ordinary citizens been effective in shaping the national immigration debate?

Considering the large role media play in drawing attention to the work of these three civil society organizations active along the Arizona/Sonora border, the function of media in this case warrants further study. Volunteers for all three groups come not just from Arizona, but from across the United States. This raises interesting questions about media flows and messages about the border and their effect on audiences outside the local area in which the activity of these organizations is carried out. What types of media messages about these organizations are being constructed, how are those messages framed, and through what channels are they most effectively being delivered? How are media used by these specific organizations to gain information or communicate ideas? Finally, how accurately do these civil society organizations feel their efforts and messages are portrayed to the wider public?

These and hundreds of other questions form the basis of my research and investigations about the Arizona/Sonora border and the daily struggles that take place there. More importantly, they continue to motivate my ongoing pursuit of stories, experiences and documents that will contribute to a deeper understanding of this very complex issue, and hopefully help members of the general public develop thoughtful, meaningful responses to the ongoing debate.

Unique Nature of the Study

From its inception, this study has focused on capturing the essence of an incredible, controversial, often misunderstood story of immigration – not from the lips of those who actually cross the border, but from the first human faces they may encounter upon entering the Arizona desert. Many accounts have been written from the perspectives of the migrants themselves, detailing the factors that necessitate their journeys, the difficulties of their journeys, and the problematic positions they find themselves in once here as people living underground, without legal protection or general social acceptance in the receiving country they risked their lives to reach (Annerino, 2009; Chávez, 1998; Martínez, 2001; Nevins, 2008; Orner, 2008; Ramos, 2005; Regan, 2010). These accounts of the migrants are critical; they offer a view into the histories and lives of the individuals whose place in U.S. society has been so vehemently debated. Such stories also create opportunities to examine the policies and practices that have led to their arrival. This study in no way attempts to underestimate the power and significance of those primary voices; they are essential to understanding the phenomenon in its current form.

However, few efforts have been made to record and analyze the impassioned responses of U.S. citizens who feel it is their duty – their calling – to create a new set of circumstances along the border that will change the course of what seems a discouraging, ongoing battle. The views, ideologies and actions of these members of civil society are a critical subsequent chapter in the saga of immigration policy, a contextual point of analysis from which diverse reactions to immigration can be considered. The volunteers who dedicate their time and efforts in the desert are acting upon a notion of obligation to respond to an issue that touches the lives of U.S. citizens both near and far from the border. Some feel that the primary obligation of the state is to provide defense and security for its people. Others feel the state is first and foremost obligated to reform the policies and practices that have cut off legal means for desperate workers to enter this country in a safe and respectable way. Both feel that federal authorities have failed to stop a disastrous course of action and they, as citizens of a democratic republic, have an obligation to *do* something to facilitate change. Both have garnered tremendous support of their work from fellow citizens through media accounts – solicited and unsolicited.

Viewing such issues through the lens of civil society organizations and the media who cover them also compels the wider public to confront its own immigration-related biases and fears. The civil society groups actively protesting the status quo of immigration policy, made up of volunteers from across the United States, are in many ways a microcosm of the U.S. population and its beliefs. The actions of such groups reflect the varied convictions of a larger receiving community and its struggle to determine an appropriate response to the arrival of officially unauthorized guests. Learning about the motivations and ideologies of the volunteers along the line enables those far from the border to identify with the patriotism, humanitarianism, loyalty and empathy that guide the organizations' efforts, and to question the sources from which those feelings come. The impassioned voices of volunteers active in border regions give rise to debate, discussion, and contemplation, thereby providing interested persons living far from the border an opportunity for involvement that might otherwise be impossible.

In summary, this is a study of the communication of a civil call to action. It is an attempt to understand the ways in which a determined civil society has, largely through media channels, shaped the nature of public response to the immigration question. Additionally, it is a contribution to a much larger inquiry into the nature of one nation's self-identification and the ways in which that identity has shaped the existing relationship with its southern neighbor.

Methodology

Participant observation, interview methods and textual analysis guide this qualitative study of media and civil society along the Arizona/Sonora border. My research was driven by the desire to become immersed in the issues at hand through study, participation, conversation and reflection. This approach to the research offered a constant reminder that the best way to develop a deeper understanding of the issues at hand was to witness the stories and voices of those most closely involved and affected by it. [5]

Participant Observation

The first aspect of my research involved participant observation within the three groups being studied: Humane Borders, No More Deaths, and the Minuteman Civil Defense Corps (MCDC). I felt that such direct participation was a critical element in establishing rapport and trust with the various groups. Participating in the organizations' activities also offered me the opportunity to gain firsthand knowledge of the structure and activities of each. Participant observation required different types of involvement with each of the three groups, depending upon the nature of their respective activities. Humane Borders and No More Deaths both hold weekly meetings, during which their accomplishments, goals and concerns are discussed. Therefore, I attended meetings of these two groups in Tucson (Humane Borders and No More Deaths) and Phoenix (No More Deaths) as regularly as possible between the months of October, 2007 and January 2008. I also accompanied the groups on various trips into the desert to assist with the work for which they are so well known. With Humane Borders, that included participating in water runs to refill emergency water stations in the desert, helping with a desert clean-up trip to clear a particular corridor of trash left behind by migrants, and joining other travelers on a day-long journey to Altar, Sonora in Mexico to view the staging area for unauthorized migrants who enter through the Tucson Sector.[6]

In addition to attending weekly meetings held by No More Deaths organizers, I also participated in a training session for volunteers wishing to assist with desert activities. One segment of that training focused on the history and mission of the movement; another segment included presentations on basic first aid and medical care for migrants. After being trained, I spent a day near Arivaca, Arizona with local leaders and a group of volunteers from Hamilton College in New York, walking migrant trails and searching for individuals who might be injured or in need of lifesaving food and water.

Although local Minuteman Civil Defense Corps (MCDC) chapters around the country hold regular meetings to discuss the goings-on of the group, the primary activities for which this organization has gained media recognition are the border watches, or "musters" held along the northern and southern U.S. borders.[7] These musters usually last for a weekend, although once or twice a year they last for an entire month. I was able to participate in two different musters in southern Arizona, spending a total of six days as a participant observer "on the line" with Minutemen volunteers in October and November of 2007. During these six days, I completed a required training session to familiarize volunteers with the MCDC's standard operating procedures, visited with group leaders and members who had traveled there from all across the United States, and participated in numerous eight hour line-watches to scope for "IAs" (illegal aliens). I also visited a lay-up area with fellow MCDC volunteers, toured the newly constructed border fence in Sasabe, Arizona with MCDC organizers, and interviewed media and politicians who had also come to participate in the musters.

Survey work

A second aspect of my research involved survey work and interviews conducted with volunteers from each of the three organizations being studied. I began by developing a 33 item questionnaire that addressed three major areas of inquiry: general demographic information, media usage and consumption habits, and information about the organization and the volunteer's involvement in it. This third section included questions asking about participants' views of immigration-related issues, advocacy efforts, personal experiences and suggestions for solutions to current problems along the border. An expanded questionnaire containing a total of 42 questions was distributed to volunteers unable to take part in personal interviews.

The questionnaire was distributed to volunteer participants in all three groups. [8] Follow-up interviews were then conducted with those who indicated a willingness to elaborate on their original answers and offer additional information. In the case of MCDC volunteers, interviews using both the questionnaire items and follow-up questions were sometimes conducted in the field, as the situation (sitting in the dark while on line watches at night) was often more conducive to oral than written questioning. In all, the questionnaire response rate among members of each group totaled roughly half the number of regular weekly participants (or, in the case of MCDC, roughly half the average number of volunteers at each muster). [9]

Developing a deeper understanding of the immigration issue required engagement in more than just participant observation, surveys and interviews. Therefore, I also attended numerous community sponsored events dealing with immigration-related themes. These included a one-day seminar in Glendale, AZ titled "Look Beneath the Surface" sponsored by local law enforcement agencies and the Greater Phoenix Area Human Trafficking Task Force, [10] a community forum in Carefree, AZ with immigration as one of three primary topics sponsored by the Spirit in the Desert Retreat Center, [11] and the International Conference on the Migrant in Tucson, Arizona sponsored by Humane Borders [12]. All three of these special events proved to be valuable sources of information, and at each of the events I made connections with officials, volunteers, and community leaders who are key players in the Arizona immigration debate.

I also felt it was critical to seek the views and perspectives of those who deal most closely with the immigration issue on a daily basis – the United States Border Patrol. To that end, I gathered information, resources and statistics from numerous officials and agents in both the

Tucson and Yuma border patrol sectors throughout the course of my research. Additionally, I made three separate trips to the new Department of Homeland Security (DHS) offices south of Tucson to personally interview three different Border Patrol agents from the Public Relations department. During the first visit to DHS headquarters,[13] Agent Gustavo Soto answered interview questions, illustrated migrant routes on maps, and displayed photographs of border fences and confiscated vehicles that had been used for drug runs. My second Border Patrol visit[14] involved a ride-along with Agent Sean King to the desert patrol areas south of Tucson, a tour of the Department of Homeland Security (DHS) facility in Nogales where migrants are processed after being apprehended, a close-up look at the wall that divides the city of Nogales, Arizona from Nogales, Sonora, and a visit to the Border Patrol's security checkpoint located along Interstate 19 between Nogales and Tucson. My third interview with the U.S. Border Patrol, Tucson Sector, was conducted in the field with Agent Michael Scioli.[15] On that occasion, I accompanied Agent Scioli on a four hour hike along a well-worn migrant trail approximately ten miles north of the border. While hiking, we spotted fresh migrant footprints on parts of the trail, assessed the extent of migrant activity in the area by the age and condition of the garbage left behind, and witnessed the brutality of the thorny plants and desert heat – even in the relatively cool month of November.

Textual Analysis

In addition to contact with the people most closely involved with the immigration issue in southern Arizona, my study involved extensive research to identify and analyze media reports of the three civil society groups being studied. Investigating the way in which immigration issues are framed involves as much study of media as it does of the civil society groups creating the frames. While a small amount of radio and television coverage was included, the most extensive source of immigration reporting analyzed for this study came from newspapers. The online database News Bank was utilized to search for all pertinent newspaper articles on the topic of immigration from Arizona's two largest daily newspapers, *The Arizona Republic* (Phoenix) and *The Arizona Daily Star* (Tucson) from March 1, 2005 to March 14, 2008.[16] Articles with a primary focus on immigration-related issues (particularly those about the civil society groups being studied) were read and the most useful or pertinent articles were printed and sorted by date or by topic (for example, immigration and crime, border patrol, fences).

Additional articles about immigration-related topics or specific people/issues being studied (for example, Minuteman Civil Defense Corps leader "Chris Simcox" or "Secure Border Initiative") were also gathered from a variety of local, state and national newspapers as mention of specific articles arose during the course of the research.[17] While texts from these additional newspapers were considered in the overall analysis of media coverage of immigration, greatest emphasis was purposely placed on articles from *The Arizona Republic* and *The Arizona Daily Star*. These are two major Arizona newspapers with the closest proximity to the border in question and to civil society groups active along that border. Given this proximity and the fact that border-related issues are highly relevant to the readership of these newspapers, *The Arizona Republic* and *The Arizona Daily Star* were logical print sources from which to gather research data. Both enjoy greater accessibility to the Arizona/Sonora line than other major publications further away, and both have arguably covered the Arizona/Sonora border with greater depth and consistency than other print sources.

In all, more than three hundred primary articles dealing specifically with the immigration-related issues previously mentioned were read and analyzed for relevant content. Additional secondary articles, not focused primarily on immigration but containing pertinent immigration-related content, were also studied.

In-depth interviews were then conducted with the immigration reporters from the two Arizona newspapers used for textual analysis. A personal interview was conducted with Brady McCombs of *The Arizona Daily* Star in Tucson, AZ and additional information was provided through an e-mail questionnaire.[18] Three telephone interviews were conducted with Daniel González of *The Arizona Republic*.[19] Three other print media professionals were also interviewed as part of the research for this study: Ernesto Portillo, Jr., a longtime columnist for *The Arizona Daily Star* who often deals with immigration issues,[20] Michel Marizco, an independent, free-lance journalist who formerly reported for *The Arizona Daily Star*,[21] and Margaret Regan, journalist for *The Tucson Weekly* and author of the book *The Death of Josseline: Immigration Stories from the Arizona-Mexico Borderlands*. The work of these journalists reflects decades of collective years of experience reporting on immigration and border-related issues.

My research also uncovered important broadcast sources that were used as part of this study. While a thorough search such as that conducted to find newspaper articles was *not* employed to access radio and television programs dealing with immigration, more informal methods were utilized to access influential voices from specific broadcast sources. Survey responses from civil society volunteers who participated in my research revealed prominent radio and television programs that served as primary sources of information about immigration-related topics. Therefore, web-based searches were conducted to locate some of the most interesting and relevant transcripts from the sources mentioned in participant surveys. These included prominent stations such as National Public Radio and well-known personalities such as Lou Dobbs.

Finally, two personal interviews were conducted with Darla Jaye, a popular radio talk show personality on KMBZ in Kansas City who frequently addresses the topic of immigration on her show.[22] These interviews took place while we both took part in Minuteman Civil Defense Corps activities during a muster southwest of Tucson, Arizona. The interviews with Darla Jaye were unique in that they took place "on the ground." Therefore, the content of the conversations covered not only information about her talk show, but also reactions to her experiences with MCDC as she toured the Sasabe border fence, hiked to a migrant lay-up area, and searched for migrants through night-vision cameras on line watch duty.

A few specific details of the study merit mention here. In order to protect the identity and privacy of the volunteers who were so generous to assist with this research, the names of all participants interviewed have been changed. However, as an exception, the names of law enforcement officials, media professionals and leaders/founders of the three organizations being studied are used with their consent. The unique public positions and/or service of these individuals and the leadership they have provided for the groups being studied necessitates the identification of each by name.

I also wish to comment on the language used throughout this work, particularly in relation to individuals crossing the border without official permission. Many terms have been used to describe such people, including (but not limited to): illegal immigrant, illegal alien, undocumented immigrant, unauthorized border-crosser, unofficial migrant, or just "illegal," used as a noun rather than an adjective. The specific application of any one of these terms has become a highly contested element of the debate about how United States citizens view such entrants. Some organizations insist on use of the term "illegal alien" while others refer to the border-crossers only as "undocumented immigrants."

I have very purposefully chosen to use the terms "unauthorized border-crossers" or "unauthorized migrants" (at times, shortened to just migrants) throughout this book when making my own references to this population. "Illegal alien" is a technically acceptable term, but it also carries negative semantic connotations or allusions to a person (or creature) somehow vastly different from the average citizen. In terms of law, "illegal" when used by itself is an adjective, not a noun, making it an unacceptable term for these purposes. "Undocumented immigrant" is not an accurate term because many of the people crossing the borders do so with false documents. Additionally, an immigrant is someone who has legal status and who arrives in a country with the intention of staying. That is not true of many individuals who come to the United States for the sole purpose of obtaining work, earning money, and returning home. Therefore, the term migrant is better suited than immigrant to refer to the wide variety of people being described. It is, in fact, migration more than immigration that has occurred for more than a century across the southern U.S. border. In summary, in describing the people who cross the border into the United States without official consent of the authorities, I choose to use the words that offer the most accurate description of the individuals in regard to their status, and the most respectful representation of these individuals as fellow human beings.

When quoting members of the civil society organizations being studied, or when explaining concepts related to these groups, however, I choose to use the terminology common to that specific group and utilized by that group's membership. Therefore, in sections where Humane Borders volunteers refer to "undocumented migrants" I will do the same; where MCDC volunteers refer to IAs (illegal aliens), I refer to IAs as well. Use of these terms is not intended to disparage anyone; instead, it is an effort to respect the choice of language and views of the organizations being researched.

Finally, I would like to clarify use of the term civil society to describe the three groups that comprise this study. Although in general terms "civil society" refers to a grouping of citizens within a state, my understanding and application of the phrase relies on the contributions of two important political and social theorists. As Antonio Gramsci described, it was through civil society institutions that the state could be effectively challenged (Gramsci, 1971). And like Habermas (1964), I view civil society as the group of active and motivated citizens whose willingness to express opinions and engage in dialogue about general matters is necessary for the successful functioning of the state. While the groups studied for this research do fit the definition of social movement organizations (SMOs) and will be referred to as such in a theoretical discussion of SMOs and their media strategies, I choose to generally use the term civil society to describe the organizations. This term encompasses a wider scope of informal networks and groupings of concerned citizens that is not limited to a singular social movement but, as may well be the case with this study, comprises individuals whose actions stem from more general concerns with social justice issues (in this case, immigration) that take on various forms.

Importance of Research

The study is important for a number of reasons. Most obvious is the fact that the issue of immigration has become such a divisive and emotional concern for much of the national populace. Few citizens of the United States are unaware or untouched in some way by the presence of unauthorized migrants, whether through prices paid for agricultural products, builders hired to construct new homes, or meals or clean rooms provided by service industry workers in restaurants and hotels. Yet public response to the presence of these unauthorized persons has in many instances been less than welcoming. In various parts of the country, rallies and demonstrations protesting "illegal aliens" and "illegal immigration" have been held by groups claiming they must defend their country against "invaders" (Madrid, 2009; Randles, 2010). Numerous state legislatures have passed laws exacerbating the legal consequences for both the unauthorized workers themselves and their employers (Vergakis, 2010). The Department of Homeland Security has gone a step further, delegating certain aspects of federal immigration authority to state and local agencies under the controversial section 287(g) of the Immigration and Nationality Act. In Arizona, this program has resulted in investigations and lawsuits against Maricopa County Sherriff Joe Arpaio for alleged civil rights abuses and abuses of power (Gutiérrez, 2009). Finally, the passage of Arizona's SB 1070 has sent a strong message to the federal government that if more is not done by federal authorities to crack down on illegal immigration, states will take matters into their own hands.

Talk radio shows and national news programs have served as both sounding boards and catalysts for a vocal, frustrated segment of the U.S. population that advocates for sealed borders and the repatriation of "illegals" to their home countries. Equally passionate are the mediated voices of activists demanding immigration policy reform that offers greater legal access for potential foreign workers and a more humanitarian approach to the treatment of foreigners in the United States without legal status. Understanding what has provoked such a strong reaction from these groups of citizens and investigating what alternative viewpoints offer to the discussion about the current state of immigration is the first step toward developing an informed opinion. Doing so is critical if we, as a nation, are serious about finding well-informed and democratic solutions to the problems currently associated with our country's southern border.

Description of the Chapters

Chapter 1, "Disorder on the Border," offers a glimpse of the U.S./Mexico border and an overview of major concerns related to changing immigration policies and patterns. The chapter also describes how the author's background and experiences relate to the nature of the research, and details the specific approach and motivations guiding the study.

Chapter 2, "Researching Immigration in Arizona" provides an introduction to the setting for this study – the Sonoran Desert of southern Arizona. This is followed by an overview of the research and a brief history of the border and border issues that led to interest in the topic. Unique considerations of language in regard to the border are discussed, and a description of the research is provided.

Chapter 3, "The History of U.S. Immigration," examines the history of immigration into the United States and the false notions of direct assimilation and acceptance of new ethnic groups from the earliest days of nationhood. The nature of immigration throughout the past century is explored, as are both popular and political reactions to the idea of "undesirables" entering into the new American populace. Mexico's unique history with the United States serves as a backdrop for an overview of the changing and continually evolving nature of immigration policies between the two countries. Finally, special emphasis is placed on the impact of the North American Free Trade Agreement on poverty levels in Mexico and the resulting changes to migration patterns into the United States.

Chapter 4, "Framing the Border: Boundaries, Illegality and Civic Engagement" offers a theoretical perspective on how the framing of the immigration issue by civil society organizations has influenced public dialogue and ideas about the current state of immigration, particularly as they are communicated through mass media. It also explores how those frames have been formed based on differing theoretical approaches to the notions of borders and legality. Particular emphasis is placed on the role of global flows in dissolving non-political borders, and the blending of societies through the natural progression of labor movement.

Chapter 5, "Shaping the National Debate," provides an in-depth look at the three southern Arizona organizations being studied and gives a brief history of their inception and growth. Through participant observation, survey and interview work, and textual analysis I studied the ideologies and actions of the organizations, the nature of the controversy surrounding their work, and the effect of this publicity on the wider immigration debate. An analysis of the organizations' media strategies also contributed to a deeper understanding of how the relationship between civil society and media shapes the discussion of immigration on a national scale. Additionally, the idea of civil society and its relationship with the state is examined through the ideas of Hobbes, Locke, and Gramsci. An analysis of the public sphere as proposed by Jurgen Habermas is also undertaken, and the possibility for such a public sphere to effectively develop in the context of the current immigration debate is considered.

Chapter 6, "Media and Civil Society: Walking the Line Together," describes how a very tenuous but beneficial relationship has evolved between the activists creating border-related stories and the reporters writing the headlines. Research involving media selection of the volunteers looks at the patterns between types of media consumed and frames created by the three groups being studied. Klapper's reinforcement theory is considered as an explanation for the parallel frames in media selected by the groups and in messages produced by the groups. The chapter considers how those frames are spread to a larger audience through mass media channels. Finally, issues of trust in media are presented, as are examples of misinformation that have broken trust between civil society groups and the media they often depend on.

Chapter 7, "Nationalist Sentiment and Mediated Messages," undertakes an examination of the frames involving national identity as conceived by the members of humanitarian aid groups and of border watch organizations. Historical examples of resistance to foreigners are provided, along with a look at how similar attitudes are infused into the language of current immigration debate. The role of both media and civil society in perpetuating those negative sentiments is described. Additionally, the notion of an American cultural identity is explored, as is Benedict Anderson's theory of "imagined communities." The importance of media in the creation of those "imagined communities" is also explained.

Chapter 8, "Pulpits, Patriotism, and the Press: How Love of God and Love of Country Motivate Action" offers an explanation of how faith-based responses to immigration issues differ from the ethno-nationalism frames guiding patriotic responses of border watch groups. The chapter examines the church's role in influencing public perceptions of the immigration phenomenon, and how the motivations of people of faith differ from those of groups who emphasize "security first." As a national public considers how it will respond to the threats and needs of an unauthorized population in its midst, faith-based organizations are calling for reactions based on compassion and acceptance. The application of religious principles to tensions involving the church and state are described, as are views of the migrant by individuals on various sides of the debate. Finally, the comparison of legal justice versus social justice is discussed in light of civil society's reaction to current immigration policy.

Chapter 9, "Bringing Order to the Border: Capturing Public Attention," offers a final look at the specific media messages being produced by civil society along the Arizona/Sonora border, and the effectiveness of specific groups in delivering those messages to a national public. The reaction of other activists and of media professionals to the present tone of the discourse about immigration is described, and opinions about which elements are missing from the media presentation of the issue are presented. Finally, the dissimilarities of civil society responses to the immigration issue are discussed in light of one particular distinguishing characteristic - personal interaction with unauthorized migrants.

Chapter 10, "Reflecting Back, Looking Ahead" summarizes the major findings of this research and offers a reflection of how such a study might contribute to the larger immigration debate. The chapter includes a final section titled "personal reflections" that outlines my own thoughts about the study and how the relationship between media and civil society affects the general public's understanding of immigration-related issues. The closing segment offers a brief explanation of key ideas for policy reform stemming from the civil society organizations studied, and concludes with the hope that an engaged and knowledgeable public, informed through mediated stories of an active civil society, will begin asking the questions that inspire just and effective solutions for all involved.

This research is important because it provokes questions about how our understanding of the "other" – largely obtained through mediated sources – shapes an understanding of ourselves. Who we are as a nation and what we stand for as a people is played out in the conversations surrounding how we choose to treat the neighbor in our midst. The immigration debate, informed largely by media coverage of activity along the country's southern border, is doing as much to challenge and shape our own national identity as it is to define the identity and place of a people who live in a liminal space between two nations.

On a personal level, this study provided an opportunity to immerse myself into the immigration issue in a way most U.S. citizens will never experience. By participating in border musters with the Minuteman Civil Defense Corps, refilling desert water stations with Humane Borders and walking migrant trails with volunteers from No More Deaths, I have seen the passions, convictions and frustrations of a civil society desperate to find answers to an alarming public injustice. Standing on the front lines with these groups, as well as with Border Patrol and other law enforcement personnel, has given me a deep appreciation of the complexity of the border and its related issues. Interviewing the major media players who have dedicated decades to covering these topics only reinforced my suspicion that there are many more layers to the issues at hand than what we often hear through the stories being told. A concerned public must think carefully about the media messages it receives, and analyze those messages in the context of a larger social and political picture. There are no easy answers, no short cuts, no quick fixes. This is an issue that requires thoughtful analysis of the arguments on all sides of the discussion. The danger of refusing such thoughtful analysis is the creation of new borders that further threaten our understanding of ourselves in relationship to those around us.

Notes

[1] Numerous references have been made to Arizona as 'ground zero' of the immigration debate because of the number of unauthorized border crossers entering through Arizona's desert and because of the nature and extent of activism that has resulted. For an example of such references, see Wagner & Bazar, 2010.

[2] G. Soto, United States Customs and Border Protection Public Relations Officer: Tucson Sector Public Affairs Office (personal interview, May 23, 2007). Statistics for migrant deaths along the border are available from Border Patrol officials in sector offices; however, there is no official Border Patrol print or electronic resource with such data available to the public. Thus, all such statistics for this research come from personal interviews or correspondence with Border Patrol officials.

[3] M. Scioli, United States Customs and Border Protection Public Relations Officer: Tucson Sector Public Affairs Office (personal interview, November 1, 2007).

[4] D. Jimarez, United States Customs and Border Protection Public Relations Officer: Tucson Sector Public Affairs Office (telephone interview, April 2, 2010).

[5] While research for this study began as early as 2005, my primary investigations involving the three civil society groups being studied were carried out between January of 2007 and February of 2008.

[6] This last trip was part of my participation in the 2007 International Conference on the Migrant sponsored by Humane Borders.

[7] Such musters were once primarily sponsored and organized by the national Minuteman Civil Defense Corps organization in conjunction with local chapters. This changed, however, in March of 2010 when MCDC President Carmen Mercer announced the dissolving of the national corporation, partly due to liability concerns prompted by the reactions of members and supporters to a call to arms for an upcoming muster and the implementation of controversial new standard operating procedures for the group. At that point, recruitment and planning of musters fell to local chapters who would then be responsible for the actions of their muster participants.

[8] The process of recruiting participants was ongoing from January, 2007 through February, 2008 for all three groups involved. Because participation in the study was completely voluntary, no formal sampling methods were used for selection of participants. Instead, I introduced myself and explained my project at weekly meetings or on-site gatherings and asked for anyone who thought they might be interested in participating to take home a consent form that explained the project in greater detail. Those who returned the consent forms through the mail or at subsequent meetings were then given a hard copy or e-mail version of the questionnaire, and were asked if they might be willing to participate in a follow-up personal interview. Spending extensive time engaged in the projects and on-the-ground activities of these organizations also provided me with an opportunity to get to know many of the local volunteers, and proved to be a fruitful means of recruiting participants.

After the questionnaires were distributed and returned by all those who were willing to complete them, the names of participants were changed and answers were studied to determine what, if any, additional questions needed to be asked. Names of organizational leaders, already considered public figures due to the nature of their work and prominence in the media, were used with their consent.

[9] Thirty-one research questionnaires were distributed to Humane Borders volunteers and 16 were completed and returned; 24 were distributed to No More Deaths volunteers with 10 of those returned, and 11 were distributed to MCDC volunteers with 8 returned. Considering there were an average of 25-30 people in attendance at the weekly meetings of the humanitarian groups, and an average of 20 per day participating in MCDC musters, the response rate reflects close to half of the average number of regular attendees for each group.

Ten in-depth interviews were conducted with members of Humane Borders, four with members of No More Deaths, and seven with members of MCDC.

[10] The date of the seminar was October 30, 2007.

[11] The date of the forum was November 3, 2007.

[12] The date of the conference was March 26-27, 2007.

[13] The interview took place on May 23, 2007.

[14] The second U.S. Border Patrol visit took place on October 17, 2007.

[15] Interview number three was conducted November 1, 2007.

[16] The following key word searches were entered into this database to find relevant articles: "immigration," "immigration AND deaths," "Humane Borders," "Minuteman Civil Defense Corps OR Minutemen NOT missile", "No More Deaths," and "migrant OR immigrant deaths." Results of the search were then sorted to determine which articles were actually focused on immigration in Arizona and related subjects, and which simply mentioned the key words as part of another broader theme.

[17] These articles were primarily accessed through Google searches, additional News Bank searches, subscriptions to newspapers such as *The Christian Science Monitor*, and many hours sorting through news archives in the Humane Borders media files room at the First Christian Church in Tucson, AZ on October 12, 2007 and November 7, 2007.

[18] Interview took place on January 21, 2008 and questionnaire was completed in April, 2010.

[19] Interviews dates were January 18 and February 12, 2008 and April 22, 2010.

[20] Interview was conducted January 21, 2008 in Tucson, AZ.

[21] Telephone interview conducted February 22, 2008.

[22] Interviews took place November 16 and 17, 2007.

3

The History of U.S. Immigration

"The responsibility of the great states is to serve
and not dominate the world."

Harry S. Truman, First Message to Congress (April 16, 1945)

Sasabe is a small town on the Mexico/United States border located 70 miles southwest of Tucson, AZ and 50 miles north of Altar, Sonora. Distinguished by a small Border Patrol station sandwiched between roughly eleven miles of fencing, Sasabe would not seem like a typical destination point for most travelers. Only one major road leads out of the town on both its northern and southern sides, and the wide expanses surrounding Sasabe are marked by vast stretches of rugged desert as far as the eye can see. In recent years, however, residents of Sasabe have been witness to hundreds of thousands of individuals from continents as distant as Asia and South America passing through the town's dusty streets.

Sasabe's recent popularity as a border-crossing point is due to its location 50 miles north of Altar, Sonora – currently the largest staging area for illegal immigration along the entire Mexico/United States border. Once a small, quiet community itself, Altar has now been transformed into a bustling "sending town" whose infrastructure has developed at a frenetic pace to keep up with the busloads of potential migrants passing through before venturing further north toward the Mexico/United States border. Altar is the last major stop for migrants typically originating from southern Mexico, Central America and South America, although increasingly more migrants from Asia are being trafficked through these same crossing sectors (Ceasar, 2010; Terrazas, 2008). From Altar, they are bused to Sasabe or a nearby area where they are dropped off and led by coyotes (human smugglers) through the desert into the United States. Robin Hoover, co-founder of the humanitarian group Humane Borders that places water stations in the desert along the border, estimates that during high season approximately

4000 migrants pass daily through the corridor that reaches from Sasabe, Sonora (MX) into the Buenos Aires National Wildlife Refuge in southern Arizona (Rotstein, 2006).

The explosion of migration through Sasabe and other desert regions in southern Arizona is a recent phenomenon. Although individuals have been crossing the geopolitical border that separates the United States and Mexico for over a century, the nature of those migratory flows has changed drastically. Prior to the mid-1990s, few migrants chose routes through isolated towns like Sasabe because of the danger and difficulty of crossing through the desert. However, changes in immigration policy over the past decade have led to subsequent shifts in immigration patterns. What was once a relatively stable and predictable pattern of migrant workers entering the United States through urban crossing areas has become a widespread inflow of unauthorized border crossers through traditional entry points[1] as well as remote stretches of previously quiescent borderlands. Militarization of the border along traditional urban crossing routes has channeled potential unauthorized crossers through less populated, more hazardous desert regions where physical borders are few but where geographical dangers, extreme temperatures, and the constant threat of dehydration or hypothermia have cost many migrants their lives (Dunn, 2010).

The shift from urban to desert crossing points is yet one additional chapter in a long history of changing relationships and continually modified immigration policies between the United States and Mexico. The political history of the United States/Mexico border illustrates a push-pull pattern that has encouraged the migration of Mexican labor into the United States during periods of economic need, particularly during eras when gaps in the U.S. workforce necessitated foreign labor, followed by efforts to "push" Mexican workers back to their home country when economic conditions change in such a way that foreign presence is seen as a threat to native-born workers. Policies designed to promote economic development while largely resisting social integration of a foreign labor pool have influenced migration patterns along this shared border for more than a century.

Although the purpose of this book is not to provide a thorough history of Mexico/United States immigration, a brief overview of the relationship between the two countries will lend greater insight into the formation of present day policies. This historical background is particularly helpful in identifying the roots of current immigration conflict and the nature of public discussion that accompanies it. An overview of the economic conditions and policies that have pushed workers out of Mexico and into the United States are discussed. In particular, an explanation of the North American Free Trade Agreement (NAFTA) and its effects on migration adds important perspectives about how contemporary border-crossing patterns have evolved based on economic and socio-political conditions in the United States and Mexico. Finally, recent U.S. border policies that have tightened security in traditional crossing areas and pushed migrants into more dangerous desert terrain have resulted in an increasing migrant death toll. Citizens along the border have become frustrated with the failure of the U.S. government to respond adequately to both unauthorized entrances and desert deaths, and their frustration has led to the formation of civil organizations dedicated to promoting mediated messages of immigration reform. Together, these histories help to clarify how policy, past and present, has affected the nature of the border and those who are willing to risk their lives to cross it.

Immigration Patterns in Early United States History

Current United States immigration policy has arisen from a long history of policies based on preference for certain groups over others. Leaders and politicians have pushed for models of immigration favoring individuals they felt were best suited for the creation and blending of the new American populace. The eloquent words of Emma Lazarus inscribed on the Statue of Liberty are often cited as an example of the young democratic nation's hospitality, highlighting its willingness to welcome "the tired…the poor" the "huddled masses yearning to breathe free" and even "the wretched refuse of your teeming shore."

Though moving, this sentiment is hardly an accurate reflection of the hostile reception many foreigners received upon arrival in the United States. In reality, there has always been a divide that has prohibited or discouraged "unwanted" people from becoming United States citizens or legal permanent residents.

For roughly a century after the establishment of the United States of America, immigration into this country remained open and virtually free of restrictions. Even as late as the first part of the twentieth century, few were denied access – especially immigrants from Europe. With the exception of socially undesirable citizens, such as those likely to become the responsibility of the public, polygamists, and the diseased (Immigration Act of 1891) and the exception of Chinese laborers and other Asians (excluded through numerous acts and laws from 1882 through the early 20th century), nearly all those who reached the shores of the United States were admitted as citizens. Of the 25 million

European immigrants who arrived in the U.S. between 1880 and 1914, only one percent was denied entrance (Ngai, 2004).

While modest restrictions were reflected in immigration laws of the late 19th century, it was not until the early 20th century that marked changes in selectivity and exclusivity began more severely limiting those who were legally admitted to the country. By 1917, various immigration acts had expanded upon early categorizations of socially unacceptable immigrants to include epileptics, the insane, professional beggars, anarchists, unaccompanied minors, "induced" immigrants, the disabled, and illiterates (Cornelius,1978; Rodríguez-Scott, 2002; Timmer & Williamson, 1998, p.766).

Certain exceptions were made to the aforementioned immigration acts and subsequent laws to ease restrictions on neighboring countries. For example, when laborers were needed for agriculture, railroads, and mining in the southwestern United States, definitions of unacceptable immigrants were relaxed, quotas were lifted for certain groups, and even head taxes were waived – all driven by the fluctuating demands of the U.S. labor market (Calavita, 1984; Timmer & Williamson, 1998).

Despite such exceptions, nativist attitudes remained and were fueled through passage of such laws as the Johnson-Reed Immigration Act of 1924, the first comprehensive restriction law in the United States. This act placed numerical limits on the numbers of immigrants admitted, as well as global racial and national categorizations that favored immigrants from certain countries over others (Ngai, 2004). Northern and Western Europeans were seen as the most desirable immigrants, while Mexicans and other non-Europeans were largely regarded with contempt.

Under the Johnson-Reed Act, land borders that had previously been regarded as open passages for flows of people back and forth between countries (particularly the U.S.-Mexico border) were now placed under state surveillance and treated as definitive, exclusive boundaries. Also, the new categorization of "illegal alien" changed the status of the migrants who were apprehended. For the first time, persons without proper documentation faced deportation if they were caught by Congress's newly created Border Patrol. This was a significant shift away from the policies in place prior to 1920, under which very few people who were already in the United States had been deported. Perhaps most significantly, the act made illegal immigration the central problem of immigration law. Entry into the United States was no longer indiscriminate; borders had become the business of the state. By 1930, "the doors to the New World were effectively closed" (Timmer & Williamson, 1998, p. 742). Or, in the words of Professor Maldwyn

Allen Jones, "After three centuries of free immigration America all but completely shut her door on newcomers. The Statue of Liberty would still stand in New York harbor, but the verses on its base would henceforth be but a tribute to a vanished ideal" (Jones, 1992, p. 238).

Mexican Immigration into the United States:
A Long History of Pushes and Pulls

"The demand for migratory workers is thus essentially twofold: To be ready to go to work when needed; to be gone when not needed."
President's Commission on Migratory Labor, 1951

In its early years, immigration policy along the Mexico/United States border was much like that of U.S. immigration policy in general – very open and unrestrictive. From the mid 1800s until the mid-1920s, workers flowed back and forth from Mexico to the United States without need for visas or other documentation. The two countries enjoyed a symbiotic relationship around the turn of the century; U.S. railroad companies, mines and ranches needed labor, and Mexicans needed jobs – particularly those who had been forced off their ejidos[2] by the Porfirio Díaz regime (Ganster, 1995).

In the years that followed, both official and unofficial guest worker programs were implemented. During World War I, Mexican laborers were recruited through mass media and word of mouth to fill jobs left vacant by active servicemen. Their labor helped to contribute to a growing, robust domestic economy as U.S. businesses profited from lower wages paid to Mexican workers. Foreign workers were welcomed as the American economy expanded.

As the 1920s approached, however, treatment of the Mexican immigrant was very much dependent on the economic status and health of the United States. Shortly after the end of WWI, a sharp recession and ensuing job losses prompted an effort to force Mexican laborers back across southern borders. During this period, Mexican workers, as well as some U.S. citizens of Mexican descent, were expelled (Ganster, 1995).

As the economy recovered in the early 1920s, Mexican labor was again welcomed by U.S. business and industry. However, by this time, Congress had begun to pass immigration laws such as the Johnson-Reed Act that produced important consequences for potential migrants. Mexicans were not assigned numerical quotas for entrance like European immigrants were, but new restrictions and paperwork requirements prevented many from obtaining legal status to cross their country's northern border. More importantly, the new restrictions were intended to penalize those entering the U.S. without proper documentation. Such laws created the category of "illegal" to describe individuals without official papers, even if they had lived and worked in the United States for many years prior.

In 1929, Congress cracked down further on illegal immigration by making a first time border crossing a misdemeanor and a second crossing a felony. That felony conviction carried with it a permanent ban from re-entry into the United States. Mexico, of course, was the country most affected by this legislation. Nevertheless, need for Mexican labor in the U.S. continued to pull laborers northward. By the late 1920s, Mexicans had become the largest group of "illegal aliens"[3] in the United States.

Slowly, Mexican identity became synonymous with the status of "illegal," leading to an ongoing exclusion of Mexicans from the national community and polity (Ngai, 2004). This "othering" through racial categorization was furthered through the language of official U.S. documents and policy. For example, in the 1920s, the U.S. census began using the term "Mexican" as a racial category for data-gathering purposes. Scientific circles perpetuated racial categorizations and blatantly discriminated against Mexicans through the newly established field of eugenics, aimed at improving the human condition by identifying weak or undesirable elements of the gene pool. Eugenic rationale prompted invasive fumigation and sanitation campaigns along the U.S./Mexico border, including "showering" groups of Mexicans with a mixture of soap, kerosene and water, and stamping their bodies with permanent ink to indicate they had been checked and/or treated for lice (Stern, 2005). Vocal proponents of eugenics and biological determinism "viewed the Mexican people as living fossils in the garden of evolutionary development" (Cardoso, 1980, p. 132). The status of the Mexican as a person who did not belong – who could never quite assimilate despite his or her legal status – was slowly taking shape.

As long as Mexican migrants could fill economic and labor needs in the United States they were welcomed as contributors to national growth. When there was no benefit to employers on the U.S. side of the border, however, or when the economy showed signs of a downturn, workers were pushed back into Mexico so as not to cause a drain on education, health care, or other domestic social programs. During periods of economic stagnation or decline, Mexican migrants were viewed as "an economic threat, an intolerable burden on the U.S. taxpayer" or "a cultural-racial contaminant" (Cornelius, 1978, p. 2). A quote from the Dillingham Immigration Commission as far back as

1911 sums up national feeling toward Mexicans in the first part of the twentieth century: "In the case of the Mexican, he is less desirable as a citizen than as a laborer" (Dillingham, 1911, p. 690).

One of the more prominent examples of such push/pull patterns was the deportation of Mexican immigrants during the Great Depression. By the 1930s, United States citizens began to attribute their increasing economic woes, at least in part, to the foreign labor pool. The economic recession and anti-immigrant sentiment that accompanied the Depression led to a "push" of Mexican workers back to their home country. Large-scale forced repatriations eased tensions among the American public (Hoffman, 1974), but simultaneously eroded the goodwill of Mexicans (and some Mexican-Americans) whose lives and work were constantly threatened by the deteriorating national sentiment toward foreigners (Ganster, 1995). Their frustration was valid; although Mexicans made up only one percent of the immigrant population during the 1930s, they made up half of the population of formal deportees (Ngai, 1999). Such a schizophrenic approach to the position of the Mexican worker in U.S. society would continue for decades.

Bracero Era

Finally, in 1942, wartime labor shortages, growth in the industrial sector and demands for foreign labor led to the next major immigration policy shift in the United States – the passage of the first *official* Bracero (guest worker) program.[4] This move recognized the value of Mexican labor to the U.S. economic system and provided a legal means by which Mexican labor could be imported for brief periods of time. Intended as a temporary emergency labor policy, the initial, official Bracero Program lasted five years. However, extensions of the original plan supported by the Immigration and Naturalization Service (INS) and other governmental agencies were continued for a total of 17 more years, making the Bracero Program one of the longest running U.S. immigration policies until its demise in 1964. It was also the largest foreign worker program in U.S. history, supplying contracted Mexican workers to employers in 26 different states (Calavita, 1992; Ngai, 2004).

The Bracero Program was both popular and successful among U.S. employers because it provided a cheap, predictable supply of laborers whose major social costs (education, homes, health care) were borne by Mexico. Indeed, one of the greatest benefits of Mexican labor to U.S. employers was the fact that Mexico's close proximity allowed freedom of movement. Agricultural and industry owners could hire Mexican workers seasonally and then send them back to their home country once the work was finished. Employers would benefit from labor contributions but the state would not have to be responsible for the welfare of the workers' families or for their ongoing needs. For this reason, U.S. policymakers saw the Bracero Program as a workable solution to the need for foreign labor in the U.S. Southwest. However, poor regulation of the Bracero Program eventually caused instability, riots, confusion and desertion. Lack of consistency with terms of the program often eroded the rights of braceros, creating distrust toward both the employers and the United States government. At the same time, American employers were angry about changes in terms of the program that limited their control over the braceros. The result was disharmony on both sides of the border.

The constantly fluctuating terms of the Bracero Program produced particular discord in the 1950s. During this time, the INS found itself between a rock and a hard place. On one hand, the government was demanding a halt to the flow of illegal aliens and on the other hand, agents understood the economic utility of migrant labor (and were often reminded of it by employers). INS agents were further incensed at the government's own willingness to circumvent the law to keep growers happy. The President's Commission on Migratory Labor devised a creative solution to illegal immigration that the INS termed "a walk around the statute" or "drying out wetbacks." Illegal aliens were rounded up, walked across the border, deemed legal braceros, and allowed to re-enter the U.S. through official ports of entry (Calavita, 1992, p. 41; Ngai, 2004, p. 154). Such actions were little more than efforts to superficially appease critics while keeping the structure of the contract labor program intact.

Despite such efforts to keep critics contented, strong public sentiment against illegal immigration remained. Cold War paranoia inspired fear that an uncontrolled border would offer easy access to "subversives" (not so different than current post-9/11 arguments that a weakened border would offer easy access to terrorists). Organized labor, threatened by "wetback labor" that was now reaching into industry and trades, published *What Price Wetbacks?* in 1953, urging a reduction in the flow of illegals.[5] Fears of increased crime, disease, and displacement of domestic workers fueled the sentiment against those in the United States without proper authorization.

In June of 1954, the Eisenhower administration and newly appointed INS Commissioner Joseph Swing responded with "Operation Wetback," a highly public campaign to deport large numbers of unauthorized migrants. Swing spoke of a "direct attack...upon the hordes of aliens facing us across the border" (1954) as he and local

Border Patrol agents set up road blocks, inspected trains and cordoned off neighborhoods for inspection (Calavita, 1992, p.55). During the campaign's first three months, 3000 undocumented workers a day were apprehended (Ngai, 2004) and the 1954 *INS Annual Report* states that over <u>one million</u> illegals were apprehended over the course of the year (Calavita, 1992). This figure, however, likely includes thousands of unauthorized migrants who left on their own due to an intensive publicity campaign advising them to do so.

The workers who were removed during "Operation Wetback" were replaced once again with official Braceros. This kept employers happy because they did not have to wonder whether their labor supply was going to "skip" to a better paying job or be deported. Over the next ten years, changes made in the Bracero Program only served to lessen Mexico's negotiating power[6] and strengthen the position of employers. And despite the publicly acclaimed "success" of Operation Wetback, unauthorized immigration continued.

The Bracero Program offered control, predictability and stability to specific segments of the United States labor system. It also affected the nature of Mexican presence in the host country. Over the course of the Bracero Program's 22 year official history, over 4,500,000 Mexicans entered the United States to work, and many times that number came illegally to find jobs (Cardoso, 1980). For brief periods of time, federal efforts to limit the quantity of unauthorized immigrants lessened the flow. Each of these periods, however, was followed by another surge in undocumented workers entering the United States, hoping to take advantage of jobs that paid more than similar work in Mexico (where jobs were often hard to find at all).

The Bracero Program officially came to an end in 1964 due to a combination of factors. The return of WWII servicemen in the 1950s resulted in a declining need for foreign agricultural labor. In addition, increasing mechanization in agriculture coupled with lack of accountability and oversight of the Bracero Program led to its demise (Martin, 2003). Even after the Bracero Program ended, however, the flow of Mexicans into the U.S. remained high because of economic imbalances between the two nations. Additionally, the policies that allowed braceros to come legally to the United States placed greater pressure on the INS to address their continued presence once the program came to a close. Subsequent laws intended to address illegal immigration have continued to wrestle with the same dilemmas of federal policies that conflict with practical labor demands, and of control over the return of guest workers to their home countries.

After the Braceros:
Changes in Migration from Mexico

Although the volume of undocumented migration into the United States and level of enforcement efforts along the U.S. border both increased from 1965-1985, the nature of migration patterns during this period actually reflected a relatively stable system. Most workers tended to come northward for seasonal work and return home when their jobs were finished. Unlike previous eras, however, these migrants were increasingly likely to be employed in service and manual labor industries rather than agricultural industries (Massey, Durand & Malone, 2002).

This "controlled" system was thrown out of balance, however, with the passage of the 1986 Immigration Reform and Control Act (IRCA) which introduced sanctions against employers who knowingly hired unauthorized workers, created a limited legalization program for undocumented persons already living in the United States, and allocated increased funding for Border Patrol and the Department of Labor. The act was largely a response to a reemergence of anti-immigration sentiment that followed the economic recession of the late 1970s and early 1980s. Once again, the nation's economic woes were blamed at least partly on immigrants. President Reagan added to the nation's fears by citing insurgencies in Central America as a potential source for a "tidal wave of refugees – and this time they'll be 'feet people' and not 'boat people'" (Cannon, 1983, p. A1).

IRCA was notable for a number of reasons. Its path to legalization for unauthorized persons already in the United States enraged critics opposing an amnesty policy, resulting in an early 1990s anti-immigration backlash (Andreas, 2009). At the same time, IRCA produced a rise in illegal immigration among the relatives of those who had been officially legalized. Families clung to the hope that potential future amnesty legislation might offer them a chance at proper, sanctioned unification.

The most notable characteristic of IRCA, however, may be that the policy was passed at the same time that Mexico entered into the General Agreement on Tariffs and Trade (GATT) and began discussing a free trade zone with the United States and Canada. Entrance into the negotiations was likely seen as an opportunity to protect Mexican labor interests and address labor issues while the economies of the three North American giants were being conjoined. However, rather than incorporating labor into the expansion and integration of markets, the United States deliberately stipulated policies based on integration with selective separation that reaffirmed its right to control its own borders (Massey, Durand & Malone, 2002).

Throughout the late 1980s and early 1990s, U.S. authorities sought to curb illegal immigration by reducing benefits and increasing costs for potential migrants. Additional U.S. Border Patrol agents and related personnel were hired to thwart attempted entries,[7] but the numbers of unauthorized immigrants slowly continued to rise in spite of these efforts. The United States government began to look for a new approach that would help the country regain an image of control over its southern border. Before that could transpire, however, the implementation and resulting consequences of the North American Free Trade Agreement (NAFTA) would have major implications for what was happening along the Mexico / United States divide.

Mixing Maize and Militarization:
How NAFTA, the Mexican Economy, and New
U.S. Border Policies Changed the Nature of Migration

The implementation of the North American Free Trade Agreement (NAFTA) on January 1, 1994 marked the beginning of a new era of hope for Mexico. The primary original intentions of this plan were to boost the economies of the United States, Canada and Mexico by eliminating trade barriers, creating fair competition in the realm of free trade, and increasing investment in the three participating countries (NAFTA Secretariat, 2010).

Sixteen years later, NAFTA was hailed as a success by the entities that enjoyed economic or social gains from the new policies. Trade among the three NAFTA countries tripled between 1993 and 2007, creating the world's largest free trade zone (Office, 2008). In the eyes of some economists and government officials, NAFTA was, and continues to be, a complete triumph. Even by NAFTA's ten year anniversary the agreement was praised by President Bush, Canadian Prime Minister Brian Mulroney and former Mexican President Carlos Salinas, with Mulroney adding that "The power of a good idea should never be underestimated. It should happen again" (Jordan, 2002, p. A27).

At the same time, the agreement produced a number of "losers" in terms of the ongoing struggles faced by both the Mexican economy and its citizens. As one researcher explains, the creation of a North American free-trade zone with three economies so markedly different in size and advancement virtually ensured an intensification of inequalities among the three participating countries (Binford, 2005). Poor states in southern Mexico with limited infrastructure and low educational rates saw far fewer benefits from NAFTA than better developed northern and central states (Easterly, Fiess, Lederman, Loyaza & Meller, 2003). Not surprisingly, the demographics of migrant populations in the years following NAFTA's implementation showed larger numbers of migrants originating from Mexico's southern region and the Mexico City metropolitan area than from traditional sending states in the northern and central parts of the country (Kochhar, 2005; Marcelli & Cornelius, 2001; Rubio-Goldsmith et al., 2006). Those who were hardest hit by the effects of NAFTA often saw migration as their best option for finding employment.

To be clear, NAFTA was not solely responsible for the emigration of individuals from any part of Mexico. Numerous factors have contributed to Mexico's northward migration flows, including detrimental effects of restructuring, insufficient domestic job opportunities, and a strong U.S. economy which has historically proven to be a major "pull" factor for migrant job seekers (Papademetriou, 2003; Passel & Suro, 2005). However, while NAFTA is certainly not wholly to blame for this phenomenon, its effect on the Mexican economy and subsequently on the financial well-being of many Mexican families whose livelihoods were adversely affected by the new trade regulations (especially those from poorer regions of Mexico) does much to explain individual motivations for migrants who risk the journey north.

Mexico and NAFTA

Negotiations between the United States, Canada and Mexico for the establishment of NAFTA actually began in 1991, but the agreement did not formally take effect until January 1, 1994 (Ramirez, 2006). Proponents of the program, keeping with the agreement's objective of increasing trade and integrating markets among the three participating countries, envisioned increased foreign investment and exports as key factors in boosting the Mexican economy (Pacheco-López, 2005). Even as late as 2006, more than a decade after its initial implementation, the Mexican government still viewed trade liberalization under agreements like NAFTA as the best hope of combating poverty and underdevelopment (Henriques & Patel, 2004).

The inauguration of the economic plan made headlines around the world – not just because of the initiation of the agreement itself, but primarily because of the massive Chiapas, Mexico-based Zapatista uprising staged to coincide with the ushering in of NAFTA (Binford, 2005). The Zapatista rebellion was largely a response to Mexico's intentional movement toward a more neoliberal economic model. Protesters, led by Subcomandante Marcos, argued that direct competition from Canada and the United States would be particularly devastating for Mexico's campesinos[8] – a population that already felt ignored by the Mexican government. The protesters' indignation was the culmination of many years of perceived mistreatment by federal authorities. They blamed the government for turning its back on the very people who provide a large portion of Mexico's wealth. The state of Chiapas, for example, is the source of 50% of Mexico's natural gas and 60% of its hydroelectric power. It also supplies substantial amounts of other natural resources, such as lumber, coffee and beef (Rich, 1997). Yet, Chiapas is Mexico's most economically disadvantaged state (Bane & Zenteno, 2009); nearly half of the population there lives in dire poverty (Howard & Homer-Dixon, 1996).

Under the leadership of Subcomandante Marcos, who waged a brilliant public relations war with the Mexican government by utilizing the Internet to engage international actors in the conflict,[9] the Zapatistas brought attention to the inequitable treatment of Mexico's poor (Almazán, 1997). Under NAFTA, argued protesters, the governance that created such poverty would now be institutionalized and justified through binding international agreements. Such contracts would only exacerbate the poverty of the indigenous population of Chiapas, "making their pitiful situation even worse" (Rich, 1997, p. 79).

Collapse and Crisis

Just eleven months after the formal institution of NAFTA, a series of domestic and political crises that shook investor confidence caused Mexico's financial system to collapse. Following a similar crisis in the 1980s, the peso was devalued by 50 percent, inflation soared, real wages dropped by 22%, and the country once again entered a severe recession – its largest economic recession since the great depression of the 1930s (Peach, 1996; Whitt, 1996; World, 1997). The situation turned from bad to worse; prices for gasoline, electricity and food staples were soon prohibitive for the country's poor (Rich, 1997). It seemed as if the Zapatistas' grim predictions were becoming reality.

International financial institutions responded by requiring Mexico to more rapidly adopt the structural adjustment and stabilization policies already in place (Heredia & Purcell, 1995). With the help of a $51 billion bailout, Mexico once again tightened its belt and pledged to embark on a strict economic recovery plan (Rich, 1997; Whitt, 1996).

The plan, however, did not bring immediate relief. Over the course of the following year, real gross domestic product (RGDP) declined by 8.7%, inflation rose to nearly 52%, the value of the peso plummeted, and unemployment reached unprecedented levels (Meza, 2008; Mishkin, 1998; Schmidt-Hebbel & Werner, 2002). In July of 1995 President Ernesto Zedillo's labor secretary challenged the state estimate that 6.3% of the population, or two million people were jobless, noting that the actual number was "closer to six million" (DePalma, 1995, p. 1).[10]

Ensuing years brought forth greater economic progress, and slowly Mexico's economy began to regain its strength. NAFTA policies increased trade and provided new opportunities for Mexican business that have helped the country slowly recover from its second economic collapse. Although the situation in Mexico since the implementation of NAFTA has improved greatly, problems remain. Instead of decreasing rural poverty in Mexico, NAFTA contributed to rising unemployment rates in the countryside and a shift of workers to urban areas where jobs were more plentiful (Henriques & Patel, 2004). In terms of income disparities, NAFTA did not have the equalizing effect that had been predicted. Former World Bank chief economist Joseph Stiglitz (2004) reported that during NAFTA's first decade (1994-2004) income disparities between Mexico and the United States actually *grew* by 10.6%. Additionally, communal landholdings (ejidos) were privatized and sold, displacing subsistence farmers and their families who worked the land (Hu-Dehart, 2003). The deep poverty that resulted placed tremendous migratory pressure on those affected to find an alternative means of providing for their families (Henriques & Patel, 2004; Stiglitz, 2004).

The effect of NAFTA on corn growers has been particularly harsh. Corn has been a staple crop in Mexico for thousands of years. Its production accounts for 60% of cultivated land and the employment of 3 million farmers, or 40% of Mexicans employed in agriculture (Henriques & Patel, 2004). Direct consumption of corn, primarily in the form of the tortilla, accounts for one-third of the country's caloric intake (Zahniser & Coyle, 2004). Since the implementation of NAFTA, U.S. subsidized corn exports to Mexico have increased by 240 percent compared 1984-93 levels (Zahniser & Coyle, 2004). In 2004-2005 alone, Mexico was second only to Japan in U.S. corn imports (Llana, 2006).

The dumping of U.S. subsidized corn onto the Mexican market creates an unlevel playing field for small farmers in poor regions who cannot with the vastly different means of production and resulting prices that subsidized products often create. With less than half the amount of government subsidies available to them than those received by U.S. farmers, Mexican corn growers are at an immediate disadvantage in a market where their domestic product competes with corn produced more cheaply and efficiently through mechanization, pest control and higher rates of government assistance (Henriques & Patel, 2004).

For more wealthy Mexicans and for many farmers on the northern side of the border, the entrance of subsidized U.S. corn in the Mexican markets is seen as a positive development. The U.S. National Corn Grower's Association does not see this move as a direct threat to Mexican farmers, because the majority of U.S. exported corn is the yellow variety used for livestock feed, not the white corn preferred by Mexicans for consumption (Llana, 2006). In fact, says the United States Department of Agriculture (USDA), this U.S.-produced yellow corn is supplementing Mexican livestock production and fostering the development of Mexican hog and poultry industries (Zahniser & Coyle, 2004). Additionally, competitive farmers who have access to land and credit have fared well by shifting from corn production to more lucrative commodities (Henriques & Patel, 2004).

But critics point out that the competitive edge of U.S. corn producers has created a market in which it is nearly impossible for Mexican farmers to compete, particularly the subsistence farmers who make up 45% of all corn-growers in Mexico (Henriques & Patel, 2004, p. 5). Most significantly, production of corn in the United States is vastly different than in Mexico. For instance, it takes an average of 17.8 labor days to produce a ton of corn in Mexico compared to 1.2 hours in the United States (ibid, pp. 3-4). Additionally, 80% of corn fields in Mexico are rain-fed plots frequently located on steep slopes with poor soil that are inaccessible to machinery even if farmers had the capital to invest in modern equipment (ibid, p. 4). Even more devastating are the large subsidies available to U.S. farmers, allowing their corn to be sold 15-20% under the cost of production and thus lowering the price of *all* corn in Mexico, not just the yellow variety (Llana, 2006).

Agribusiness in Mexico saw an advantage to large imports of lower-quality U.S. corn that could be used in sweeteners, processed foods and flour. The pressure these industries placed on the Mexican government resulted in imports even larger than NAFTA's quotas, further hurting the ability of Mexican producers to compete (Wise, 2003). Additionally, the Mexican government cut its own tariff revenues for crops such as corn and beans by allowing tariff-free imports above quota long before the agreed-upon fifteen-year adjustment period (Carlsen, 2003). In fact, within four years of NAFTA's passage, tariffs were eliminated altogether for corn and dry bean imports (Hufbauer & Schott, 2005).

Circumstances like these prompted poor farm families to develop survival strategies, including migration to larger Mexican cities or into the United States (Henriques & Patel, 2004; Llana, 2006; Medrano, 2005).

Migration after NAFTA and Official Policy Responses

The passage of NAFTA opened the U.S./Mexico border to the flow of commercial goods, but not to the flow of labor between the two countries.[11] However, critics say, pre-existing official barriers for labor have not stopped thousands of Mexican citizens from entering the United States in search of work. According to *Washington Post* reporter Harold Meyerson (2006, p. A19), NAFTA "could not have been more precisely crafted to increase immigration."

Ironically, one of the Clinton Administration's justifications for intervening after the 1994 Mexican peso crisis was that if the situation worsened further, U.S. borders could be flooded with even greater numbers of unauthorized migrants (Whitt, 1996). "There will be less illegal immigration because more Mexicans will be able to support their children by staying home" Clinton told Americans in 1993 (Meyerson, 2006, p. A19). Both Mexico and the United States shared this vision that NAFTA would initiate job growth in Mexico, thus lessening the number of migrants trying to illegally enter the United States in search of work (Mowad, 2006).

Instead of creating adequate jobs within Mexico's borders, NAFTA's provisions converged with other challenging factors for the Mexican population that made immigration into the United States (both legal and illegal) appear an attractive option, despite potential risks (Oliver, 2007). For middle to high-income families, legal immigration was a way to escape becoming a target for kidnapping, violent crimes, and other existing socio-political problems. For poorer families, jobs in *el norte*[12] made illegal immigration a viable alternative to the unemployment and poor economic conditions at home (ibid). The benefits produced under NAFTA were not distributed evenly throughout the Mexican population (Villarreal & Cid, 2008), and David Bacon (2004) argues that the population that has paid the highest price of trade liberalization under NAFTA is the country's poor. Research on sending communities seems to reaffirm this finding. Data from a 2005 study show that migration had expanded beyond traditional sending states in central parts of Mexico to include southern states as well (Kochhar, 2005) where the majority of Mexico's corn and bean crops are grown.

Net migration from Mexico to the United States nearly tripled during NAFTA's first ten years (NACLA, 2005).

It is critical to note that NAFTA alone is not fully responsible for post-1994 emigration trends out of Mexico and into the United States. In fact, two critical historical factors affecting immigration from Mexico into the United States are the interdependence of the two countries' labor markets and the social networks between Mexican families in the United States and those in Mexico – neither of which was significantly affected by provisions of NAFTA (Oliver, 2007). However, the implementation of NAFTA's neoliberal economic trade policies in conjunction with domestic economic, social and political problems created a situation in which many segments of the Mexican population felt emigration was the most viable solution. The trade agreement was implemented amidst an already challenging social and political environment in Mexico, and one in which there was insufficient work available for an expanding Mexican labor force (Alvarado, 2008). Effects of the policy were likely exacerbated by additional "push" factors that included this existing unemployment as well as crime, ongoing distrust of and frustration with the Mexican government and general socio-political unrest (Oliver, 2007). Thus, argues Oliver, even if NAFTA performed up to its original expectations, the trade agreement was unable to produce both the economic and personal security that might have prevented immigration into the United States. Even if long-term gains from the treaty's provisions might one day reduce the number of illegal immigrants into the United States, Oliver says, its short-term effect has "significantly contributed to the wave of (mostly illegal) Mexican immigration in the United States" from 1994-2006 (ibid, p. 61).

"Funnel Effect" Legislation and Deaths in the Desert

By late 1994, the number of migrants crossing the U.S. border illegally was rising, as was public sentiment in the U.S. favoring immigration restrictions and boundary enforcements (Nevins, 2002). Despite the fact that NAFTA was opening borders to the trade of commercial goods, migration was treated as a *border security* issue rather than an *economic* issue related to labor market regulation (Andreas, 2006). With the rise in illegal immigration came a corresponding increase in the intensity of attempts at border enforcement by U.S. authorities (Orrenius, 2001). In an effort to curb the influx of unauthorized border crossers, the U.S. government instituted a series of border enforcement policies designed to stop the flow at the busiest crossing points.

In 1995, the U.S./Mexico border was one of the most asymmetrical in the world in terms of economic disparities from one side to the other (Ganster, 1995). At the same time, however, the U.S. government began earnest efforts to stop the flow of unauthorized migrants by allocating large sums of money for the fortification of the border. Programs such as Operation Hold-the-Line in El Paso (1993), Operation Gatekeeper in San Diego (1994), Operation Safeguard in central Arizona (1995) and Operation Río Grande in south Texas (1997) were designed to fortify traditional crossing areas in an effort to prevent illegal entry through these popular zones (Cornelius, 2005).

The "prevention through deterrence" approach carried out by federal government agencies *was* successful in reducing the numbers of unauthorized crossers in the most heavily trafficked areas. In the case of Operation Gatekeeper, security enhancements, including the construction of a border fence separating San Diego from Tijuana, reduced migrant flows in that sector by more than 75% in the two years following its implementation (U.S. Customs, 2010).

However, Operation Gatekeeper and similar policies had an additional effect – that of channeling the flows of migrant crossers away from urban zones into more dangerous desert regions. Migrants who choose or who are directed through these more remote, less heavily patrolled desert routes face life-threatening dangers such as extreme desert temperatures, dehydration, poisonous animals/insects, and disorientation that often leads them far off their intended course. As a result, since the implementation of these programs, the number of unauthorized border crossing deaths has risen dramatically (McCombs, 2009, May 17; Ufford-Chase, 2005a). Conservative estimates conclude that a total of 3,600 bodies were found on U.S. soil between 1995 and 2005 (Nevins, 2006, p. 1). In total, more migrants died trying to cross from Mexico into the United States between 1995 and 2005 than the number of people who were killed in the World Trade Center attacks on September 11, 2001 (Cornelius, 2005).

The Tucson Sector is currently considered "ground zero" for the influx of hundreds of thousands of migrants from Mexico, Central America and South America (Rubio-Goldsmith et al., 2006). The number of crossers through this corridor has increased drastically over the past two decades (ibid). By 2006 thirty-six percent of all border apprehensions took place there (Department, 2008). In December 2010, Tucson Sector was described by Randy Hill, Chief Patrol Agent, as "the busiest Sector in the country in both illegal alien apprehensions and marijuana seizures" (Department, 2010). According to unofficial Border Patrol statistics for fiscal year 2010, Tucson Sector was responsible for

47 percent of total apprehensions – the highest percentage in a decade (Department, 2011).

Because of the Tucson sector's current designation as the leading corridor for illegal entry (Cornelius, 2005, p. 783) it is not surprising that the majority of migrant deaths also take place there. These deaths within the Tucson Sector have reflected changing trends in immigration patterns. Fatalities in the Tucson Sector were minimal in the late 1980s and early 1990s. However, after restrictive policies and militarization were implemented along the border in the mid-1990s, the death toll skyrocketed. A recent study by the Binational Migration Institute (BMI) as well as a statement by the U.S. Government Accountability Office (GAO) concluded that the "funnel effect" resulting from federal legislation beginning in the mid-1990s has been the primary factor underlying the dramatic increase in known unauthorized border crossing deaths in the Tucson Sector (Rubio-Goldsmith et al., 2006, p. 58). Most of these border crossing-related deaths were the result of heat exposure.

The agency charged with handling and processing the bodies of migrants who perish in their attempt to cross into the United States from Mexico through the Border Patrol's Tucson Sector is the Pima County Medical Examiner's Office (PCMEO) in Tucson, Arizona. Conservative estimates state that this office processes approximately 90% of all the known unauthorized migrant deaths in Arizona's Tucson Sector (Rubio-Goldsmith et al., 2006). A study carried out by the BMI documents nine known unauthorized border crosser deaths handled by PCMEO in 1990. But in 2005, the number increased to 201 – more than twenty times the original figure. Total cases handled by the office from 1990-1999 totaled 125; the number of cases from 2000-2005 was 802 (ibid).

These figures revealed in the BMI study do not match the official death counts of the Border Patrol. The BMI report, published in October of 2006, revealed serious discrepancies between official Border Patrol death counts and counts by various human rights organizations. Authors stated the reason for the differences in numbers was due to a very narrow set of criteria used by Border Patrol to classify a fatality as an unauthorized border crosser (UBC) death.[13] Because of the limited criteria, they said, many bodies were left out of counts, such as those found on reservation lands or those decomposed to the point of being only skeletal remains.[14]

Local media also complained that Border Patrol statistics of unauthorized border crosser deaths were inaccurate or incomplete. An analysis by the *Tucson Citizen* newspaper found that Border Patrol had undercounted the number of deaths from October 2002 through July 2003 by 43% (LoMonaco, 2003). *The Arizona Republic* newspaper gathered information from medical examiners offices and foreign consulates in 2004 and concluded that 219 people had died that fiscal year – a figure significantly higher than the Border Patrol's 172 (González & Carroll, 2005). "It's not that officials in Washington, D.C. have the information and are refusing to give it out" said Susan Carroll, then reporter for *The Arizona Republic.* "They don't track all the deaths. To arrive at a more accurate count, journalists have to take on an independent watchdog role and pull together the statistics from medical examiners, foreign consulates, and law enforcement along the border" (Carroll, 2006, pp. 48-49).

Border Patrol representative Gustavo Soto said the agency has since corrected the practices that led to such discrepancies in statistics. For example, skeletal remains are now included in the official count. According to Soto, the disparity in numbers was due to the fact that Border Patrol used to count only those bodies the agency found – not bodies brought to the Pima County Medical Examiner's Office for processing that had been found by other law enforcement agencies or by individuals. Now, he says, the agency works more closely with the Medical Examiner's Office and other law enforcement agencies to reach a more accurate count of total UBC deaths.[15]

This change in Border Patrol counts was seen as a step forward by media and activists alike, as have other changes that have improved the relationship between the agency and the public. In 2004, the *location* of migrant deaths was considered a national security position, and Border Patrol and other federal authorities declined to release that information (Calderon, 2007). However, in 2007 the agency changed its policy and made the information public. Statistics about migrant deaths which used to be difficult to access are now sent directly to media and civic groups that request them.[16]

However, certain tensions still remain. In 2007, humanitarian groups and news agencies were angered by an announcement by the U.S. Border Patrol that it would no longer provide death and apprehension statistics on a daily basis. Instead, the information would be most often released as a part of the Border Patrol's end-of-month reports. The editorial board of the *Tucson Citizen* criticized the move, saying federal public records laws require public information to be made available in a timely manner, and that with increased national attention on border security the Border Patrol has an obligation to provide the public with more information – not less (Tucson, 2007).

Additionally, both media and civic groups acknowledge that death counts only provide statistics about the numbers of bodies actually found. They point out that decomposition in the desert occurs very rapidly due to harsh conditions, that the vast expanses of desert leave many areas unexplored, and that many missing persons reports are filed by families in Mexico whose relatives headed north across the border and are never heard from again. Given these facts, it is likely that the number of unauthorized border crosser deaths is actually much higher than any current figures show.

Statistics and indicators such as these prevent any obfuscation of the shortcomings – and tragic consequences – resulting from recent border policies. Despite mounting evidence of a malfunctioning system, the federal government continues to allocate more money and/or resources each year for border enforcement. National Guard troops were stationed along sections of the border in 2006[17] and again in 2010[18], and subsequent legislation paved the way for construction of a 700-mile protective fence. By April 2011, 646 miles of various types of barriers had been erected along the southwestern border, nearly half of them in Arizona (Associated, 2011, April 29). In spite of this, the State Legislature of Arizona created a fund in 2011 soliciting private donations to pay for fencing along the additional 82 miles of border that still lacks a protective physical structure (Lacey, 2011).

Finally, policies that have emphasized securing the border have had an additional effect on immigration. What were once circular migration patterns among undocumented migrants have now become more permanent settlement patterns in the United States. Fortification and militarization of the border have made it too risky for those who successfully make it to the United States to journey home if they think they may someday wish to return northward. Furthermore, few can afford the costly human smuggling fees charged for each crossing.[19] Finally, given the rising death tolls, many already in the United States feel that the risks associated with returning home and then re-entering the country through the desert are just too great. Thus, a policy designed to reduce the numbers of unauthorized migrants has actually succeeded in encouraging many to remain within U.S. borders.

To summarize, border policies and immigration legislation since the mid-1990s have not only been largely ineffective in reducing the flows of migrants who enter without authorization, but they have created unprecedented dangers for potential migrants. Rather than deter migrants from crossing, the effects of these policies have led to large scale migrant deaths and injuries, creating what 2006 Senate Majority Leader Bill Frist called a humanitarian crisis (Rubio-Goldsmith et al., 2006) and what Centers for Disease Control & Prevention researchers have termed a "major public health issue" (Sapkota et al., 2006, p. 1).

Perhaps the greatest irony in this tragedy is that the number of persons attempting to enter the United States without documentation increased drastically in spite of massive efforts to prevent their successful crossing. Border security expenditures quintupled between 1993 and 2004, from $750 million to $3.8 billion, and nearly tripled *again* between 2004 and 2009, when the proposed budget for Customs and Border Protection reached $10.94 billion (U.S. Customs, 2008). The number of Border Patrol agents tripled to over 11,000 between 1993 and 2004 (Cornelius, 2005). Yet, in spite of these efforts, the Pew Hispanic Center estimated that as of March 2008 there were 11.9 million unauthorized immigrants living in the United States (Passel & Cohn, 2008), and 11.2 million as of March 2010 (Passel & Cohn, 2011). It is estimated that 80-85% of the Mexicans who came to the United States between 1995 and 2005 were undocumented (Binford, 2005).

Reflections on U.S. Approaches to Mexican Immigration

If the effectiveness of administrative agencies created to manage Mexican immigration is measured by their ability to balance the sentiment of anti-immigrant public factions with economic labor needs, then it can be said that the official Bracero Era (1942-1964) was a period of success. Although the program was not without problems, the INS and other federal agencies found creative ways to sidestep laws, overlook illegal immigration trends, and grant employers the labor they demanded while at the same time keeping public criticism of the program to a manageable level. Thus, employer demands were satisfied while public criticism was appeased with periodic efforts to "crack down" on the problem of illegal immigration.

Operation Wetback (1954) is perhaps the greatest example of a government response to public demands that official action be taken to send unauthorized migrants back home. As a public relations campaign, the effort was brilliant. Due to both its own actions and the decision of many migrants to return home voluntarily rather than face legal or political consequences in the United States, the U.S. government was able to claim victory in its effort to remove hundreds of thousands of "illegals" from U.S. soil. Then, by simply replacing unauthorized migrants with legal braceros, the government successfully kept the labor needs of growers in balance with the desire of Mexican workers to find employment in the United States.

The publicity generated by Operation Wetback served an important function in controlling the fears of the American public. The federal government, through widely disseminated reports of its "roundups of wetbacks," crafted an image of itself as a strong, competent force that was in control of immigration issues. This was particularly critical during a time when Cold War fears inspired paranoia about foreigners, and when nationalist sentiment was on the rise.

If the effectiveness of federal agencies is measured in terms of preventing illegal immigration, however, then nearly all of the policies and programs that have been implemented since the early part of the twentieth century would be considered failures. Nearly every new law that has been passed or policy that has been implemented to restrict illegal immigration into the United States has been followed by a rise in the number of unauthorized migrants entering the country. Both the Bracero Program and IRCA, for example, exacerbated the very problems they were designed to solve by actually encouraging unauthorized workers to come to the United States. Not all of these spikes take place immediately, but eventually the tensions of economic imbalance between the U.S. and Mexico combines with the dynamic of labor needs in the U.S. and availability of laborers from Mexico to overwhelm formal efforts aimed at stopping the flows. Cultural and familial ties formed by migrants who have relatives in the United States have also contributed to increases in the numbers of unauthorized entrants. As immigration scholars continually remind us, immigration is a cultural, not just a political or economic phenomenon.

Finally, while NAFTA was not an immigration policy, it did have an effect on Mexican migration patterns into the United States. Although Mexico's economic problems were largely in place before the signing of NAFTA, the treaty has in many ways intensified their negative effects for specific sectors of the Mexican population. Mexico originally saw its NAFTA-inspired trade concessions as necessary steps toward developing a stronger economy and reducing poverty. More than a decade of NAFTA policies, however, has shown that while NAFTA has produced many gains for Mexico's economy in general, its effects on already poor populations has intensified their struggles to earn a living.

Furthermore, the simultaneous institution of NAFTA and militarization of the U.S. border seems to have created additional, unforeseen problems. As the economic situation (particularly for the poor) and the rights of workers grew more dismal at home, many Mexicans saw no other option but to cross illegally into the United States. New border security policies pushed those migrants from traditional entry points near larger cities to remote, desert crossing areas where increasing numbers of migrants lost their lives.

Ironically, one of the greatest indicators of failure in terms of restricting illegal immigration flows is that so many individuals have continued to attempt to cross into the United States at a time when more resources than ever before have been poured into border security and enforcement measures. Starting with border militarization efforts such as "Operation Hold-the-Line" and "Operation Gatekeeper" in the mid-1990s, federal resources allocated toward border enforcement have risen to unprecedented levels.[20] Yet despite these huge allocations, efforts to restrict and reduce illegal flows were largely unsuccessful in the early part of the new millennium (Cornelius, 2004; Montgomery, 2005).

Recent years have seemed to indicate a change in that trend. Official Border Patrol statistics for fiscal year 2010 showed a seventy percent reduction in the number of individuals apprehended while attempting to cross the border compared to fiscal year 2000 (Fisher, 2011). However, even with the dramatic reduction, nearly half a million people were still apprehended in 2010 (ibid), and that figure does not represent those who cross successfully without being caught.

For some, statistics pointing to lower numbers of apprehensions serve as proof that border security measures work in stemming illegal immigration. Officials such as Pinal County Sheriff Paul Babeu, Senator John McCain and various border patrol personnel, among others, have credited construction of fences and military presence at the border with a reduction in migrant flows (Jeffrey, 2010; Wood, 2008). Recent government data citing fewer persons living in United States illegally seem to support that assertion. According to the Department of Homeland Security, the number of unauthorized immigrants in this country dropped from an estimated 11.8 million in 2007 to 10.8 million in 2009 (Hoefer, Rytina & Baker, 2011). Similarly, Pew Hispanic Center research estimates that unauthorized immigrants in the United States totaled 12 million in 2007, but only 11.1 million and 11.2 million in 2009 and 2010, respectively (Passel & Cohn, 2011). Experts maintain, however, that any declines are likely the result of a combination of factors rather than one single effort or circumstance, and that enforcement alone does not seem to be driving unauthorized migrants back home (Preston, 2011). Other likely factors for their decreased presence include lack of employment due to the U.S. recession, (Passel & Cohn, 2011), restrictive state laws such as Arizona's controversial SB 1070 (Fischer, 2011) and similar legislative efforts in other states that would make life difficult for persons with illegal status (Clark, 2011). Additionally, an increase in the number of immigrant visas issued by the United States to Mexican citizens in the years 2008-2010 has given Mexicans greater opportunity than ever before to enter legally with proper papers in hand (U.S. Department of State, 2010).

Nevertheless, while total numbers of unauthorized crossers have dropped, the number of migrants still traversing the Mexico/U.S. border is significant. In spite of life-threatening dangers, increased smuggling fees and growing awareness of deaths in the desert, traffic in remote border regions has continued to remain high. Hopes of finding jobs or reuniting with families drive many to make the perilous trek. In the words of one Mexican migrant, "If the economy is bad in the United States, it's worse in Mexico... .The economy in the United States is always better" (McCombs, 2009, April 19). Taking action by journeying through a desolate desert is deemed preferable to remaining in a stagnant environment with few jobs or opportunities. Unfortunately, scores have died making the effort.

Civil society organizations frustrated with federal policy have observed the situation on the border and stepped in to take action on their own. Groups as ideologically disparate as the Minutemen Civil Defense Corps (MCDC) and Humane Borders share one sentiment in common: current immigration policy is not working. The system is broken and needs reform. Members of MCDC argue that reform should require the upholding of federal law to prevent unlawful persons from entering the country (The Official, 2007) while humanitarian organizations and religious groups call for comprehensive immigration reform that addresses deeper social issues of family unity, economic inequality and human rights (Humane, n.d.; No More, n.d.; Interfaith, 2005). Voices on all sides of the debate have stirred the interest and concern of the public, and sentiments both sympathetic to and opposed to the unauthorized migrant have caused immigration concerns to rise toward the top of the national political agenda.

Immigration scholar Peter Andreas argues that the expansion of border policing in the past decade has been less about deterring border crossers and more about politically re-crafting the image of the border to reaffirm the state's authority over its territory. He points to the clandestine labor market that serves as the impetus for current illegal immigration trends, and argues that "[t]he current immigration policy debate remains conveniently afflicted by historical amnesia" (Andreas, 2006, p.68).

Amnesia or not, the status of current immigration policy is not reflective of a successful system. Increasing amounts of money are being spent on deterrence, yet undocumented persons continue to cross the border in surprisingly large numbers. Pew Hispanic Center studies estimate that each year between 2002 and 2006, half a million unauthorized immigrants entered the United States (Meissner et al, 2006). According to Mexico's National Commission for Human Rights, "only about 60,000 Mexican nationals immigrate to the U.S. each year with their documentation in order" (La Comisión, 2007, p. 5).[21]

Busses and vanloads of hopeful crossers making their way from Altar, Sonora (Mexico) to Sasabe, Arizona each day defy claims by federal authorities that greater investments in border deterrence and prevention will keep unauthorized border-crossers out of the United States. The migrants themselves know better, and they are willing to risk their lives to take the chance of successfully making the trip. These migrants are proof enough that if any policy is to be successful in curbing illegal immigration, it will have to acknowledge the human lives and needs of those travelers, and the reasons they are willing to risk so much to make so little.

Until the foci of domestic policies on both sides of the border are realigned to consider the well-being of all people, including the impoverished, the gap between Mexico's rich and poor will continue to increase and the country will lose its most valuable resource – citizens who are forced to emigrate in search of a better life. Inherently, it is the combination of economics, social ties and immigration-related policies that most influences migration patterns. As pushes and pulls continue to draw people toward jobs and opportunities, issues of identity, citizenship, and national security in the receiving country present their own challenges to those who feel threatened by the migratory movement. In the words of Harold Meyerson of *The Washington Post* (2006, p. A19), "So long as the global economy is designed, as NAFTA was, to keep workers powerless, Mexican desperation and American anger will only grow. Forget the fence. We need a new rulebook for the world."

Notes

[1] Those who do not want to risk desert crossings often pay higher fees to be smuggled through official ports of entry, often by being concealed inside a vehicle or by using false documentation to pass through. For more information on the type and nature of human smuggling, see the extended interview with Wayne Cornelius at Mexico: Crimes at the Border (2008, May 27). *Frontline World, PBS.* Retrieved March 12, 2010 from http://www.pbs.org/frontline world/stories/mexico704.

[2] Ejidos are communal lands, usually used for agricultural purposes, in Mexico.

[3] This terminology, while controversial in today's context, was the legal definition used in the early part of the twentieth century to describe non-citizens whose presence in the United States was not officially authorized.

[4] Actually, the Bracero Program was not officially endorsed until April 29, 1943, when Congress passed Public Law #45. By this time, however, the program had already been operating for seven months and few people paid attention to the formal passage of the law. In the words of researcher Kitty Calavita, "The Bracero Program was born virtually overnight and with remarkably little fanfare" (1992, p. 18).

[5] However, the terms 'wetback' and 'Mexican' were often used as a general racial stereotype to describe people of Hispanic descent *regardless* of their legal status. This made life very difficult for legitimate Mexican American citizens, who were subjected to discriminatory actions as well (Ngai, 2004).

[6] Under the initial terms of the Bracero Program agreed upon on April 4, 1942 (before Congress officially endorsed the program), the Mexican government was granted certain rights in its representation of Mexican workers. Under what was termed a collective bargaining situation, braceros were to be paid the same as domestic workers with a minimum wage of thirty cents an hour, and employers from Texas were deemed ineligible for the program because of a history of abuse and discrimination against Mexican workers there (Calavita, 1992). However, terms included in the passage of Public Law 45 on April 29, 1943 took the bilateralism out of the original bracero agreement and lessened the influence of the Mexican government to help oversee the program. Additional changes in subsequent years further eroded the role of Mexican authorities to regulate the treatment of braceros in the United States.

[7] This happened largely through the passage of the 1990 Immigration Act.

[8] Individuals from rural areas, often used to refer to farmers or peasantry.

[9] It is somewhat ironic that the very technology that, in essence, symbolizes the growing digital and information divides between Mexico's rich and poor, was precisely the medium through which Marcos garnered international support for the peasants of Chiapas. The peasants themselves would have no access to such technology or means of communication; it was only through the application of such communication channels by Marcos that their plight was publicized worldwide.

[10] Calculating precise rates of employment (and unemployment) in any developing country has always been problematic due to such factors as limited channels in which to exchange job-related information and large rural sectors of the population that may be self-employed or employed in agricultural work. In fact, the very definition of unemployment in developing countries can pose a challenge to researchers. For more information, see Byrne & Strobl, 2004.

[11] In fact, the issue of labor migration is not addressed at all in the actual wording of the agreement (Bean, 1997).

[12] "The North," referring to the United States.

[13] The study lists the following criteria as necessary for inclusion in Border Patrol statistics of unauthorized border crosser deaths: 1) the death must occur during furtherance of an illegal activity 2) the death must occur within a specific "target zone" specified by the Border Safety Initiative (BSI). This zone includes nine of the twenty Border Patrol Sectors. 3) if the death occurs

outside the BSI target zone, to be included in statistics the Border Patrol must have been directly involved in the case.

[14] In such a case, Border Patrol would not be able to prove how the death occurred or that the deceased was an unauthorized border crosser and not a citizen of the United States.

[15] G. Soto, United States Border Patrol: Tucson Sector Public Affairs Office (personal interview, May 23, 2007).

[16] R. Hoover, personal interview (February 21, 2008).

[17] Under President George Bush's Operation Jump Start, as many as 6,000 National Guard troops were deployed to the border from 2006-2008. The troops, not authorized to make arrests, filled many administrative and clerical roles in addition to helping build roads and infrastructure in border areas.

[18] In the fall of 2010, President Obama sent approximately 1,200 National Guard troops to the U.S.-Mexico border. Nearly half were stationed in Arizona.

[19] The price of hiring a coyote, or human smuggler tripled to $1500-$2000 U.S. dollars per person during the period from roughly 1993 to 2003 (Cornelius, 2004). In 2008, the average cost of crossing the Mexico/U.S. border was nearly $3000 U.S. dollars (Mexican Migration Project, 2009).

[20] For instance, the expenditures for border enforcement have quintupled from $750 million in 1993 to $3.8 billion in 2004 and $10.2 billion in 2008 (Cornelius, 2005; U.S. Customs, 2007).

[21] Although nowhere near the half a million figure, the number of visas issued to Mexican nationals has increased slightly since 2007. For more information on the types and numbers of visas, please see the U.S. Department of State 2010 Report of the Visa Office, found at http://www.travel.state.gov/visa/statistics/statistics5240.html.

4

Framing the Border: Boundaries, Illegality, and Civic Engagement

"Before I built a wall I'd ask to know
What I was walling in or walling out"
Robert Frost, Mending Wall (1914)

It's a symbol of division. A reassurance of security. A representation of fear. A medium of artistic and political expression. An enormous waste of taxpayer money. A successful law enforcement expenditure.

It is a sounding board of sorts for the varied voices of the immigration debate. Exactly how the border fence is viewed depends in large part on how it is framed.

Border fence separating San Diego, USA, and Tijuana, MX. Coffins displaying the yearly migrant mortalities have been placed side by side along the fence. January 2006 (Eastman photo)

Framing and Its Role in Immigration Discourse

What exactly is framing? While the concept has taken on slightly different meanings in different disciplines, frames are most broadly defined as "principles of selection, emphasis and presentation composed of little tacit theories about what exists, what happens, and what matters" (Gitlin, 1980, p. 6). The term originated with Erving Goffman, who defined a frame as "schemata of interpretation" that aids in the perception, identification and understanding of an occurrence (1974, p. 21). Viewed another way, frames are the structures that surround a communicative message, indicating what factors within that message should stand out as most important or most noteworthy[1].

Perhaps even more influential than the on-the-ground actions undertaken by civil society organizations along the Arizona/Sonora border are the frames they utilize to define the focal points of the current immigration debate. These frames, disseminated to the general public through media coverage of the groups' activities, go on to influence public sentiment and understanding far from the actual border. The frames perpetuate larger, deeper ideologies about what borders represent, what constitutes "belonging" in terms of legality and illegality and what place individuals without official documentation have in U.S. society.[2] Some frames resonate more effectively and deeply with the general public than others due to the nature of the frames themselves as well as the contemporary context in which they are reproduced – in this case a post–Sept. 11 context in which national security is foremost in the minds of many U.S. citizens. Furthermore, among the sectors of society that choose to become actively involved in the immigration issue, frames are sustained and even strengthened as members of activist groups seek out, identify with, and are galvanized by media sources that reinforce their pre-existing beliefs.

The study of framing processes and their influence on social movements has gained increasing currency in sociological studies. One recent example is the research by Kathleen Staudt on framing strategies used by human rights activists and feminist activists protesting the femicides and domestic violence of Ciudad Juárez (2008). Social movement leaders often utilize collective action frames which, in addition to creating meaning and helping recipients make sense of an issue, mobilize adherents and garner support for the cause in question (Snow & Benford, 1988). Prognostic and motivational elements may be incorporated as well to emphasize human agency, or the ability of individuals to change the circumstances of the issue at hand (ibid). In terms of the immigration issue, the different ways collective action frames are used by civil society organizations in southern Arizona help to explain why various populations across the United States have reacted so emphatically to immigration and border-related reports. At the same time that they present a perception about the current status of immigration, these frames offer remedies, providing an impetus for involvement to those willing to move from internalization of an idea to action.

While there are as many frames as there are nuances and understandings of the word immigration, specific master frames (Benford & Snow, 2000) guide the messages of civil society groups along the border. In general terms, both Humane Borders and No More Deaths rely on master frames focused on rights (Valocchi, 1996; Williams & Williams, 1995) and injustice (Gamson, Fireman & Rytina, 1982) to explain the current situation in southern Arizona. These master frames "fit" the two groups partly because they are broad and inclusive enough to be culturally resonant to both groups within the present historical setting (Swart, 1995). The Minuteman Civil Defense Corps, on the other hand, tends to use more oppositional master frames (Coy & Woehrle, 1996) and to a smaller degree master frames related to the right of exercising choice (Davies, 1999) to relay their messages about immigration. Each of these master frames encompasses ideas about the role of borders, the notion of illegality, and the role of an engaged citizenry. They have united certain populations as effectively as they have divided others. The frames serve two purposes: they define the civil society organizations and their calls to action on the immigration issue, and they serve to attract support from members of the general public who share or are willing to adopt similar master frames.

How do individuals who do not live near the border adopt such frames? In part through media reports of these groups and their often controversial activities. Organizations like Humane Borders, No More Deaths and the Minuteman Civil Defense Corps can function as "pressure groups" that utilize mass media for purposes of constructing realities and establishing frames of reference, (Edelman, 1977, p. 51; Scheufele, 1999) – in this case, about the immigration issue. That is not to imply that media professionals pander to the press releases, calls, faxes and encouragement of any of these civil groups. On the contrary, media professionals must determine for themselves what the "reality" of the border is and how they will present it to the public. In essence, they select their own frames. However, the very nature of the three groups being studied and the ideas they wish to promote are inherently intertwined with the groups' activities. These endeavors, intentionally or unintentionally, have drawn attention from numerous sources, including media. It is nearly impossible, for example, to report on the Minuteman Civil Defense Corps without mentioning that the group's primary objective is to secure America's borders and prevent illegal entry. That frame, which automatically insinuates that national boundaries are presently insecure and require additional defenses, affects the way media report on their activities and consequently how media consumers perceive the border.

Likewise, a story about No More Deaths would undoubtedly include a humanitarian frame including information about the group's dictum that "humanitarian aid is never a crime," particularly because the events attracting the most media attention to this group have involved volunteers charged with criminal activity for conducting what they interpret as humanitarian acts of compassion. The idea of humanitarian aid, too, provides a frame through which a different set of emotions or opinions is evoked regarding the problems resulting from current immigration policies. Humane Borders, like No More Deaths, draws on frames of altruism and compassion. The group's very name suggests a need to change a border environment that is currently "inhumane," and the efforts of volunteers to place life-saving water in remote desert regions creates a frame that promotes active response to people at risk as opposed to protective responses linked to personal or national security.

What evidence reveals that specific frames about immigration are employed in media reports, and that they are influential to media audiences? Textual and content analysis of media sources is one way to identify the presence of frames. Although the purpose of this study is not to analyze the wide types and frequency of media frames, a textual analysis of articles about the three civil society groups from Arizona's two largest newspapers indicates that immigration-related frames are discernible in coverage of the organizations and their activities. In regard to the influence of the frames, this study does not attempt to quantify the reach or intensity of frames on the general population. However, it does purport that such frames are internalized, adopted and repeated by certain members of the population, particularly those who are motivated to act on their convictions about the immigration issue. Evidence of this lies in the makeup of volunteers for all three organizations being studied. Participation in these groups is not limited to residents of the border region. Each year, thousands of individuals travel to Tucson, AZ from all across the United States to take part in border activities with fellow group members. Some stay for a few days, some stay for years. Sympathizers who are unable to physically come to the border engage in meetings, rallies, or fundraising efforts in their home states to support the organizations they favor. For a good number of these participants, media coverage was the link between themselves and the civil society organizations they joined. During the course of personal interviews, many volunteers cited media reports about the border region as their primary source of information about the current state of immigration and the reason they decided to become involved in one of the organizations trying to make a change in the status quo.

Identifying Movement-Specific Frames

Unlike collective action master frames which paint rather broad generalizations about topics, generic, movement-specific frames serve to narrow concepts of the issue at hand toward more concrete ideas and approaches. In terms of being attractive to media, the issue of immigration is ideal because it covers all three of the generic frames that tend to dominate media discourses: conflict, human interest and economic consequences of a particular issue (deVreese, 2002; Price, Tewksbury & Powers, 1997; Semetko & Valkenburg, 2000). These three frames are vividly apparent in the terminology used by Humane Borders, No More Deaths and the Minuteman Civil Defense Corps to present themselves and the issue of immigration to media. Minuteman Civil Defense Corps members most often frame illegal immigration in terms of conflict, using terminology that presents the unauthorized individuals as threats to society. Humane Borders and No More Deaths, on the other hand, most often use justice frames to further the idea that economic disparities can promote migration. They also rely on humanitarian frames to remind audiences of the commonalities they share with individuals seeking better lives, but lacking official documents to enter the United States.

Why are some frames more effective than others? Partially due to the degree of narrative fidelity they convey.[3] Minuteman Civil Defense Corps (MCDC) members who have been victims of a crime committed by an "illegal alien" relate well to frames that portray unauthorized border crossers as criminals and dangers to society. Those frames hold a high degree of narrative fidelity because personal experience creates a direct connection. Volunteers for No More Deaths or Humane Borders may feel motivated by frames of injustice or compassion because they have either experienced or witnessed unjust situations in their own lives that impacted them. Becoming active in these organizations gives them direct opportunities to not only provide for physical needs of people at risk, but also to advocate for justice in what they feel are unjust policies.

Just as strong as narrative fidelity is the power of empirical credibility to "sell" a frame to an audience. Although not all people have had a direct personal experience that is congruent with a specific frame, most people do feel involved in an issue because of their perceived experience with that issue, often through media consumption as well as the nature of ongoing world events (D'Anjou, 1996; Snow & Benford, 1988). Using the previous example, even if someone has never been the victim of a crime committed by an "illegal alien," internalizing media reports that cite large "illegal" prison populations or that portray border crossers as criminals may foster a perspective equating the frame "border crosser = criminal" with a notion of victimhood. Thus empirical credibility, like narrative fidelity, functions to create connections between audiences and relevant issues presented through deliberately crafted frames.

***

Citizens have gathered. They are fed up with the status quo and want to see changes in immigration policy. What impact can this type of active civil society have on the immigration debate through mediated frames? Why are these frames so important to the wider discussion about immigration? A closer look at two specific border-related issues, together with the histories and theories that have helped form the basis of the organizations' frames of these issues, highlights the complexity of the resulting discourse. Differing theoretical views of borders and notions of legality shape distinct frames used by the three groups being studied and exemplify how issue-specific frames can create alternative dialogs that can then influence public opinion.

Physical Fences:
Framing Borders as a Means of Security

The boundary that separates San Diego, CA from Tijuana, MX represents many different things to many different people, depending on which side of the border – or the border debate – one is currently standing. While reactions to the barrier are varied, what is indisputable is the imposing nature of the fence itself. Where there was once a single strand of cable to serve as a marker between the two countries, there is now a two-layer, and in selected areas a three-layer fence, with space between the sections wide enough for Border Patrol lights, cameras, and surveillance roads (Robbins, 2006). The first section of fence, ten feet high, is made of recycled military airplane landing mats that have been welded together. Just 150 feet away from the primary wall is a second fence, this one fifteen feet high, made of steel mesh and angled sharply at the top to discourage climbing attempts. Finally, another 150 feet away in selected high-traffic areas stands a third chain-link section topped with barbed-wire (Robbins, 2006b).

At one end, the fence rises out of the Pacific Ocean and intersects the popular Imperial Beach. The barrier then crosses fourteen miles of bustling urban sprawl and rolling countryside - traversing hills, valleys and wide fields along the way – and ends up at the foot of the Otay Mountain Range. Completion of the fence required clearing a number of physical and political hurdles. Construction of just the last 3.4 miles of the barrier required filling a valley known as "Smuggler's Gulch" with 5.5 million cubic feet of dirt, raising the total cost of the 14-mile fence to $74 million, or more than $5 million per mile (Pomfret, 2006).

Imperial Beach section of the San Diego/Tijuana border fence. January 2006 (Eastman photo)

This border fence, built as part of Operation Gatekeeper in the mid-1990s, has been considered a huge success by law enforcement agencies determined to reduce unauthorized immigration through this area.[4] Since the fence was built and additional security enhancements were put into place, apprehensions in the U.S. Border Patrol San Diego Sector declined from 1300 a day in 1996 to roughly 275 a day in 2002 (Nuñez-

Neto & García, 2007). According to government officials, increasing personnel and various forms of security at the most popular urban crossing areas was intended to deter potential migrants from attempting illegal crossings. The Southwest Border Strategy, which included plans known by the names Operation Hold-the-Line (TX), Operation Río Grande (south TX), Operation Gatekeeper (CA), and Operation Safeguard (AZ), was an effort to cut off the most popular crossing areas to those without authorization. This was considered a "prevention through deterrence" approach (Bach, 2005, p. 3; U.S. Border, 1994). Officials felt that the dangers inherent in more remote spaces would thwart attempts at entering the United States through those areas. Journalists who have covered the policy point to early Border Patrol promotional videos in which agents say the rough terrain of the desert would deter potential crossers because of the harsh natural barriers (Frontline, 2004).

But those predictions were wrong. Instead of reducing overall entries of unauthorized migrants into the United States, the fence in San Diego/Tijuana and other border militarization efforts in the 1990s simply pushed determined migrants into more remote, dangerous crossing areas such as the deserts of Arizona. This phenomenon, referred to by scholars as the "funnel effect,"[5] has had major consequences for subsequent border policy. So many border-crossers began appearing on the desert trails of southern Arizona that by April of 2010 the number of Border Patrol agents stationed in the Tucson Sector alone skyrocketed to over 3000,[6] compared with 401 agents in the same sector in 1995 (Marizco, 2005). Additionally, The Pima County Medical Examiner's Office, which handles approximately 90% of all unauthorized border crosser (UBC) remains in the Tucson Sector, examined the corpses of 927 UBCs between 1990 and 2005 (Rubio-Goldsmith et al., 2006). According to the U.S. Government Accountability Office, this reflects at least a 78% increase in known UBC deaths along our country's Southwest border from 1990-2003 (ibid; U.S. GAO, 2006).

This funneling of migrants through the desert has been decried by human rights groups as an inhumane approach to border policy that policy-makers were well aware of when they made the decision to close off urban crossing areas. Even T.J. Bonner, President of the National Border Patrol Council, explained it this way: "Imagine the border as a big, long, skinny balloon. When you squeeze in one part, it comes out in another" (McCombs, 2006, Sept. 25, p. A4). By the late 1990s, it was becoming clear that death counts in the Arizona desert were increasing, and in 2001, Immigration and Naturalization Service[7] reports provided hard documentation that the number of migrant-crossing deaths resulting from extreme heat or extreme cold had risen after implementation of the Southwest Border Strategy (U.S. GAO, 2001). The Border Patrol responded with rescue beacons in the most dangerous desert crossing areas, Border Patrol Search, Trauma and Rescue (BORSTAR) teams, and new databases to collect detailed information about the location of migrant deaths.

Despite these efforts, the number of deaths has continued to grow. With the exception of 2006 and 2008, when the number of border-crossing fatalities dropped slightly,[8] death tolls rose every year between 1998 and 2009 in the Tucson Sector, the Border Patrol's busiest sector.[9] As of February 16, 2011, Border Patrol was unable to provide the number of UBC deaths for fiscal year 2010 which ended September 30, 2010. However, data from the Pima and Cochise County Medical Examiner's Offices (which cover the Tucson Sector) indicate that 2010 deaths reached a record high of 252 (McCombs, 2010, Oct.5). This increase in deaths occurred in spite of the fact that unofficial Border Patrol statistics for fiscal year 2010 show apprehensions down for the sixth straight year in a row, indicating that fewer people are attempting to cross the border (Department, 2011; McCombs, 2011, Feb. 9). Additionally, data from *The Arizona Daily Star* border death database shows that when the number of unauthorized border crosser deaths is compared per 100,000 Border Patrol apprehensions, the risk of dying has never been higher than it was in FY 2010 (McCombs, 2011, Feb. 4). This data supports the argument that current policies, while perhaps discouraging illegal crossing on the whole, have pushed those who do cross into increasingly remote and dangerous desert regions, resulting in unprecedented death tolls. Deputy Chief of the Tucson Sector Robert Boatright, however, attributes the increased death count to more thorough record-keeping and improved methods of recovering bodies (McCombs, 2009, May 17).

The following figure illustrates the number of unauthorized border crosser (UBC) deaths in the Tucson Sector as recorded by both the U.S. Border Patrol and by *The Arizona Daily Star* border death database. As previously noted, there are discrepancies between the death counts of the two sources in part due to a very narrow set of criteria used by Border Patrol to cite UBC deaths. *The Arizona Daily Star* border death database data is collected from Pima and Cochise County Medical Examiner's Offices. These offices are responsible for bodies found in Santa Cruz, Pinal and Pima Counties (all located within the Tucson Sector).

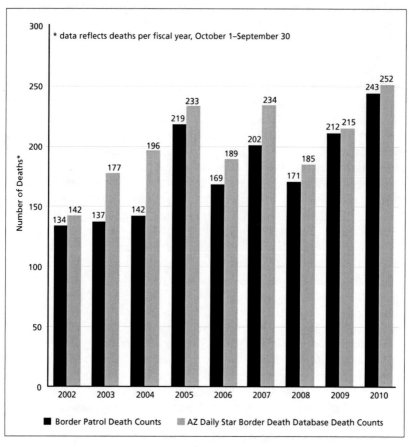

**Figure 4.1 Border Death Statistics for Arizona's Tucson Sector
(Based on remains recovered)**

Humanitarian groups, through frames that emphasize the destructive impact of enforcement efforts on human lives, have argued that not only has increased border enforcement along the Arizona/Sonora line not prevented crossing-related deaths, but it has also created a humanitarian disaster by pushing migrants into more hazardous desert terrain (Humane, 2007; Welch, 2007). Volunteers from the organization Humane Borders have documented the locations of migrant deaths and found that each year from 2000-2007 the distance from a recovered body to a major road has increased (Humane, 2007). Thus, instead of portraying fences and enforcement strategies as means of protecting national borders, they frame them as sources of human suffering. Groups such as these call on officials to revise current policy by providing more *legal* opportunities (through visas and official documentation) for workers to enter the United States. By doing so, they argue, workers who are a vital part of the U.S. economy will be allowed to enter with dignity and protection under a proper system of documentation rather than having to risk their lives crossing through the desert. Furthermore, they say, such a system would reduce the number of migrants who send for their families or choose to stay permanently because under the current system, they cannot afford the coyote[10] fees necessary to make the frequent trips back and forth across the border.

The government, however, has reacted to the new channeling of migrants through the desert with a very different strategy: strengthen the border with more security and more fences.

In September of 2006, Congress passed the Secure Fence Act, authorizing the building of a 700-mile-long double layer fence along one-third of the U.S.-Mexico border.[11] In addition to the physical fence in specified areas (similar to that used in the San Diego area), other portions of the border were to be fortified with vehicle barriers and/or a virtual fence that uses radar, cameras, unmanned aerial vehicles, satellites and other technology to detect crossers[12] (Garreau, 2006). By the end of 2008, the government hoped that 370 miles of fencing and 300 miles of vehicle barriers along the 1,950 mile-long border would be completed (Holstege, 2008, Feb. 10). Roughly 650 miles had been completed by July, 2011 (Johnson, 2011).

Reaction to the fence and the increased enforcement accompanying it has been mixed along the Southwestern border. Some landowners have welcomed fences on their property. They say life is much more peaceful there now that some barriers have been erected (Robbins, 2006). One farmer outside of Mission, TX hopes the eventual border fence will cut down on the number of people running through his land – people he fear may be involved in drug trafficking (Cohen, 2007).

Ranchers south of Tucson, AZ said they were glad to hear of fencing being erected around the tiny border town of Sasabe. They hoped the fence would diminish instances of cut fences, litter, smuggling of drugs, and general feeling of fear among families in the area because of the heavy flow of migrant traffic.[13]

But not everyone is thrilled with the idea of fences being erected, and federal agencies faced many obstacles in trying to implement the Secure Fence Act. Arizona Tribal Chairman Ned Norris Jr., for example, is not necessarily opposed to vehicle barriers or high-tech monitoring towers on Tohono O'odham lands, but he resents the idea that the government could construct a physical fence there. "[H]ave they consulted with us on this permanent 15- to 20- foot iron fence? No. Do they think they are just going to come out here and do that? Not over my dead body," he said (McCombs, 2007, August 19, p. B1).

Some property owners along the Southwestern border were also resistant to the idea of physical fences being built on their properties. In Arizona, California, and Texas, the government prepared 102 court cases against landowners who refused to allow a fence to be built on their property (Feds, 2008). In Texas, federal plans called for 85 miles of fencing and alternative barriers, but these projects were delayed by numerous lawsuits over the government's seizure of private property[14] (Holstege, 2008). The mayor of Brownsville opposed a physical fence because it would hurt the local economy, which depends on tourists from the United States and Mexico. He also worried about how the fence would be interpreted. "Symbolically it's the wrong message to send to our neighbors," he stated (Cohen, 2007, p. 1). Other Texas mayors agreed, and argued that border security does not necessarily have to involve physical fences like those planned near their towns. Laredo Mayor Raùl Salinas said, "I think when you build a wall, it's a wall of shame" (NPR.org, 2007, p. 2). These mayors pushed for other aspects of the border security plan to be implemented, like stadium lighting and paved roads that parallel the Río Grande River. Such improvements would create illuminated thoroughfares that would allow law enforcement to patrol the area in vehicles and increase security without necessitating the construction of divisive fences.

Technological problems have provided the biggest challenges to federal agencies in the Grand Canyon state. Much of Arizona's virtual fence, contracted to Boeing Corporation under the name Project 28, was found to be flawed and in need of replacement almost immediately after Boeing completed the $20 million project (Holstege & Marrero, 2008).

The original hope was that this combination of physical fencing, vehicle barriers, and border security technology would drastically facilitate the identification and apprehension of border-crossers by Border Patrol officers. However, the virtual fence system in particular was riddled with problems. Numerous attempts were made to remedy the problems on a 28-mile test section in the Arizona desert. Nevertheless, after three years and a price tag of over $1 billion, the system was still not working correctly. Plans to complete the border-wide fencing project were cut short in March 2010 when Department of Homeland Security chief Janet Napolitano announced she was freezing funding for the Secure Border Initiative Network program (Robbins, 2010). On January 14, 2011, the Obama administration ended the southern border fence project which had yielded only 53 miles of high-tech fencing[15] at a cost of roughly $1 billion (Powell, 2011) or $15 million per mile according to testimony in congressional hearings (Associated, 2011, January 14). Napolitano added, however, that although plans for the original high-tech fence have been dropped, ongoing border protection plans still include some 700 miles of pedestrian and vehicle fencing, as well as the use of aerial surveillance by unmanned drones (Powell, 2011).

An ironic addendum to the fence-building saga is that shortly after the Secure Fence Act was passed in 2006, a fence-building company in southern California was fined nearly $5 million for hiring unauthorized workers to construct part of the border between San Diego and Baja, Mexico. The company had been warned twice about hiring illegal immigrants, but subsequent checks in later years found many unauthorized persons still working there. The company's attorney said the case proves the need for a guest-worker program (Horsley, 2006).

Are these efforts worth the cost? Will fences be effective? Not fences alone, say both advocates and critics of the barriers. In places like the desert of Arizona, some segments of the border lie as many as 80 miles away from a major road. In areas like this, traditional fences just don't make much sense, says Sean King, a Border Patrol agent who has spent many hours enforcing these vast stretches of desert.[16] Another Tucson Sector agent, Gustavo Soto, agrees that barriers are of little use where there are no roads or infrastructure to support them. "So if you have a wall out there in the desert and no agent to protect it or camera to look at it, if a person just jumps over the wall – I mean, why build it if you can't protect it?"[17] To address this issue, Department of Homeland Security spokesperson Russ Knocke says officials have tried to place the most appropriate barriers in the most appropriate locations, based on terrain, climate and Border Patrol needs in the area (Cohen, 2007). However, former Immigration and Naturalization Service director Doris Meissner says that focusing *only* on fences is the wrong approach to immigration reform; physical or virtual, these barriers are not going to stop determined border-crossers. "The border is not the single answer to the problem of illegal immigration," she stated (Robbins, 2010). Thus, even law enforcement officials frame the idea of fences not as a national security solution, but as tools that are part of a more complex strategy to prevent unauthorized entry into the United States.

It is indisputable that in many sections where fences have been built, the number of migrant crossings has diminished. What is not clear, however, is whether the fences have any effect on the overall numbers of border-crossers considering that many just shift their routes and attempt to cross in other locations. A three week independent investigation along the southern U.S. border conducted by *The Arizona Daily Star* in 2006 concluded that it would take ten times the number of border patrol agents in place (roughly 100,000) to slow crossings across the entire border as effectively as the El Paso and San Diego sectors did in the late 1990s (McCombs, 2006, September 24). And even in these two major urban areas, the walls did not prevent crossings altogether. As more border enforcement personnel were added to Arizona sectors in recent years, some of whom were transferred from San Diego, flows of migrants began to return to the Tijuana/San Diego region. In fact, by 2006, apprehensions in the San Diego Sector had risen once again to nearly 400 per day, making it the second-busiest sector along the border (McCombs, 2006, Sept. 25).

For all the publicity that border fencing has received in recent years, public understanding of the barriers is still somewhat incomplete. Much of the general public came to believe that a single, imposing fence would be built across the entire border (Cohen, 2007). Groups that support sealing off the border such as the Minuteman Civil Defense Corps (MCDC) or American Border Patrol (ABP)[18] advocate construction of a tangible fence, arguing that permanent, physical fencing along the entire border is necessary to keep unauthorized persons out of the United States.[19] Some of these groups, frustrated at the government's pace and approach to constructing physical barriers, have begun building their own border fences on private lands. Their success in framing the idea of fences as a means of fortifying national security has garnered a great deal of public support and financial contributions for such efforts, although reaction to the fences they actually built was largely critical (Boudreau & Shiffman, 2007; Clark, 2007;).

What many do not understand is that the proposed fences were not intended to be the answer to national security. In fact, the fences were never intended to prevent border crossings, says Border Patrol agent

Gustavo Soto.[20] Agents fully recognize that determined individuals will find ways over, under, or through the barriers. In San Diego, a tunnel spanning a half mile was found below the border fence that separates the city from Tijuana[21] (Soto; Pomfret, 2006). While riding along with Border Patrol agent Sean King near Nogales, King pointed out a section of fence on "Hamburger Hill" where every night, a man on the Mexican side is paid to bring his blow torch and cut holes in the fence for smugglers to get through.[22]

Instead of stopping all illegal passage across the border, the border fences are designed to either deter or slow the crossers enough to allow Border Patrol or other law enforcement to be in place, ready to apprehend them once they do breach the barrier. Department of Homeland Security spokesperson Russ Knocke agrees, saying that the fences are particularly useful in this regard in urban areas (Cohen, 2007). Furthermore, added technology along specified areas of the border, including sensors, cameras, and unmanned aerial vehicles give enforcement officers enough warning to know where people are crossing, how many are crossing, and where they are most likely to successfully intersect their route to make an arrest. For example, cameras along a fence in Nogales may pick up activity of people attempting to climb over, giving agents time to position themselves so they can make an apprehension immediately when a crosser scales the fence. "If he is deterred, we have done our job," says agent Gustavo Soto. "If he crosses over and gets arrested right there, we've done our job." Either way, the effectiveness of the fence without agents to patrol it would be minimal at best.

Finding a way to physically fence off access to the United States might be politically popular because it creates the image of a secure boundary, but its effectiveness as an overall border strategy has been called into question. The widespread use of fences and technology as crossing barriers indicates an understanding of the borders as geopolitical boundaries in need of fortification and protection for purposes of control. Not everyone sees them as such. Political Science Professor Peter Andreas dismisses the idea that the U.S./Mexico border can ever be "controlled" because, he says, it has never been "under control" (2006, p. 67). He warns that a narrow focus on policing a physical borderline distracts from pursuing more effective border policy solutions – solutions that, he adds, must consider additional factors that contribute to border activity, including the handling of labor market regulation.

El Paso Representative Silvestre Reyes, a former Border Patrol officer and major architect of the Southwest Border Strategy, says people need to understand that the border will be chaotic until the disparities between the Mexican and United States economy are lessened. Development in the Mexican economy and society, he maintains, is one component that would relieve pressure on the U.S. southern border. Raised, educated, and employed along the U.S./Mexico divide nearly all his life, Reyes also understands borders as more than just fences or walls. "If we learned anything from the Berlin Wall, it's that you can't build a wall to keep people in or out. We need to recognize that," says Reyes. Not a proponent of open borders, Reyes instead advocates restricted access to the United States and says that controlling traffic on the border is a matter of compromise. At the same time, however, Reyes calls on those who advocate "sealing the border" to understand the "economic diversity and vitality the border region represents to the two countries" (Laufer, 2004, pp. 87-89).

Other border experts and scholars also point to dynamics outside the realm of security and control that shape border regions into unique zones of human interaction. Their assessments make clear that the notion of what constitutes a border is as diverse as the functions of borders themselves, and the nature of border environments is often understood very differently by those who have lived their lives along the line. Various scholastic and literary conceptions of the border add a rich perspective and important insight into the nature of the immigration question. It is to these concepts that we now turn.

Secure or Symbolic?
Alternate Views of Borders and Belonging

The United States/Mexico border is one of the busiest and most heavily policed borders in the world. It is unique in that nowhere else on earth is there an equally long and dramatic meeting point between a rich and a poor country (Andreas, 2009). Like many other borders, however, it is also the site of an amazing diversity of culture, trade, language, ideas, history, and human interaction. Viewing it simply as a territorial boundary overlooks the rich complexity of its function and the historical character of the regions it flanks.

For instance, when labor is not considered part of the transnational framework that guides economic flows across borders, it is easy for the state to paint international migration as the result of individual decisions rather than economic linkages between the receiving and the sending countries (Sassen, 1999). Instead of being viewed as an economic or political process, migration is therefore relegated to the realm of border control (ibid).

The current pervasive dialogue on fences, border security, and plugging the holes in our international boundary reflects a security-based framing of the issue of migration along the United States/Mexico border. This approach places full responsibility for the "illegality" of crossing the border on the migrant, rather than taking into consideration the policies, economic regulations, and natural pushes and pulls that have contributed to large numbers of workers headed northward. Borders become a distraction, focusing attention on the *result* of policy – unauthorized crossings – rather than the *nature* of the policy itself.

Globalization has blurred the definition of what constitutes a boundary and even of whether or not borders remain important as transnational identities that bypass the role of the nation-state (Sassen, 2006). In instances where there is a potential blurring of the citizen subject and the alien subject, citizenship may no longer be connected exclusively to the nation-state and does not always result in full, equal membership rights for recognized subjects. Rather, a destabilization of traditional state actors or figures of power allows alternative, informal practices of membership to develop. These "practices of the excluded" are partly responsible for the production and definition of citizenship (Sassen, 2005, p. 8). Such practices include informal contracts of belonging between undocumented immigrants and the communities in which they live and interact, even though they are formally unauthorized subjects and do not have political status as citizens. This is certainly true of U.S. cities where undocumented families have lived, worked, and participated in the community for many years. Often, families are assumed to be part of the community precisely *because* of their involvement and contributions to the society. This has recently been launched as a major argument among those who support a path to citizenship for unauthorized persons already in the United States. Critics, however, point to political, legal definitions of citizenship and counter that amnesty should not be allowed for people who have broken the law. The divide between the two camps underscores the tensions that shifting boundaries – political, physical, or social – create for notions of belonging and nationhood.

An alternative view of the border's function proposed by Peter Andreas maintains that the southern U.S. border is less about deterring unauthorized persons than it is about creating an impression of security and order along the demarcation line (2006). In this view, the border's symbolic purpose is to reaffirm the state's territorial authority as well as the traditional political boundaries of an "imagined community" such as that described by Benedict Anderson (1991).[23] While actual successes in preventing unauthorized crossings have been marginal, Andreas argues that policing of the boundary has offered an opportunity to present the border to the public, often through media, as a secure, ordered site. Even when efforts to provide a sense of control fail, he says, border policing can be seen as a ritualistic performance in which law enforcement saves face by promising a "bigger and better show" of narcotics seizures or arrests (2000, p. 144). When news is released of major drug busts or record numbers of apprehensions, public fears are once again soothed and faith is resumed in the idea of control. Perhaps even more importantly, emphasis on policing and enforcement divert attention from the larger issue of the state's failure to formally recognize a clandestine cross-border labor market.

The situation along the border and public reaction to state policing of the boundary have changed a great deal since 2000 when the first edition of Andreas's book *Border Games: Policing the U.S.-Mexico Divide* was published. Civil society organizations who feel the government has not done its job along the border have raised national awareness and re-framed immigration issues to highlight both humanitarian concerns and problems of security and border management, making the public dialogue about immigration and borders very different from the conversations centered on importation of drugs and cheap labor prior to the new millennium. Their actions and means of framing the issue of border security have also raised *fears* – not just concerns – among U.S. citizens about the number of unauthorized persons crossing the border and the number of those persons perishing in the desert. In a post-9/11 environment where anxiety over future terrorist attacks still drives much official policy, such fears lessen the likelihood that publicity about major drug busts or arrests of human smugglers will pacify the public.[24] As one former public relations director for MCDC stated, "The border is open and we're going to have another 9/11 if we don't watch what we are doing. ... National security is our #1 concern."

However, Andreas's thesis remains important for its observation about the role of the state and its relationship to the border. By effectively emphasizing the importance of border enforcement and security, both the state and activist groups favoring tougher border enforcement draw attention away from questions about treatment of unauthorized labor and United States business interests. Historically, the state has always played a major role in either the recruitment or expulsion of undocumented workers. Recent years are no exception, but today's state turns a blind eye to both the fact that far more undocumented persons are entering than there are legal entrance visas allotted, and that those workers who do successfully cross the border have little trouble finding jobs in "*el norte*." Addressing these issues would require re-evaluating border and immigration policy from the inside-out, taking into consideration the needs and practices of employers, domestic workers, and the foreign labor pool. Adding difficulty to this already tough task is a growing national anti-immigrant sentiment fueled by media personalities and civic groups who frame immigration as a security issue by drawing attention to the "holes" in the border and in border policy.

Andreas's sentiments about the symbolism of the border are not limited only to the U.S.-Mexico divide or to recent history. The symbolic role of border walls can also be likened to representations described by Jurgen Habermas in *The Structural Transformation of the Public Sphere* (1991). In this work, Habermas describes the efforts of the manorial lords and rulers to legitimate their power through public displays. Habermas writes, "The *publicness* (or *publicity*) *of representation* was not constituted as a social realm, that is, as a public sphere; rather, it was something like a status attribute...[T]he manorial lord...displayed himself, presented himself as an embodiment of some 'higher' power...Representation in the sense in which the members of a national assembly represent a nation or a lawyer represents his clients had nothing to do with this publicity of representation inseparable from the lord's concrete existence, that, as an 'aura,' surrounded and endowed his authority" (p. 7). As with the ceremonial displays of power of feudal lords, the power of the U.S. government is put on display through its construction of border fences. Furthermore, deliberate publicity of the fences grants a token of legitimacy for that display of power. Activist groups such as MCDC benefit similarly from such displays of power as they go one step further by proclaiming government responses inadequate and taking on the task of fence-building themselves.

As perceptions about U.S.-Mexico relationships have changed, so have notions of the boundary itself. This shift in perspective has "entailed an evolution of the U.S.-Mexico divide from a border (or zone of transition) to a boundary (or a strict line of demarcation)" (Nevins, 2002, p. 13). This change transforms those crossing the border without official permission from workers or individuals into "illegal aliens." Doing so has moved the notion of boundaries beyond the terms of political debate, essentially ceding power over management of such divides to the state and severely limiting the terms of discussion about boundary and immigration enforcement. In doing so, the nation as a whole has accepted the role of boundaries almost entirely as political units separating geographical territories, and has overlooked their importance as sites of formation for diverse social relationships (ibid).

This border protectionist view can be readily observed in the reaction of civil groups favoring 'sealed borders' who have created their identities around the idea of preservation of an American culture, language, and way of life. Such perceptions assume that within a small geographical area (for example a span of 10 miles north to south as is the case of Nogales, Sonora and Nogales, Arizona) a physical boundary creates a valid distinction between people living on both sides of the line. Those from the United States are presupposed to adhere to 'American' philosophies and behaviors, while those south of the line are portrayed as different, foreign, somehow not sharing similar lifestyles or ideological convictions. MCDC volunteer Philip states it this way: "What is of primary importance to me is the preservation of our way of life. This is the United States of America and I believe that English should be the primary language ... but what I see now is a lot of people trying to make it their own country, trying to make it Spanglish. And culturally wise, it's the culture of the United States. That's what you have to assimilate to."

While there is certainly diversity among people from the two different countries, it is not the border itself that demarcates or establishes those distinctions. A visit to the border – physically or through the stories of those who have been there – illustrates this point. Residents of border communities or of tribal nations that span the southern U.S. boundary are clearly connected in many ways, not the least of which is through shared histories and culture. The economic situations of residents may differ from one side of the border to the other, but the line does not separate the relationships that have formed over centuries between such neighbors. Communities separated by a border are not suddenly divided into two dissimilar cultures. On the contrary, it is the interaction between the two communities that enriches both – economically, socially, emotionally, spiritually, and physically. The danger of a physical boundary, however, is that it creates opportunity for people to think differently about one another *because of* this artificial line of demarcation. Geopolitical boundaries have their purpose, but when that purpose is equated with a need for social and cultural separation, countries on both sides of the line lose out.

"Borders: Scars on the Earth" graffiti along the Arizona/Sonora border fence at Nogales, Arizona. May 2008 (Eastman photo)

Notions of Legality

One of the most gripping issues of the immigration debate is the problematic notion of illegality faced by those who cross a physical boundary without permission. This vexing question of illegal status/entry into the United States is a problem not only for the migrant, but also for the receiving state and society. The term "illegal alien" was formed as a consequence of restrictive immigration practices and policies. It created a "new legal and political subject, whose inclusion within the nation was simultaneously a social reality and a legal impossibility – a subject barred from citizenship and without rights" (Ngai, 2004, p. 4).

The development of that new legal distinction is directly tied to the evolution and representation of the border, argues Joseph Nevins. In *Operation Gatekeeper: The Rise of the "Illegal Alien" and the Making of the U.S.-Mexico Boundary* (2002), Nevins examines the changing character of the U.S.-Mexico dividing line. He contends that today's militarized border separating Mexico from the United States evolved alongside the progression of political, cultural and economic trends, including the development of the American nation-state and the creation of an "illegal" immigrant whose presence was a threat to the concept of the American "nation" [25] (p. 10). The idea of fluid, permeable borders under the notion of Manifest Destiny once justified United States intervention into Mexican territory (ibid). However, with territorial expansion came a new notion of separation and demarcation that gave rise to rigid national boundaries as well as the idea of an "illegal alien" – one who is unwelcome on the wrong side of the divide. State regulation of southern U.S. boundaries changed perceptions of both territory and social identities in those areas. For instance, Nevins points out that construction of the fence separating San Diego from Tijuana heightened the sense of difference between "Americans" and "Mexicans," and between "citizens" and "aliens" (p. 59).

Treatment of the unauthorized migrant by the receiving nation has been varied. Even throughout the history of U.S.-Mexico relations, the presence of the "illegal alien" has been a boon to businesses wishing to take advantage of cheap foreign labor. Thus, those who make it to the United States are often hired by employers looking for a way to maximize profits, and their legal status is either never questioned or is ignored. Not everyone is willing to turn a blind eye to such practices, however. In January of 2008 Arizona became the first state in the nation to impose employer sanctions laws. Following passage of the laws, employers were required to run information on their employees through a federal database to ensure they have legal status. Those caught hiring persons in the country without authorization were subject to stiff fines and even revocation of their business licenses.

In many places, however, the presence of migrants lacking official papers signifies low-cost labor to businesses, high wages to the workers (compared to wages in the home country), and mounting discontent among the populace over the fact that people are entering the United States "through the back door." Because "illegal aliens" technically have very limited rights as citizens, guests, or lawful residents, they are often exploited by employers or corrupt individuals who recognize their lack of legal recourse. Most common are cases of sub-minimum wages being paid to willing workers who are in the country without authorization. Less common but more disturbing are cases of these workers being physically abused, sold into human-trafficking schemes, or forced into prostitution.[26] Although in these extreme cases there are legal measures by which those designated as illegal aliens can seek help and apply for legal status, most are either unaware of such avenues, hindered by language barriers that would enable them to understand the help available, or are simply too frightened to leave the abusive situation.

Formally, however, the United States has yet to determine how "illegal aliens" should be handled. Proponents of comprehensive immigration reform legislation (which would likely include a path to citizenship for certain persons in the United States without official documentation) say it would be impossible to locate and deport all of the nearly 11 million[27] people in the country without authorization. Furthermore, they state, in many cases doing so would tear apart families comprised of both "legal" and "illegal" members, and the economic and social impact on communities where many have lived and contributed for years would be damaging. However, numerous attempts to pass comprehensive immigration reform in recent years have been halted, largely because of public opposition to the notion that persons in the United States illegally could be granted a path to citizenship. Frames used by MCDC and likeminded groups characterize "illegals" as a danger to the United States and focus on the idea that citizenship for those who have entered illegally would be unjust. These frames have been widely disseminated to the general population, largely through media personalities such as Lou Dobbs and Glenn Beck who have made tougher immigration laws part of their public platform. The passage of restrictive immigration laws on local, state and national levels[28] as well as increased federal expenditures for border enforcement indicate that, at least to some degree, these border security frames have been successful.

Thus, the border and the frames that surround discussion of it – whether political, geographical, cultural, symbolic or economic – have a tremendous impact on the lives of those who cross it and the lives of those across it. The power to define belonging, restrict access, reflect policy and create a sense of security (or insecurity) all lies along an imaginary line that separates one of the world's wealthiest nations from a country where hope and progress seem more likely to come from the north than from within. Those who dare to cross find new borders awaiting in the land of opportunity, and their presence challenges the perceptions and acceptance of those who understand borders in strictly political-legal terms. If history is any indication, the construction of more physical fences along the geopolitical division separating Arizona from Sonora will do more than create a physical barrier for those wishing to cross; additional fences will redefine the relationship between two neighboring countries – and peoples – who have, for centuries, had great reason to share the best of what they have to offer.

*Memorial crosses along the U.S./Mexico border fence between
San Diego, CA and Tijuana, MX. January 2006 (Eastman photo)*

*Border fence separating Nogales, AZ from Nogales,
Sonora, MX. October 2007 (Eastman photo)*

Notes

[1] For example, suppose a man slips in a puddle of spilled soda in a restaurant and breaks his leg.   For some passers-by, the mental frame they construct of the scene would emphasize the look of pain on the man's face and capture his physical agony.   For others, the frame could emphasize the irresponsibility of the person who spilled the soda and neglected to clean it up. The frame most immediate to the owner of the restaurant, on the other hand, might accentuate the possibility of a lawsuit or legal repercussions of the accident.   All three frames are valid ways of viewing the situation, but they are different based on the life experiences and values of the people observing the scene.

[2] The distinction between frames and ideologies, for purposes of this study, is an important one.   Frames are means of presenting an issue in a certain light by focusing on specific aspects or details over others.   They normally provoke reactions to immediate circumstances, and are designed to resonate with individuals as they attempt to explain what matters most about a particular situation.   Ideologies, on the other hand, are ideas about the world that require deeper thinking about the values and norms of a society and/or theories that help explain the issue at hand.   Ideologies, because they are more general, can be applied to a variety of situations and are learned over time through education or socialization.   For more about the distinction between frames and ideologies, please see Oliver & Johnston, 2000.

[3] If an individual can relate closely to a frame because he or she has had similar direct life experiences, that frame is said to hold great narrative fidelity (Gamson & Modigliani, 1989; Oberschall, 1996).

[4] Various types of fences and barriers were in place prior to the mid-1990s. The building of the current fence, much more formidable than what had previously been in place, is part of the evolution of increased border fortification that began in the early part of the twentieth century and continues into the twenty-first century.

[5] Although the term has been used by numerous scholars, its widespread use can be credited to the work of Rubio-Goldsmith et al. and the major study carried out by the Binational Migration Institute in 2006.

[6] D. Jimarez, United States Border Patrol Public Affairs Officer: Tucson Sector Public Affairs Office (telephone interview, April 2, 2010).

[7] When the Department of Homeland Security (DHS) was created in 2003, the Immigration and Naturalization Service (INS) and 21 other federal agencies were brought together within DHS.   United States Customs and Border Protection (CBP) then assumed the responsibilities that formerly had been assigned to the INS.

[8] Border Patrol Officials credit this drop to increased enforcement efforts. Humanitarian groups argue that milder than average temperatures that year decreased the likelihood of dying of exposure or dehydration.

[9] D. Jimarez.   United States Border Patrol Public Affairs Officer: Tucson Sector Public Affairs Office (telephone interview, April 2, 2010).

[10] Human smuggler.

[11] The Secure Fence Act did not include funding for the project, but Congress authorized $1.2 billion for the fence in October of 2007.

[12] Officials estimate that a virtual fencing project, tested in Arizona, could be extended across the Southwest border by 2014 for approximately $6.7 billion (Gaynor, 2010).

[13] Notes from personal interviews, spring and fall 2007.

[14] The Department of Homeland Security can invoke national security interest laws and eminent domain laws to obtain private property for purposes of building the border fence. The land needed to complete the last section of the fence near San Diego was acquired this way.

[15] The 53 miles of invisible, high-tech fence were located in Arizona.

[16] S. King, U.S. Border Patrol: Tucson Sector Public Affairs Office (personal interview, October 17, 2007).

[17] G. Soto, U.S. Border Patrol: Tucson Sector Public Affairs Office (personal interview, May 23, 2007).

[18] The American Border Patrol (ABP) is in no way affiliated with the U.S. Border Patrol Agency. It is an independent organization with similar objectives as the Minuteman Civil Defense Corps that advocates sealing the border and recruits volunteers to patrol border areas for illegal aliens.

[19] For more information about the fences constructed, built, and advocated for by these groups, see their websites: http://www.americanborderpatrol.com and http://www.minutemanhq.com/bf.

[20] G. Soto. U.S. Border Patrol: Tucson Sector Public Affairs Office (personal interview, May 23, 2007).

[21] Although this particular tunnel appeared to be used for drug smuggling, it has been recognized that such tunnels can be utilized by human traffickers as well. ICE Special agent Michael Unzueta stated, "Whether they are designed to smuggle drugs, people, weapons or other contraband, these tunnels pose a threat to our nation's security" (Pomfret, 2006).

[22] S. King, U.S. Border Patrol: Tucson Sector Public Affairs Office (personal interview, October 17, 2007).

[23] This concept described communities based not on face-to-face contact, but on groups of people connected through a shared ideal or notion of common shared experience. Anderson felt it was the advent of print capitalism that connected geographically distant populations with a common experience, and thus made imagined communities possible. For more, see Anderson, B. (1991). *Imagined Communities.* London: Verso.

[24] Personal interview (November 17, 2007).

[25] Use of the term "American" here reflects the widespread acceptance of the term as referring to the United States. It is a term frequently used by citizens of the United States today, particularly those who wish to classify cultural and social practices unique to this country. In actuality, "American" refers to the Americas – North, Central and South – and does not apply specifically to the United States. Use of the term reflects a lack of sensitivity to both geographical truths and socio-political relations with other nations of the Americas. While context does dictate the use of the term from time to time because of its widespread historical acceptance and application (as is the case in Nevins's book), every effort has been made to avoid the use of the term in other

sections of this work so that the status, significance, and contributions of our neighbors to the north and south will not be trivialized and the inaccuracy of this linguistic connotation will not be perpetuated.

[26] Summaries of such cases were presented by law enforcement officials at the "Look Beneath the Surface" training seminar in Glendale, AZ on October 30, 2007.

[27] The United States Department of Homeland Security estimated the unauthorized population living in this country at 10.8 million in January 2009. For more information, see Hoefer, Rytina & Baker (2010).

[28] Examples include local restrictive immigration-related laws in Arizona and Missouri in 2008 (Preston, 2008), a huge increase in tougher immigration laws and bills in a number of states across the country in 2009-2010 (Romano, 2011Seattle, 2010), and the passage of Arizona SB 1070 in 2010, thought at the time to be the strictest law in the nation (Jordan, 2007).

5

Shaping the National Debate

"The humblest citizen of all the land, when clad in the armor of a righteous cause, is stronger than all the hosts of Error."

William Jennings Bryan, Speech at the
National Democratic Convention, Chicago (1896)

Civil Society in Arizona: Taking a Stand

When Daniel Strauss and Shanti Sellz signed up to volunteer for the humanitarian organization No More Deaths during the summer of 2005, they knew their work would bring them face-to-face with the grim realities of Arizona/Sonora border. They knew they would likely meet migrants who had risked their lives, and suffered greatly, for the chance to cross into the United States in search of work. And they knew that although they could not "fix" the situation, they could at least help ensure that those migrants making their journey through such inhospitable terrain received life-saving water and medical care.

What they didn't know is that their desire to help prevent deaths in the desert would potentially land them in prison for fifteen years.

Strauss and Sellz, while patrolling a remote sector of the southern Arizona desert with No More Deaths in July 2005, came upon three migrants who were vomiting and exhibiting symptoms of severe dehydration. After consulting via phone with a medical professional and a No More Deaths attorney, the 23-year-old volunteers loaded the men in their car and proceeded to transport them to the nearest medical facility.[1]

Before they arrived, however, Strauss and Sellz were pulled over by the Border Patrol and charged with two felonies: transportation in furtherance of an illegal presence in the United States and conspiracy to transport in furtherance of an illegal presence in the United States (Medrano, 2006). If convicted, those felonies could have resulted in a maximum of fifteen years in prison and $500,000 in fines.

Strauss and Sellz, who did not call the Border Patrol, argued that they were only trying to bring the migrants to a hospital where they could receive treatment. The Border Patrol argued that the migrants were not severely ill, and any decision to transport undocumented individuals – regardless of the circumstance – is a violation of federal law.[2] Over the course of the next year, Strauss and Sellz were offered a plea bargain to avoid imprisonment if they admitted committing a crime. Both refused, saying that providing humanitarian aid to people in need is not a criminal act (LoMonaco, 2007, April 17a).

In September, 2006 a federal judge threw out the charges against the volunteers, citing the fact that the protocol established and followed by No More Deaths members for providing aid had never been challenged in the three years prior to the arrest (Grossman, 2006). While the ruling was considered a victory for supporters, the precedent of arrest had now been established, leaving the legality of future aid in question.

Strauss and Sellz received both support and condemnation for their actions. Their story sparked a widespread "Humanitarian Aid Is Never a Crime" campaign throughout southern Arizona and other parts of the state. While their trial was in progress, supporters sent 18,000 postcards of protest to U.S. Attorney Paul Charlton (Innes, 2005). In April of 2007, Strauss and Sellz were named recipients of the 2007 Oscar Romero award for their unwavering convictions and dedication to human rights (The Oscar, 2007). However, while many praised the duo, numerous website blog entries and letters to the editor in local newspapers denounced the actions of the volunteers as an effort to facilitate the entrance of illegal aliens into the United States (LoMonaco, 2007, April 17b).

In many ways, the story of Daniel Strauss and Shanti Sellz is not unique. Their volunteer efforts with No More Deaths reflect a widespread rise in the presence of civil society organizations along the Arizona/Sonora border, as documented by research from Doty (2009), Sabet (2008), Staudt & Coronado (2002) and others. The steady increase in migrant flows through the Arizona desert in recent years has alarmed both the federal government and those non-governmental and humanitarian organizations who view current border policy as a broken system in desperate need of change (Medrano, 2005; Shields & Nieves, 2006). While debates about migration policy echo through the halls of Congress in Washington, D.C., numerous civic groups working on or near the border have begun taking action of their own. Humanitarian groups have decried the huge increase in migrant death rates and have rallied to action to prevent more migrants from perishing in their attempts to cross, while opponents of current immigration practices have decried the failure of the federal government to stop the flow of migrants crossing illegally and have taken matters into their own hands by forming volunteer civilian border patrols.

As different as their approaches and responses may be, these organizations have adopted a common public proclamation – that current border policy is broken and the system needs to be repaired. Additionally, all have been effective at garnering public support for reform proposals that challenge the legitimacy and effectiveness of the current U.S. immigration policy. Such groups have successfully framed the issue of unauthorized border crossing in unique ways that highlight the concerns most relevant to that organization's own ideologies and efforts as well as those of its participants, a process known as frame alignment (Snow & Benford, 1988). The effectiveness of the frames developed by organizational leaders has relied partly on their ability to identify the problems inherent with current immigration policy, offer solutions to those problems and motivate citizens to become involved (Snow & Benford, 1988).

The result of such framing and recruitment efforts can be considered a social movement aimed at transforming not only immigration law but also the treatment of immigrants in this country. Movements such as this often function as catalysts necessary to engage the public in social issues that otherwise may go relatively unnoticed. While the civil rights struggle is one of the most well-known examples of a successful social movement, public consciousness has also been jarred through efforts of community organizers to protest conditions or draw attention to a host of other issues including race, the environment, women's rights, gay rights and use of nuclear power.

Research on the brutal murders of women in and around Ciudad Juárez, Mexico offers a recent example of how a social movement can raise public knowledge and influence public perceptions of an issue. Kathleen Staudt (2009) points to the impact of transnational social movements and coalitions in the El Paso/Ciudad Juárez region on creating public awareness of the femicides in Juárez. Staudt states, "At the U.S.-Mexico border, dramatic, sustained social movement activism brought local, regional, national and international attention to femicide and ultimately and belatedly to the broader issue of violence against women" (p. 112). Ideally, she says, this episodic attention directed toward the issue through social movements should complement sustained efforts by nongovernmental organizations working to create widespread awareness of the atrocities taking place.

What differentiates a well-intentioned effort to create social change from a successful movement? Resource mobilization theory maintains that the effectiveness of a movement depends largely on the resources available to participants (including communications, finances and political means) as well as the capability of movement leaders to gather and utilize those resources (McCarthy & Zald, 2001). The ultimate goal for such a movement is to take action politically in an effort to bring about change. Under this theoretical umbrella, the successful work of civil groups along the Arizona/Sonora border is apparent. Leaders of Humane Borders, No More Deaths and the Minuteman Civil Defense Corps have all effectively garnered civic participation and response by utilizing the channels mentioned above. Through savvy use of media, extensive educational campaigns, and political advocacy, the groups have exerted notable influence over the management of an issue whose governance once belonged exclusively to the nation-state.

One resource in particular, however, has proven critically important in furthering debate about immigration, particularly the discussion of the events taking place in the Arizona/Sonora corridor. Media have played an integral role in offering a public platform for the grievances and ideologies of movement leaders. Research by Gamson and Wolfsfeld (1993) indicates that general social movements rely on media to: attract widespread political support, validate mainstream discourse about the issue (which also provides credibility to the movement), and broaden the scope of the conflict to attract otherwise unlikely allies. Undoubtedly, leaders of Humane Borders, No More Deaths and the Minuteman Civil Defense Corps have received both attention and support as a result of media coverage of their organizations. They have depended largely on newspaper stories, radio interviews, television coverage, film production, blogs, distribution lists and other media extensions to voice their opinions about the problems inherent in current immigration policy. Those media channels have also provided a means of recruitment and have, perhaps most importantly, infused immigration-related language and discussion into the national conversation. Certainly movement leaders would have done important work without media intervention. With it, however, they have been able to create a platform and outreach large enough to attract attention worldwide.

Humane Borders, No More Deaths and the Minuteman Civil Defense Corps are not the only groups working to create change in immigration policy. Numerous civic and nongovernmental organizations make up the complex network of activists who have worked along the Arizona/Sonora border – some for many years and others for just a few. The ongoing efforts of Border Links, the Samaritans, Derechos

Humanos, American Border Patrol,[3] and other comparable groups have brought the topics of immigration and border policy to the public eye and have served as an inspiration for similar civic endeavors across the entire span of the border.[4] The contributions of these organizations are not to be overlooked, for they are an important component of a concerned civil society that has committed itself to promoting policy changes.

Three particular groups, however, have drawn national attention to the Arizona/Sonora immigration phenomenon through utilization of media and somewhat controversial on-the-ground activities that have captured the attention of media professionals around the world. These three groups were selected for study because of the extensive recognition and media attention they have received for their actions in recent years. Humane Borders, No More Deaths, and the Minuteman Civil Defense Corps (MCDC) have played a crucial role in making a national and even global audience aware of the current migration phenomenon playing out in southern Arizona. Their activities and advocacy efforts to promote immigration reform have successfully identified the failures of current U.S. policy and focused public attention on the need for alternative solutions to the immigration issue. In some cases, the founders and volunteers in these groups claim patriotic duty as the reason for their work along the border; in other cases, their actions are inspired by religious or humanitarian motivations. Either way, their involvement provides an interesting context for the immigration debate as these members of non-governmental organizations (NGOs) publicly challenge the state's authority. Although they seek very different outcomes, each of these organizations has made a meaningful impact on public understanding of the border and the disasters occurring daily in the southern Arizona desert.

It is important to briefly mention that classification of these organizations is somewhat complicated because of varying definitions of what it means to be a non-profit or non-governmental organization. Non-profit status varies from state to state, so what may be classified as a non-profit organization in one state is not necessarily classified as such in another. Definitions of NGOs in recent scholarship range from simple political classifications to descriptions of the organizations' activities and social roles: NGOs as citizen organizations (Najam, 1999), humanitarian NGOs as watchdogs of the state (DeChaine, 2002), NGOs as advocates or as service-delivery organizations (Jordan & Van Tuijl, 2000), NGOs as agents of accountability (Brown & Fox, 1998) and NGOs as private, nonprofit, self-governing organizations dedicated to improving the quality of life of disadvantaged people (Vakil, 1997).

All three of the activist groups on the Arizona/Mexico border could be considered NGOs under a wide definition of the term. However, relationships between some of the organizations and state or federal agencies (for example, the county funding that supports Humane Borders efforts) create a gray area, placing the non-governmental affiliation in question. In this study, designating any of the groups as NGOs indicates a behaviorally descriptive definition of the term, (referring to a group's humanitarian focus, for example) rather than referencing an economic or legal definition. To avoid this ambiguity and uncertainty, however, I will primarily refer to the three organizations under a broader umbrella, as representatives of civil society. In doing so, I borrow concepts of civil society from Hegel, who saw human needs as civil society's defining feature and who believed that civil society functions as a mediator between the needs of the family and those of the state (Hegel, 1821). I also rely on Gramsci's view of civil society as that place outside of both the state and the market where the public acts to challenge existing powers (Gramsci, 1971).

A closer look at each of the groups selected for study reveals the distinctive approaches they have chosen to address a common issue, the reasons for their widespread notoriety, and the important roles they have played in creating national awareness of the immigration phenomenon, starting in southern Arizona.

Fountains in the Desert: Creating More Humane Borders

Reverend Robin Hoover of First Christian Church in Tucson, AZ is no stranger to border-related issues. Originally from Texas, Hoover was born and raised in the state with the longest stretch of U.S.-Mexico border and an equally long stretch of border history. His education about the border came from both life experience and formal training; he gained an understanding of migrant labor by growing up in a state where "wetbacks" were part of the social landscape, and he earned his Ph.D. in political science with a dissertation on migration policy and religious nonprofit groups.

However, within five months of moving to Tucson, AZ to serve as pastor of First Christian Church, Reverend Robin Hoover found himself facing a new set of immigration issues. Here, just a short drive south of the city, increasing numbers of migrants were dying of dehydration and exposure as they tried to cross through the Sonoran desert into the United States. By June of 2000, the growing death toll in the desert prompted Hoover and two other faith leaders in Tucson to sit down to discuss how the Christian church could respond. That group decided to invite other interested persons to take part in the discussion. At the subsequent meeting, over 90 representatives of faith communities from both the U.S. and Mexico – many of whom had participated in the Sanctuary Movement[5] of the 1980s – gathered and began to brainstorm. This delegation, led by Reverend Hoover, decided that in order to save lives in the desert the group would somehow need to fill the desert with water. By the end of that meeting, the bi-national, interfaith movement/organization Humane Borders had been established, along with a creative plan for bringing water to desolate stretches of the desert.

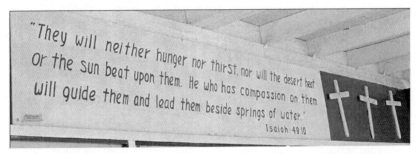

Sign at Humane Borders headquarters. May 2007 (Eastman photo)

In March of 2001, the organization placed its first two water stations in Organ Pipe Cactus National Monument. Volunteers recycled empty 40 gallon Coca-Cola syrup barrels, turned them into mobile water stations, painted them blue, and marked each with a flag that waved high above the desert floor. The organization began with twelve water stations in 2001, but by 2010 the number had grown to more than 35 in multiple locations throughout the Arizona desert. During the summer of 2005, close to 30,000 gallons of water from those stations were consumed by migrants (Fife et al, 2005). The organization has 65 trained drivers who make regular trips to the desert with specially designed water trucks. On average, Humane Borders volunteers make 70 trips per month to service water stations from May through September (the hottest desert months), and 30 trips per month from October through April.[6]

This unique approach to saving lives in the desert has garnered the support of the Pima County Board of Supervisors who, each year from 2005 to 2011, has granted Humane Borders a $25,000 contract for the purpose of maintaining the water stations. The Pima County Health Department has also supported the group's efforts, granting $25,000 in 2005 toward an expansion of lifesaving efforts (Fife et al., 2005;

Meltzer, 2006). Not everyone is happy with such contracts. Members of the Minutemen Civil Defense Corps and other critics have protested the allocations, claiming the presence of water stations encourages migrants to make the trek through the desert and that federal law prohibits such a misuse of public funds from the county (Duffy, 2007). However, as one Board of Supervisors member explains, supporting the water stations is "sound fiscal policy" because it prevents the county from being burdened with additional migrant death-related costs down the road (Meltzer, 2006, p. B2). In fact, Pima County Medical Examiner Bruce Parks says that autopsies on the bodies brought into his office cost taxpayers between $100,000 and $200,000 a year. Additional costs are incurred for the burial of unidentified bodies in the Pima County Cemetery. Thus, despite protests, the county continues to support the efforts of the faith-based humanitarian group at least in part because preventing deaths is a significant cost-saving strategy compared to processing human remains.

Humane Borders sparked controversy in 2005 for publishing and distributing maps and posters of the southern Arizona desert that marked the location of the group's emergency water tanks, as well as highways, cell phone reception spots and rescue beacons in the area (Mexico to, 2006). The Mexican government originally agreed to distribute 70,000 of the maps, but within days withdrew their support after deciding the maps might put migrants in danger of watchdog groups who might target the highlighted areas (Seper, 2006). Critics charged that the group was encouraging migrants by highlighting possible routes; members of the organization replied that the intent of the map was simply to provide information that could save lives for those who make the trek through the desert. Debate also swirled around survival tips included on the map that advised what to wear and how much water would be required to survive a desert trek. However, the organization's leaders pointed out that the map also highlighted the locations of known deaths in the Tucson Sector (many of them close to water stations) and includes a large Spanish script warning potential migrants not to make the trip because the dangers are too great.

Humane Borders reports that it has benefitted from the contributions and assistance of a total of 10,000 volunteers from all over the United States. In addition to maintaining water stations, Humane Borders sponsors trash pick-ups, provides public education programs, escorts faith leaders and other interested parties to border areas, and interacts with elected officials and public administrators as a means of implementing the group's mission of establishing a humane borderland. Humane Borders also works with families, the consulates of sending countries, and Border Patrol personnel to help locate missing persons. Humane Borders was founded with 501(c)(4) IRS status, reserved for non-profit organizations[7] operating only to promote social welfare (Internal Revenue Service, n.d.). In 2011, the group changed its IRS status to that of a 501(c)(3) charitable organization. The new designation makes it easier for donors to contribute directly to Humane Borders (rather than donating money through a sponsoring church) but it also restricts the form and amount of political activity in which the group can engage. With the 501(c)(3) status, Humane Borders cannot lobby or participate in political campaigns. The organization receives its financial support from a combination of government, faith communities, businesses and individuals.

In addition to the primary project of placing water in the desert to save lives, volunteers dedicate themselves to advocacy efforts for humane, comprehensive immigration reform. Under the 501(c)(4) status the organization held for most of its first decade of existence, volunteers participated in legislative advocacy efforts such as testifying before Congress. They also raised public awareness of the situation in the desert through speeches, educational presentations to schools and civic organizations, and participation in public events. According to co-founder Hoover, the group's deliberate efforts to tell the story of the migrant through the media play an important educational role in the wider community.[8]

The work of Humane Borders is dominated largely by religious convictions, but not all volunteers are people of faith. Regardless of their backgrounds, all are driven by a moral code of ethics that motivates them to offer assistance to those in need. Their outreach reflects a Gramscian view of civil society as an ethical or moral society.

Under the leadership of Robin Hoover, Humane Borders received international attention for its unique humanitarian work. In 2006, Mexico's Commission for Human Rights presented Reverend Hoover with the highest humanitarian award ever bestowed upon a non-Mexican national – the National Human Rights Award. In late 2007, however, Hoover stepped down as President of Humane Borders and by December of 2009 he officially separated himself from the day-to-day operations of the agency to focus on other personal and academic interests related to migration. With Hoover's departure, the organization underwent a period of reorganization and restructuring, emerging in mid-2011 with Juanita Molina as the new Executive Director and with members of the board taking on additional responsibilities.

Justice Through Civil Initiative: No More Deaths

While migrant testimonies indicated that the Humane Borders water stations undoubtedly saved lives, desert death counts in 2001 and 2002 continued to rise. In July of 2002, minister John Fife united with other activists to form a new faith-based group that would provide more direct assistance to migrants in need. Fife was no stranger to faith-based activism. As minister of Tucson, Arizona's Southside Presbyterian Church in the 1980s, Fife's congregation was the first to offer sanctuary to Salvadorian refugees. This action spearheaded a national Sanctuary Movement, later involving over 500 churches and synagogues across the country that offered protection to thousands of Central American refugees fleeing political persecution in their home countries (Goodman, 2007, April 23). The U.S. government infiltrated Fife's group of volunteers to gather evidence on the movement and, in 1986, Fife and seven other activists were charged and convicted with smuggling aliens (ibid).

Just after serving his five years probation, in 2002, Fife gathered like-minded citizens together to form the Samaritan Patrol – "people of faith and conscience who are responding directly, practically and passionately to the crisis at the U.S./ Mexico border" and whose objective is to bring food, water and medical assistance into remote stretches of the desert.[9] The group uses four-wheel drive vehicles to transport doctors and nurses from local churches, as well as other volunteers, into critical desert stretches. There, they search for sick or dying migrants and try to provide assistance before it is too late (Fife et al., 2005). For nine years, the group has made desert runs every day during the summer and two to three days a week in the winter. They have encountered victims with heatstroke, head wounds, broken limbs, and severe burns from walking through the sand after their shoes had fallen apart. When the situation they encounter is critical, volunteers use their satellite phones to call for a helicopter (ibid).

According to Fife, today's crisis on the border has been caused by a border enforcement policy, outlined in an August 2001 United States General Accounting Office report (INS', 2001), that uses death of migrants in the desert as a deterrent to other potential crossers. "That's a gross violation of human rights, this policy, this strategy of deterrence by death," Fife says (Democracy, 2007, p. 3). To resist this official strategy, Fife and others began a movement in coordination with Samaritan efforts that they called No More Deaths.

No More Deaths is unique in that it describes a *movement* – not an organization – initiated in 2004 to unite the various humanitarian efforts already underway along the border in Arizona. It is a faith-based effort, but many of the volunteers come from non-religious backgrounds. As one volunteer described it, the group is "made up of people of faith <u>and</u> conscience."[10] There are no formal leaders; any decisions that are made are made with the input of the entire group at weekly meetings and responsibilities are rotated among various committees that work on specific projects.

While No More Deaths volunteers engage heavily in advocacy efforts through lobbying, public speeches and presentations, and organized media campaigns, the primary work of the group takes place on the ground in the southern Arizona desert. No More Deaths volunteers are most active during the summer, the deadliest season for migrants because of the extreme heat and lack of water. From June through September, hundreds of participants from Arizona and across the United States set up camps in the desert where migrants who cross their path can receive food, water, and medical aid. Volunteers map migrant trails throughout the winter, and these maps are then used to lead search and rescue patrols – small groups equipped with food, water, and basic first aid supplies who search for migrants in distress.

In addition to the desert camps, No More Deaths volunteers organize aid stations at the ports of entry in Nogales, Sonora and Agua Prieta, Sonora to address the physical needs of dehydrated, weak, hungry or injured migrants who have been apprehended and sent back across the border. One volunteer says 500-600 people pass through the Mariposa station in Nogales each day; in the spring, the number can jump to as many as 1,200 daily (Robbins, 2007). She sees people in bad condition coming to the aid station – people with pus-soaked socks from blistered feet, with festering cactus spine injuries, and with severe exhaustion after walking for days through the desert. A grateful migrant who received food and aid from the volunteers did not mince words when describing them. "These people are angels from heaven," he said (LoMonaco, 2006, p. 4A).

Besides offering food and physical assistance to migrants who come to the aid stations, the group also interviews these individuals in an effort to develop statistical evidence of abuses by Border Patrol and flaws in the detention apprehension process. The stories they hear are often heartbreaking, but they are determined to continue recording the migrants' accounts in hopes of using them to change the system and ensure that others are not mistreated. As one volunteer described, "I have been instilled with a gigantic urge to fight for social justice and each sad and traumatic experience I have while talking to someone else only instills the urge in me even more."[11] John Fife agrees. "Our

Following the arrest of two No More Deaths volunteers, "Humanitarian Aid is Never a Crime" signs appeared throughout Tucson and the surrounding area. March 2007 (Eastman photo)

responsibility out there is to do everything we can within the law to save lives."[12]

The No More Deaths movement was founded on the idea of using civil initiative to try to bring about immigration reform. Civil initiative, according to No More Deaths co-founder Rick Ufford-Chase, was a guiding set of principles established by Arizona rancher, activist, and ideological founder of the Sanctuary Movement Jim Corbett (Ufford-Chase, 2005b). Corbett's definition of civil initiative rested on the idea that there must be balance between accountability to law and the protection of those being persecuted, and that protest of unjust laws must be non-violent, truthful, catholic, dialogical, germane, volunteer-based and community-centered (Corbett, 1991b). Corbett distinguished this course of action from other forms of protest by explaining that civil initiative "extends the rule of law unlike civil disobedience, which breaks it, and civil obedience, which lets the government break it. The heart of a societal order guided by the rule of law is the principle that the nonviolent protection of basic rights is never illegal" (Corbett, 1991a).[13]

The civil initiative approach favored by No More Deaths volunteers is reflective of the theory of negative resistance proposed by Immanuel Kant (1996). Kant felt it was important for individuals to engage in a sort of social contract system with the state to produce an ordered, productive structure for governance. While he did not advocate resisting the state and its laws through revolution or revolt, Kant felt that citizens must argue against perceived injustices because open criticism of the state among its citizens would promote public reason and contribute to a healthy society. Negative resistance – refusing to accede to every government demand – is a moral resistance and is not inconsistent with the purpose of maintaining an ordered, effectively-governed society (Anderson-Gold, 1988; Calabrese, 2004; Kant, 1996). No More Deaths volunteers actually move one step beyond Kant's civil debate and dissent as they exercise both their moral responsibility and legal right to provide direct aid to the victims of government violations of human rights (Fife, 2009).

Within the No More Deaths movement, great care is taken to distinguish between the definition and ideas of civil initiative and those of civil disobedience. In fact, all No More Deaths volunteers are trained in a detailed protocol of action based on civil initiative designed by the movement's legal counsel. While civil disobedience involves assuming the consequences of disobeying what is seen as an unjust law, civil initiative operates under the premise of an individual's *legal* right to act in protest of human rights violations and to protect victims of those violations when government is the violator (Fife, 2009). In practical terms for movement participants, civil initiative involves providing direct aid to victims of unjust border policies (particularly in the desert) and then using that experience and credibility to be more effective political advocates.[14]

At times, however, the distinction between lawful and unlawful action (and thus, civil initiative vs. civil disobedience) has not been entirely clear, and people of faith have come head to head with government officials over what they regard as violations of human rights principles. The most well-known example was the controversial arrest of Strauss and Sellz during the summer of 2005 and the subsequent "Humanitarian Aid Is Never a Crime" campaign that drew national media attention. Although charges against the two were eventually dropped, this was not the last time the group's volunteers would find themselves in a quandary with officials. In February of 2008, No More Deaths volunteer Daniel Millis was fined $175 by a Buenos Aires National Wildlife Refuge law enforcement officer for placing water jugs in the desert for migrants. The officer said that trash left in the desert, particularly by illegal entrants, was becoming a serious problem. Millis, who had found the body of a 14-year-old girl two days earlier in a nearby area, said he was trying to save lives by leaving water for people who could otherwise die of dehydration. He argued that he had also been picking up trash as he walked the trail. In September of 2008, Millis was convicted of littering and given a suspended sentence. That conviction was overturned in September, 2010 by a federal appeals court.

Three months after Millis's original conviction, Claremont School of Theology seminary student and No More Deaths volunteer Walt Staton was cited for littering as he left water jugs on migrant trails. He was sentenced to one year probation which was later dropped. No More Deaths members responded to these incidents by again engaging in civil initiative (that bordered on civil disobedience) to draw attention to the outcome of the trials and to highlight what they felt were unjust policies. In July, 2009 thirteen more volunteers placed water jugs on trails in the refuge and were cited for littering (McCombs, 2010, Feb. 7). Immediately, Tucson media reported on the citations and the ongoing conflict between No More Deaths volunteers and Buenos Aires National Wildlife Refuge personnel. This incident and the ensuing publicity led to meetings between No More Deaths volunteers and Interior Secretary Ken Salazar, as well as with officials from Buenos Aires National Wildlife Refuge (BANWR). All charges against the thirteen volunteers were dismissed by the U.S. Attorney's Office before trial.

While both Humane Borders and No More Deaths volunteers have engaged in numerous cases of criticism against current policies, No More Deaths has generally gone one step further by engaging in "negative resistance," finding creative alternatives to federal regulations that would otherwise prevent them from assisting migrants in need. Perhaps the most memorable example was the massive public campaign "Humanitarian Aid is Never a Crime" that followed the arrest of Strauss and Sellz in 2005. Through yard signs, postcards, letters to the editor, and many other public displays of resistance, supporters of the movement made public their refusal to accept the state's view that a humanitarian action could be treated as a criminal offense. Another example was the placing of water bottles on national wildlife refuge land even though volunteers knew they could face legal repercussions for doing so. Walt Staton protested his original sentencing, sending a letter to the judge that stated, "When a government fails to respect and protect basic human rights—or, worse, is itself a violator—it is the responsibility of citizens to act in defense of those rights."[15]

The problem with an application of Kantian philosophy to the No More Deaths strategy is determining where negative resistance ends and civil disobedience begins. After the 2005 Strauss/Sellz court case, for example, a legal precedent was established making the furtherance of migrants into the country, for *any* reason, illegal. However, early in 2008 Border Patrol introduced a new apprehension strategy called Operation Streamline that eliminated voluntary repatriation as a choice for migrants who had been arrested. Until that point, unauthorized persons who were apprehended and chose voluntary repatriation were processed and taken back across the line to Mexico rather than being held in the United States and formally charged in a court of law. The new strategy, however, ensured that a target number of migrants who were caught would be incarcerated for 10-15 days, brought to court and charged with/convicted of a crime (at the time, entering the U.S. without authorization was a misdemeanor), and then formally deported.[16] No More Deaths volunteers who disagreed with the moral grounds of the new strategy and who had also documented numerous cases of migrant abuse by Border Patrol and other officials were outraged. At subsequent meetings, participants discussed the possibility of transporting migrants who were sick or ill *south* – back *to* the border – so they would not be apprehended and processed as part of what volunteers see as an inhumane system. Technically, they would not be furthering entry of unauthorized persons into the country, but clearly they would be acting in opposition to the principle of the new Border Patrol strategy. Whether they will act on the idea or resist in other ways remains to be seen.

No More Deaths volunteers have won every legal case they have faced; thus members of the movement have not engaged in civil disobedience. As the Sanctuary Movement of the 1980s exemplified, however, interpretation of what constitutes a human rights violation is not always clear, and it can be difficult to prove that government policies are in violation of human rights principles. To their benefit, the Inter-American Court of Human Rights ruled unanimously that the migrant deaths resulting from Operation Gatekeeper are strong evidence that the United States has violated human rights. The United Nations Human Rights Commission, Amnesty International and other international organizations came to the same conclusion (Fife, 2009). Thus, in spite of the challenges they encounter, No More Deaths volunteers are committed to the protection of victims of immigration policy, even if that means it may be necessary to defend their actions within a court of law.

On a final note, the guiding principles of Humane Borders and No More Deaths may seem quite similar to one another. Indeed, the strategy of using civil initiative to respond to deaths in the desert was the philosophical basis for the founding of both Humane Borders and the Samaritans whose establishment (by many of the same leaders) preceded No More Deaths. Perhaps the primary difference between Humane Borders and No More Deaths can be found in the methods each currently uses to draw attention to border and immigration-related concerns. While members of Humane Borders have sparked controversy over the placement of water stations in the desert and distribution of maps previously described, the group has always made a concerted effort to act, and protest, within the boundaries of the law. Their approach has remained one in which a relatively non-confrontational form of civil initiative guides direct action. The No More Deaths movement also functions primarily on the basis of the principals of civil initiative. However, in recent years members have found themselves teetering on the brink of civil disobedience as their actions have been legally challenged by government agencies that disagreed with their legal right to act out of protection and compassion for victims of abuse. The conscientious decision to remain engaged in activities for which volunteers have been harassed and charged by authorities makes the approach of the No More Deaths movement unique and contributes to the attention the movement has received from media sources.

Musters and Media:
Minuteman Civil Defense Corps (MCDC)

Shortly after the terrorist attacks of 9/11, former Los Angeles kindergarten teacher Chris Simcox decided to do some vacationing at Arizona's Organ Cactus Pipe National Monument. What he saw there changed the course of his life. While hiking and camping, he encountered numerous migrants and drug smugglers – all making their way from Mexico northward through the park. His experience at Organ Pipe sparked an epiphany: if he could bring national attention to the borders and demand that the government do something to secure them, he would be helping to save his country.[17] So Simcox began a massive campaign to make the media – and the public – take note of what he felt was lax security along U.S. borders. What happened during the ensuing years captured headlines across the country.

In 2002, Simcox bought the *Tombstone Tumbleweed* newspaper. "To get the media to pay attention, I decided I had to own a piece of the media," he said (Egan, 2005, p. 14).[18] In October of 2002, he printed a headline titled "Enough is Enough" that stated his intent to form a civilian border watch militia. "I used militia, too, on purpose" Simcox stated during a personal interview. "I knew "militia" would bring the media running because of the bad name that militias had earned, unfortunately, over the years. And we wanted to 'right the ship' on that."

Some media did pay attention over the next year and a half as Simcox gained support for his Civil Homeland Defense border watch group in Cochise County, AZ. But it was not until October of 2004 when Simcox was approached by Jim Gilchrist, a retired accountant from Southern California, that the idea for a 30-day protest on the border was born.

Simcox and Gilchrist co-founded the Minuteman Project in December of 2004. The two launched their first major publicity campaign in April 2005 near Tombstone. Volunteers from across the country were invited to join the group in southern Arizona for a month-long border watch for illegal immigrants. Turnout was low – numerous reports indicate that volunteers were outnumbered by the local, regional, and national media – but the goal of the campaign was a tremendous success. As media flocked to southern Arizona to report on a group of gun-toting civilians searching the desert for migrants, the nation's attention was captured, just as Simcox had originally envisioned. The Minuteman Project was described in one instance as "a national coming-out party, less an effort to capture Mexicans crossing the border than to capture airtime on the cable news channels" (Scherer, 2005, p. 50). An *Arizona Republic* newspaper headline, "Border Volunteers Basking in Attention" summed up the effort (Carroll, 2005). Suddenly, Arizona's southern border was the topic of conversations – and the subject of headlines – across the country. The debate over illegal immigration was heating up.

Immediately after the April event, Simcox and Gilchrist split due to differences in their goals for the organization. Two distinct subgroups were formed: the Minuteman Project headed by Gilchrist, and the Minuteman Civil Defense Corps (MCDC) led by Simcox. The branch most active on the Arizona border has been the Minuteman Civil Defense Corps.

Before continuing further, it is critical to note that in late March of 2010 the Minuteman Civil Defense Corps dissolved as a national corporation. On March 16, 2010, MCDC President Carmen Mercer sent an email to the organization's members, urging them to gather at the border with other MCDC volunteers "locked and loaded and ready to stop each and every person they encounter" (Mercer, 2010). Roughly one week later, she called for the dissolution of the organization, citing the overly strong responses of thousands of individuals ready to come to the border with arms, as well as liability concerns (partly due to a new standard operating procedure just enacted) as reasons for the breakup of the group. "It only takes one bad apple to destroy all the good that we have worked for in the last eight years," Mercer stated (Martin, 2010). Critics pointed to failed leadership and mistrust within the organization as reasons for the group's demise (McCombs, 2010, March 25).

Mercer added that "The movement itself, the organization itself, is not going to go away, just the dissolving of the corporation" (Wallace, 2010). She indicated that although the national group was disbanding, independent Minutemen chapters in various states would continue the organization's work through legislative efforts and on the ground action, and be responsible for their own members' behavior (ibid; Martin, 2010). References to MCDC in subsequent chapters will reflect the thought, actions, and quotes of members prior to the dissolution of the national organization, while research for this project was being conducted.

The MCDC, under the leadership of Simcox and later Mercer, cited its purpose as doing "the job the government should be doing" – securing the nation's borders to "protect the United States from invasion by enemies foreign and domestic."[19] Minuteman volunteers came from across the country to take part in citizen patrols along the border. These patrols most often consisted of participating in eight-hour "line watches" –human chains of eyes and ears spread out across a mile or two, watching for border crossers and reporting the activity they saw to the Border Patrol. Most often, these line watches were uneventful; volunteers sat in silence in their lawn chairs, scoping the dark desert for any signs of movement. Many used sophisticated technological devices to assist in their watch: infrared cameras, night vision goggles, enhanced listening devices and radios to communicate with other people on the line. All dressed in dark colors so as to blend in with the landscape; many wore camouflage. In fact, MCDC founder Chris Simcox estimated that half or more of the volunteers came from military or law-enforcement backgrounds.[20] When the volunteers' cameras, goggles, or ears picked up movement in the brush, line leaders radioed the location information to Border Patrol. While they waited for agents to arrive, volunteers sometimes "lit up" crossers with high-powered million candle power spotlights. Some offered food or water while they waited.

According to the organization's standard operating procedure, if illegals were spotted, volunteers were to radio information about their location to the Border Patrol and maintain a no contact policy.[21] Some of the volunteers carried guns or weapons; Simcox claims this was necessary for self-defense in a dangerous area (Well-meaning, 2006). The Border Patrol expressed mixed emotions about this practice. A statement was issued by the Laredo Sector Border Patrol Chief stating that while the Border Patrol appreciates the help, securing the border is a dangerous job and "should be left to the highly trained law enforcement personnel" (Castillo, 2006, p. 1A). Agent Gustavo Soto indicated concern that one of the armed MCDC volunteers could be easily mistaken for an armed drug runner at night, and this situation would place both the agents and volunteers at risk.[22] However, another agent pointed out that MCDC's publicity about the border resulted in much-needed increases in funding for the Border Patrol. In that sense, he felt the organization had been a great help.[23]

One immigration scholar referred to Minuteman efforts as a "border publicity stunt designed to embarrass the federal government" (Andreas, 2006, p. 68). Stunt or not, the Minutemen undoubtedly attracted national attention with newspapers, television stations and other media outlets across the country taking note of the group's controversial activity along the U.S./Mexico line. In fact, the primary success of the group lay not so much in its policing of the border, but in its efforts to garner publicity and advocate for tougher immigration and border control. Simcox encouraged volunteers to talk with media who came to investigate their activity along the border. Indeed, media who contacted the organization were rarely left hanging. Staff trained in public relations handled media-related issues at MCDC headquarters, and leaders eventually hired an official spokeswoman and media consultant, Connie Hair, to help manage publicity for the organization (House & Kamman, 2005). The MCDC also established just over 100 local chapters across the country, with members of these chapters involved in protests, media campaigns and other activities in their communities. According to Mercer and Simcox, in 2010 there were 12,000 active (and therefore screened) members of the organization (McCombs, 2010, March 25).[24]

The Minutemen's emphasis on securing the border by taking matters into their own hands through border watches reflects a lack of confidence in traditional channels of policy change. Chris Simcox stated on the official MCDC website that "composing letters, e-mails and faxes did not make an impression on our public servants. Now we will assert ourselves as citizen representatives of the government. We are citizens who set the example, of the people for the people and by the people."[25] Simcox expounded upon that statement during a personal interview[26] when he described his desire "to embarrass the federal government and expose their duplicity, their dereliction of duty, their absolute abrogation of duties when it comes to securing the borders. We'll expose it, we'll demand reform, and we'll educate the rest of the country." To that end, he says MCDC has been absolutely successful.

MCDC volunteer on line watch duty. November 2007
(Eastman photo)

The Minutemen's efforts have received mixed reviews from the wider public, as evidenced in numerous news reports. Supporters of strict border enforcement measures such as Colorado Representative Tom Tancredo have called the Minuteman volunteers heroes (Carter, 2005). California Governor Arnold Schwarzenegger, who himself admitted to working illegally when he first came to the United States, said the Minutemen had done a "terrific" job and commented that the border with Mexico should be sealed (Glaister, 2005, p. 12). Not everyone is pleased with the organization's efforts, however. Opponents of the group include former U.S. President George W. Bush, who called the Minuteman volunteers "vigilantes" (Lakley, 2005, p. A01),[27] and Mexico's former President Vicente Fox, who referred to them as "migrant hunters" (Ramírez, 2005, p. 3). Positive or negative, the extensive publicity the organization received has drawn international attention to its cause and inspired public participation in this highly contentious issue.

Members of MCDC (and its resulting independent Minuteman chapters), like volunteers for No More Deaths, call into question the state's authority in regard to the handling of immigration-related issues. However, unlike the negative resistance strategy employed by No More Deaths that requires the state to take on an ethical nature and situates its laws within moral principles of justice (Anderson-Gold, 1988), MCDC views the state's role almost exclusively in terms of sovereignty, responsibility, and protection. For members of MCDC, the distrust of the government to effectively control the border and the desire to take matters into their own hands more closely reflects the philosophy of Thomas Paine, who proposed to limit state power in favor of civil society (2000). Paine stressed that citizens must resist state power when the state begins to encroach upon the liberties of individuals (Paine, 2006). This notion has been the basis for numerous civil resistance movements from the 18th century onward, and it is the primary notion that guides the actions of MCDC volunteers. Many of the members with whom I spoke talked about feeling a violation of privacy and witnessing disrespect for personal property when "illegal aliens" had literally walked through their backyards. These individuals feel it is the responsibility of the state to ensure that unauthorized persons, especially mass quantities of them, are not allowed to enter the country at will and cause problems or create fear among United States citizens. Because numerous attempts by the state have failed to secure the border, they see it as their mandate to do this job in place of the federal government – at least to the point of shaming federal authorities into getting serious about their responsibilities.

Civil Society, the State, and the Immigration Debate

How can we best understand the nature and purpose of the organizations dedicated to changing current immigration laws? The histories of the three organizations selected for study exemplify how U.S. immigration policy and its consequences have produced a vibrant, active civil society along the Arizona/Sonora border – one that is unafraid to voice its discontent with federal governance of the immigration issue. In the words of one Humane Borders volunteer, "A nation of compassionate people is depending on [Congress] to bring compassion into our policies." Or, as a Minuteman Civil Defense Corps member states, "[Our goal is] to raise public awareness of impacts and to force elected officials at all levels to enforce the law."

This is a total turn from the relationship that Thomas Hobbes felt civil society shared with the state. In his mid-seventeenth century publication of *Leviathan*, Hobbes portrays natural society as warlike and wrought with disorder, a place of "continuall feare, and danger of violent death; And the life of man, solitary, poor, nasty, brutish, and short" (Keane, 1988, p. 186). This society, unable to rely on human nature to promote ideals of respect and tolerance, depends on a powerful state to establish order. Without this "security state," peace, harmony and stability in society can never be established because individuals will resort back to their natural violent condition.

In such a society, civil society is seen as indistinguishable from the state, which theoretically holds unlimited power. Any type of division in state power could result in its weakening and perhaps spark a crippling civil war; therefore, state power is considered absolute and is in no way transferred to citizens. The actions of the state, because they are supposed to represent the greater interests of the society, are not to be challenged. Thus, no form of collective resistance is permissible *unless* the sovereign rulers are no longer able to protect their subjects.

John Locke's proposal of a constitutional state reflected a much more optimistic view of man than that of Hobbes. Rather than acting as a negation of man's natural condition, Locke believed the state was a cure for the imperfections of the social processes within it (Keane, 1988). Locke believed that society could effectively be managed by a state with limited power that governed civil society only through mutual trust of the governed and those governing. Leaders must always be subject to their own laws, and they must not infringe upon household (private) affairs. When such mutual trust is broken, the governed (members of civil society) have a right to resist.

It is this critical point that explains the reaction to official border policy of the three civil groups being studied. From a Lockean perspective, members of civil society organizations along the border feel the state has broken the trust of its citizens. For humanitarian groups, the state has failed to modify the policies that funneled migrants from urban crossing areas into the desert, leading to large numbers of needless migrant deaths. For Minuteman Civil Defense Corps volunteers, the state has failed to provide security and protection for its citizens by allowing a porous border to remain uncontrolled. In both cases, because this mutual trust has been betrayed, the citizens exercise their refusal to accept the status quo.

The resistance of such organizations, however, has been problematic partly because it does not always fit neatly within distinct categories that separate civil society from the state. Religious and political beliefs have spawned activity that at times challenges the distinction between legal and illegal. What's more, the law itself can be interpreted broadly enough to create a subjective space within which legalities are difficult to define. For example, does the civil liberty to practice religious beliefs advocating care of the poor and suffering exclude the provision of care when those who are suffering happen to be border crossers without legal status? And does the right to protect personal property justify the formation of armed citizen watch groups guarding corridors normally enforced by the federal Border Patrol? What about when members of such watch groups accidentally trip sensors intended for unauthorized border crossers? Such activities create tensions for state institutions that must then re-evaluate their roles as enforcers of immigration law, and determine to what extent civil activity is allowed to impact the responsibilities of federal border-protection agencies.

This relationship between civil society and the state has become even more tenuous as members of civil society, seeing no progress on political or geographical immigration fronts, take on issues themselves that once belonged exclusively to the nation-state. These groups maximize opportunities to utilize the media for purposes of highlighting the ineffectiveness and "broken" state of current policies. They also very resourcefully use media to disseminate their own immigration-related ideologies. By effectively harnessing media attention, civil society organizations have demonstrated an amazing ability to focus public attention on the power of *active citizens* – not the state – to "solve" the immigration problem. Thus a federal issue, through intense media exposure and national debate, becomes an issue debated in political circles *and* in small, private circles. Citizens who might have previously entrusted the issue to the legislative branch are now strapping on their firearms and joining fellow supporters on border watch operations like "Operation Stand Your Ground."[28]

Most remarkable about this entire process is that a policy once considered the responsibility of the nation-state is now being challenged and adopted by members of civil society. This is deemed by some as a threat to the dominion of the state (nation) in supposedly federal matters. Failure of the state to effectively address the issue of immigration and secure the southern U.S. border has prompted action among members of nongovernmental organizations who believe they have better, alternative solutions to offer.

One branch of scholarship argues that this weakening of the state has been partially caused by the recent implementation of global networks. Saskia Sassen feels that a transformation of the state has taken place in immigration policy developments since global economic systems gained strength and power. She believes an analysis of these developments signals "the beginning of a displacement of government functions to non-governmental or quasi-governmental institutions" (Sassen, 1997, p. 15). Sassen writes that "Economic globalization has created a new geography of power in which the state finds its sovereign power reconstituted and often diminished. By contributing to the formation of the new legal regimes and many legal and policy innovations, the state has, to a great extent, transferred authority away from itself" (pp. 2-3).

Peter Andreas's perspective on border policing as a symbolic representation of state authority also indicates a loss of control on the part of federal authorities (2006). Where once the public may have taken for granted that the Border Patrol and related agencies held effective jurisdiction over the border, these authorities now must "perform" by highlighting numbers of arrests or publicizing spectacular busts in order to gain the public's confidence. Even then, certain segments of the public have become so accustomed to hearing about the state's failures in this area that they show greater faith in organizations such as MCDC to "fix the border" than they do in the federal government.

The work of Antonio Gramsci reinforces this potential of a mature civil society to challenge or redefine the role of the state. For Gramsci (1971), civil society was an element of society separate from both the political sphere and the economic sphere. It was a third dimension, a sphere within which capitalists, workers, and other citizens could engage in political and ideological struggles. This third dimension also provided a space for the formation of political parties, religious bodies and other organizations. Gramsci felt that civil society was inherently a moral society because it was through civil society that the ethical roots of the state were created and, through political and ideological struggles, the hegemony of the dominant class was formed.

While Gramsci clearly envisioned the state to be a separate entity from civil society, he also saw the relationship between the two as a methodological one. By this he meant the two should be viewed as separate entities, but at the same time, one must recognize that they are effectively intertwined in practice. Even civic institutions such as schools or newspapers operate as a part of a political society, thus illustrating that civil society cannot ever be completely separated from the state (Gramsci, 2000).

Gramsci also saw civil society as the sphere of "cultural politics" that provides a site for struggle for legitimate use of state power (Calabrese, 2004). He felt the hegemonic position of ruling groups prevented the aims of subaltern groups from being achieved; therefore, it was up to the masses and their use of good reason or "common sense," to confront this state power (and if need be, to seize it). Among the key players in this effort to challenge state hegemony were members of a "thinking class" that Gramsci termed "organic intellectuals" (1971, p. 302; 2001, p. 1138). This was a group of citizens that had been educated and united through institutions of civil society such as newspapers[29] and public education systems. As he stated in the *Prison Notebooks*, "The mode of being of the new intellectual can no longer consist in eloquence, which is an exterior and momentary mover of feelings and passions, but in active participation in practical life, as constructor, organizer, 'permanent persuader' and not just a simple orator" (1971, pp. 9-10). The organic intellectuals, inspired and uplifted by the press, would bring about social change through their active engagement in those civic matters traditionally dominated by the state.

The educational outreach promoted by both Humane Borders and No More Deaths is largely dependent on this class of "organic intellectuals" who, upon learning of the dramatic effects of current immigration policy, will be motivated to shift the balance of power by encouraging other citizens to replace security-driven policy with humanitarian, globally-focused laws. The state may be the entity that determines immigration law, but for these two groups, its hegemony to dictate the nature of that law can and must be challenged by well-informed citizens.

The role of organic intellectuals in Gramsci's writing also mirrors the role that a broader civil society plays in southern Arizona's immigration debate. These members of the citizenry who become active along the border are not considered intellectuals because of class privilege. Instead, they are intellectuals from average backgrounds whose knowledge and leadership inspire fellow citizens to action. Media play an important part in their formation and civic participation, as these organic intellectuals rely on information provided by media (in Gramsci's time, by the press) for both information and inspiration.

Gramsci described a function of the press as leading the masses from "common sense to systematic thought" (1985, p. 413). In a similar fashion, media messages today have influenced public thought about immigration policy to such a degree that likeminded receptors of those messages from across the nation have decided to organize and take action. In doing so, they challenge the nation-state's authority to adequately manage an issue that has, from the time of its inception, fallen under the jurisdiction of federal authorities. Their effectiveness, and the sheer fact that leadership in this civil society movement comes not from elite classes but from average citizens, makes Gramsci an integral part of this research.

Finally, the writings of Jurgen Habermas provide great insight into the idea of civil society and its functions relative to the state – an idea with direct application in the public immigration-related controversies addressed in this study. His emphasis on the importance of discourse relies on an engaged citizenry willing to address topics of concern from divergent points of view within a community setting. While today's public sphere is much more media-centered than the coffee-house feudal era public sphere Habermas originally described, his concepts still offer hope for a strengthened democracy through citizens who are willing to think critically and engage in thoughtful public discourse with one another.

In *The Structural Transformation of the Public Sphere* (1991), Habermas outlines the developments of the public sphere, a site of rational discourse that grew out of the Enlightenment. Prior to this time, during the feudal era, there had been no public – only public display. The notion of sovereignty was embodied in the monarch, who was in turn the embodiment of the state. His will was the public's will, and publicity or displays of power were tokens of his legitimacy.

With the Enlightenment came a separation of private and public and the emergence of critical reasoning. The development of periodicals and rise of new social centers in Europe led to the formation of what came to be known as the public sphere (1964). Private individuals (members of the bourgeois public sphere) began to gather in coffeehouses to engage in public discourse about matters of civil society and the state. The public sphere was the place in which civil society flourished through its active participation in reason and discussion. This was viewed by Habermas as an ideal form of public engagement, because he felt a vibrant civil society that tested out ideas in a public setting was necessary for a successful state.

Although Habermas's theory of the public sphere and the role of civil society within that sphere have been criticized for their idealism (discussion might be valuable, but what happens after the discussion?) and exclusion of women and working classes (though it is important to remember the 18th century context of Habermas's original ideas) they are concepts that continue to provoke discussion among media scholars today. Habermas sees the press as critical to an active, reasoning public. In fact, he distinctly states that "today newspapers and magazines, radio and television are the media of the public sphere" (1964, p. 49). As media technologies have expanded, contemporary researchers point out emerging ways in which blogs, chat rooms, webcams and other forms of communication have augmented the traditional print and broadcast forums for debate such as those described by Habermas in *Structural Transformation*. While some criticize Habermas for paying too little attention to the *mediated* public sphere (Goode, 2005), his designation of media as a critical element of public debate holds great implications for its role in supporting the participation of the masses in public matters.

Habermas believes that an informed and active civil society is critical to healthy community discourse. He suggests that a rise of state involvement in private affairs and lack of public participation have weakened the public sphere (1964). The immigration phenomenon on Arizona's southern border, however, has turned Habermas's theory on its head. In this case, there has been a rise of private (civic) involvement in state affairs, and a growth in public participation in an issue that was once exclusively state-driven. While the swap certainly reflects a changing landscape in terms of the roles of state and society in an increasingly globalized world, it also demonstrates the power of a strong, involved populace that refuses to tolerate what it views as dysfunctional state policies.

Habermas's conceptions of civic participation in public discussion are central to my inquiries about activism and media strategies among border activists. I examine not only the importance of media as a forum for public debate and discussion, but also the ways in which media messages encourage such discussion among members of civil society. Habermasian coffee house discussions may not be the primary means of debating the immigration issue, but blog entries, letters to the editor, talk radio, and other forms of media certainly generate public discussion about immigration across the United States and beyond. Additionally, the information presented in newspaper articles and on television broadcasts stimulates discourse among families, between neighbors and within communities. This study looks critically at how perceptions of media by members of civil society influence their resolve to initiate discussion and engagement among the wider citizenry – even among citizens who are geographically distant from the border.

Although not focused specifically on mediated civic engagement, the theories of Alexis de Tocqueville also contribute a great deal to this study as they address issues of power and negotiation between the state and its citizens. De Tocqueville (2003) acknowledged that a strong state and its correlating political institutions are necessary in order for civil society to function effectively. However, he also feared the tyranny of a state with unchecked power and excessive political authority that would take freedom away from the populace. He was primarily concerned with preserving democratic equalizing tendencies without allowing the state to abuse power and usurp freedoms. To prevent the formation of power monopolies, he recommended that political power should be placed in many and varied hands, citizens must be active within state institutions, and civil associations must be active, grow and develop beyond state control. Only then can they act as a barrier against despotism. Through their active involvement in trying to bring about justice for migrants or in demanding the government seal its borders, civil society volunteers in southern Arizona feel they are helping to define the limits of state power which otherwise might grow beyond its intended scope. Additionally, to the extent that they have chosen legal means for addressing injustices (for example, the effort of No More Deaths volunteers who take affidavits to formally document abuses experienced by migrants at the hands of Border Patrol) members of these groups have exhibited a willingness to not only resist state institutions – but also work within them – to bring about the desired changes.

De Tocqueville's model illustrates how an active civil society can contribute to the balance between state and individual power. It is an ideal democratic model, recognizing the activity of political institutions for the success of democracy while providing a means by which citizens can ensure that state powers do not encroach on individual needs. Although the reality is that citizen interest groups can also create divisive political atmospheres in which problem-solving and dialogue are hindered rather than enhanced, the ideals espoused in this model highlight civil society's important role in balancing state powers with citizen interests. Ideally, according to de Tocqueville, citizens and the state engage in a symbiotic relationship – each ensuring the other's success.

***

The philosophies, ideologies, and active efforts of volunteers for Humane Borders, No More Deaths and the Minuteman Civil Defense Corps make it clear that citizens have invested great energy and passion to making a change in immigration policy. As the aforementioned philosophers and theorists have suggested, if the state won't take action, civil society should – and will. Differences in their approaches are primarily evident in the way the three groups have chosen to view effects of recent immigration policy. The resulting messages about immigration that they have formed and the way those messages are framed and relayed to the public are the topics we turn to next.

Notes

[1] No More Deaths official website. *Humanitarian aid is never a crime: Summer desert work.* Retrieved April 13, 2007 from http://www.nomas muertes.org.

[2] One of the most severely ill migrants later testified at his deposition that without the volunteers' intervention, he would not have been able to make it to a place to receive medical help, and would have likely died (Espinoza, 2006).

[3] Again, American Border Patrol is not to be confused with the U.S. Border Patrol.

[4] For a list and brief description of other border and immigration-related organizations in southern Arizona, please see Appendix 2.

[5] During the 1980s, individuals from Central American countries plagued by civil conflict (particularly Guatemala, El Salvador, and Nicaragua) sought refuge in the United States. However, laws at the time made it difficult for many to obtain asylum. In response, over 500 congregations from churches of various denominations across the country declared themselves sanctuaries for the refugees, opening their doors to the asylum-seekers and providing assistance in open defiance of federal law. Many leaders of the Sanctuary Movement were later arrested and tried for their actions.

[6] Humane Borders Official Website. Retrieved July 24, 2011 from www. humaneborders.org.

[7] An additional item of note is the fact that recognition of many civil society organizations has changed from nongovernmental organization (NGO) to non-profit organization. Such a change mirrors the broader global emphasis that has shifted from state to market.

[8] R. Hoover, Humane Borders, Tucson, AZ (personal interview, October 31, 2007).

[9] Samaritan Patrol website. *Samaritans – who are we?* Retrieved April 1, 2010 from http://www.samaritanpatrol.org/ABOUTSAMARITANS.html.

[10] Zac, No More Deaths, Tucson, AZ (questionnaire).

[11] Abby, No More Deaths, Tucson, AZ (questionnaire).

[12] Fife, J. No More Deaths, Tucson, AZ (Personal interview, November 12, 2007).

[13] The concept of civil disobedience was developed by Henry David Thoreau in his essay "Resistance to Civil Government" published in 1849 (and later re-titled "Civil Disobedience"). In this essay, Thoreau says it is the duty of individuals to act upon their consciences and protest injustices of government, even if that means defying the law (Thoreau, 2009). Thoreau's essay later

influenced the philosophies and actions of such leaders as Martin Luther King, Jr. (See Washington, 1991) and Mohandas Gandhi (See Hunt, 2005).

[14] Fife, J. No More Deaths, Tucson, AZ (Personal interview, November 12, 2007).

[15] Statement taken from No More Deaths website, press release database. Retrieved April 2, 2010 from http://www.nomoredeaths.org/index.php/Press-Releases/federal-judge-threatens-humanitarian-aid-worker-with-25-days-imprisonment.html.

[16] Voluntary repatriations are not considered formal deportations. A person who is formally deported, however, is then subject to a felony charge if he or she attempts to re-enter the United States.

[17] C. Simcox, Minuteman Civil Defense Corps, MCDC muster site (Personal interview, October 22, 2007).

[18] The newspaper has since ceased publication.

[19] Minuteman Civil Defense Corps official website. *About us.* Retrieved April 13, 2007 from http://www.minutemanhq.com/hq/aboutus.php.

[20] C. Simcox, Minuteman Civil Defense Corps, MCDC muster site (Personal interview, October 22, 2007).

[21] Minuteman Civil Defense Corps official website. *Standard operating procedure.* Retrieved April 13, 2007 from http://www.minutemanhq.com/hq/sop.php.

[22] G. Soto, U.S. Border Patrol: Tucson Sector Public Affairs Office (personal interview, May 23, 2007).

[23] M. Scioli, U.S. Border Patrol: Tucson Sector Public Affairs Office (personal interview, November 1, 2007).

[24] MCDC standard operating procedures specify that all applicants and volunteers must undergo a screening process before being granted membership. Simcox says this vetting is important to prevent racist extremists, criminals, or other unwanted persons from becoming part of the organization.

[25] Minuteman Civil Defense Corps official website. *About Us.* Retrieved March 25, 2008 from http://www.minutemanhq.com/hq/aboutus.php.

[26] C. Simcox, Minuteman Civil Defense Corps, MCDC muster site (Personal interview, October 22, 2007).

[27] Both media and politicians who disagree with the aims of MCDC have publicly referred to members as vigilantes. This label infuriates the volunteers, who say they follow strict operating procedures that require them never to take the law into their own hands. They also claim that not one incident of illegal action among members has been reported since the volunteers started their border watches.

[28] Minuteman Civil Defense Corps Official Website, *Operation Stand Your Ground Scheduled for April.* Retrieved March 3, 2008 from http://www.minutemanhq.com/hq/article.php?sid=206.

[29] Gramsci felt the role of newspapers should be to provide cohesion, educate the general public and unite communities. These ideals form the foundations of today's community journalistic practices.

6
Media and Civil Society: Walking the Line Together

"Without criticism and reliable and intelligent reporting,
the government cannot govern."

*Walter Lippmann, Address at the International Press
Institute Assembly, London (May 27, 1965)*

A Beneficial Interaction

The relationship between media and civil society along the Arizona/Sonora border is in many ways a symbiotic one. Without media reports on the activities of these civic groups, the public might know about the problems along the border but not the people who are working to see those circumstances change. Groups such as Humane Borders, the Minuteman Civil Defense Corps (MCDC) and No More Deaths would have a much harder time delivering their messages to a wider public and recruiting support from people both near and far from the border if it were not for the help of media.

These organizations benefit greatly from media, but they also contribute greatly to it. The actions of these civic groups give reporters and journalists context and content for their stories on border-related issues. While media are in no way dependent on civil society for survival, they do benefit from the human interest and controversy created through the actions of these groups. The dedication and determination of these organizations adds richness and depth to the story of immigration, a story that also in many ways highlights struggles of the human condition. Furthermore, the passion of a citizenry that is willing to roll up its sleeves and take action on an issue that should under normal circumstances be handled by the federal government provides excellent substance for front page or lead stories.

This chapter explores the delicate, contentious, and collaborative ways that media and civil society interact with one another along the

Arizona/Sonora divide. It begins with a look at the media selection patterns of the activists in the three groups being studied. Emphasis is placed on the idea that members of these civil groups, recognizably among the most extreme and/or passionate populations in their immigration-related views, largely fuel their own convictions and ideologies through media sources that reinforce their pre-existing beliefs. The volunteers then perpetuate their beliefs through the frames they create to present their border and immigration ideas to media. This generally happens through coverage of their activities or of a major event; nonetheless, those frames are consequently communicated through media to a wider public where they contribute to national discourse and understanding of the immigration issue. Starting with media selection and ending with media controversy, the following sections examine consumption patterns, levels of trust, and obstacles along the long, uneven line that media and civil society have walked together.

The Selective Process of Media Consumption

The extent of media's potential for mass persuasion and power of influence has been the subject of research dating back to the early part of the twentieth century. Accepted views of media evolved from the "magic bullet" theory that media have a direct influence on audiences to limited effects theories acknowledging the role of human agency and recognizing additional factors playing a role in people's interpretation of media messages (Davis & Baron, 1981). Instead of granting media the power of direct influence over individuals, the empirical studies conducted during this limited effects era provided evidence of various personal, social and environmental factors that influence decision-making. They also emphasized that media's primary influence comes from the way individuals *choose* to use media (ibid).

Researcher Paul Lazarsfeld and his student Joseph Klapper, through research investigating the link between people's media consumption habits and their views of the world, concluded that people tend to gravitate toward media that reinforce their pre-existing values, ideas and beliefs about the issues at hand (Baran & Davis, 2006). Klapper in particular concluded that individuals employ selective processes when choosing various forms of media (1960) and that media's influence (if any) was to reinforce preexisting beliefs (ibid).

This theory of reinforcement holds great implications for research about media and civil society along the Arizona/Sonora border, because it provides a framework for understanding the media consumption choices of the civil society volunteers being studied. Widespread generalizations can never be made about a diverse population, nor can assumptions be formed about the psychological influences that draw people to certain types of media messages. Whether individuals select specific media sources because they reinforce pre-existing beliefs, or whether they develop their ideas and beliefs based on the media messages they consume is a separate study in itself. However, research for this project did point to definite media selection trends indicating the content of media selected by group members generally mirrored their internalized and reproduced messages about immigration. This was particularly true regarding selection of media sources for news-gathering purposes. Although the subject populations were small and these test populations represent groups of people with intense opinions about immigration, it is still noteworthy that members' selection of media sources seems to aid in the formation and reinforcement of the frames used by such groups to promote their messages about immigration.

Sources and Perceptions of Reliable Information

Questionnaires addressing media selection and usage were distributed to volunteers from all three civil society groups being studied.[1] The first page of the questionnaire listed questions related to demographics and media consumption patterns. For example, participants were asked what (if any) newspapers they read, which magazines they subscribed to, which news or talk programs they watched/listened to, and which websites they regularly visit to gather news or information. They were also asked to indicate the number of hours they spent each day gathering news, and which factors (from a designated list) were most important to them when considering the sources from which they obtain news. (Examples included: easily accessible source, convenient times, trusted reporters or news personalities, similar political beliefs of the source to their own views and beliefs, etc.) Later questions provided the opportunity for participants to expound upon their previous answers and list reasons why they like or dislike specific media sources.

Analysis of the questionnaires indicated specific media consumption trends that stood out for each of the three separate groups being studied. Volunteers for Humane Borders, for example, were more likely to use radio than any other media source for gathering information. Of the 18 interviews and questionnaires that were evaluated, eleven listed radio as a source of news. National Public Radio (NPR) was the most common news source – listed by all eleven of the radio listeners. Many also specified NPR programs such as *Democracy Now!, All Things Considered* and *Talk of the Nation.*

The second most common source of news information for Humane Borders volunteers was local newspapers. Ten respondents indicated that they regularly read *The Arizona Daily Star*, and some also read the *Tucson Citizen*. Mona, a 4-year Humane Borders volunteer, says media mostly hinder the group's efforts to educate the public, but adds that "the stories in the local newspaper do personalize the issue and that helps." Muriel, who moved to Tucson in order to be regularly involved in border work, agrees that local media cover the immigration issue well. "*The Daily Star* here is probably one of the best mainstream newspapers around to try to get immigration news. And then things that are in the news here don't even get touched on elsewhere in the U.S.; national news often doesn't pick it up. I mean, for instance, I don't think there's anybody on the national level who is reporting the number of deaths, but we know the number of deaths."

Humane Borders volunteers also tended to subscribe to a wide variety of magazines (although not necessarily for border-related information), and they indicated accessing a number of different websites for news. The importance of television as a source of news information for this group was, however, surprisingly low. Of the 18 respondents, eight said they do not gather *any* news from television, and two of those do not even own a TV. One explained that she relies on written media more than television "because with TV there is still a show to be put on. For example, *60 Minutes* lost a lot of credibility to me because after the '70s and '80s they tried too hard and became more about sensationalism and less about neutral reporting. So printed media seems to be more accountable." Those who do watch television news programs listed primarily the major networks (NBC, CBS, ABC) as well as CNN and MSNBC as their sources. Three also said they watch FOX News. Brian, a retired Air Force Master Sergeant, says he listens to Bill O'Riley, Chris Matthews, and Hannity & Colmes in order to understand opposing points of view. "Doesn't mean I agree with them," he says. "We need to know what these dangerous people are thinking."

Humane Borders founder Robin Hoover does not fit neatly into any of the categorizations listed above because he consumes from a wide variety of media sources. In fact, as I conducted a personal interview with Hoover in his office, a satellite television news program was playing in the background and various newspapers were lying on his desk.[2] In addition to accessing global channels on the television, he subscribes to XM satellite radio so he can stay informed while driving around town or in the desert. Hoover says he also listens to local air play on talk radio. When asked about how he selects these sources he replied, "I want the full breadth of ideological presentation. I don't listen to people that I *want* to listen to – I listen to *all* of them."

Hoover's interest in global sources may also stem from the fact that Humane Borders has been covered so extensively around the world. As Hoover describes it, "We've been in every media market on earth. We've been in the Manchurian Chinese news agency, the Pakistan news, the Pacific Rim, Japanese TV, Chile live interviews. We've had foreign film crews from 25 nations here. ... We've had every network in the United States of any size here and in Mexico with us."

With the exception of Robin Hoover and Brian, the choices Humane Borders volunteers make about their media sources of news and information tend to support Klapper's reinforcement theory. In response to a question asking respondents to choose the most important factors they consider when selecting a news source, five people checked the box that stated "the political beliefs of this source reflect my own views and beliefs." Trends in the nature of coverage also link the beliefs of the respondents to the media sources they choose. Textual analysis of transcripts from approximately ten NPR programs from December 2006 to February 2008 and more than two hundred local (Phoenix and Tucson) newspaper articles about immigration and/or border-related issues from March 2005 to March 2008 demonstrates broad coverage of these issues that often combines factual information with personal stories highlighting the human condition. In contrast to conservative media outlets that stress border security and legalism, the news sources accessed by Humane Borders volunteers tend to be more far-reaching in their efforts to explore the current state of unauthorized immigration as an economic, labor, and social issue in addition to presenting security concerns. For example, analysis of coverage from *The Arizona Daily Star* revealed numerous stories related to border safety issues and the building of the fence, but also a large quantity of stories that explained the hazards of desert crossing, the number of deaths in the desert and the efforts of groups like Humane Borders, No More Deaths and the Minuteman Civil Defense Corps to increase public awareness and participation. NPR coverage was similar; reporters found unique story angles about the families of migrants, the impacts of migration on the economy and the cost incurred by counties to pay for the processing of bodies found in the desert. Thus, in general terms, news sources selected by Humane Borders volunteers tended to reinforce their own beliefs that the issue of immigration cannot be reduced to just security or illegal entry, and that effective reform dictates a more extensive and inclusive understanding of the complex problems at hand.

The media consumption trends of No More Deaths volunteers were very similar to those of Humane Borders volunteers. National Public Radio was again listed as the most common source of news (nine of the eleven respondents indicated this), with local newspapers such as *The Arizona Daily Star* following close behind (7 of 11 regularly read this paper). In addition to these sources, however, the *New York Times* was listed by five as a regular source of information, and indymedia (independent media) was popular among three. Abby, a No More Deaths volunteer from New Hampshire, said, "*The New York Times* has had some good articles on immigration issues in Phoenix recently and I think these are vital. Media sources that use terms such as "illegals" and discuss "amnesty" as if it is a four letter word greatly hinder efforts to educate the public about what the border is really like."

These last two sources mentioned, *The New York Times* and indymedia, are considered examples of liberal media by MCDC members as evidenced by responses to survey questions and comments during interviews. This designation, particularly of *The New York Times*, has been debated in blogs and various public forums. However, a search for "Immigration and Refugees Editorials" on *The New York Times* website produced 157 results between March 1, 2005 and March 28, 2008. Many of these editorials highlight the problems with current policy, describing the present "harsh-enforcement virus" and "immigration zealotry" affecting the country,[3] discussing this nation's "neurosis" about the border[4] or commenting on "rational debate about immigration policy that went beyond xenophobia and the fear of disorder."[5] Other editorials retrieved during the search held titles such as "Pass the DREAM Act"[6] and "They Are America."[7] While the language and content of these editorials do not make *The New York Times* a liberal newspaper, they do indicate an unfavorable view of security-first approaches to immigration and a willingness to view the issue through a critical lens that considers the human element of the debate. Such views correspond well with the more humanitarian convictions of No More Deaths and Humane Borders members.

No More Deaths volunteers also relied very little on television as a source of news. Five of the eleven respondents do not use television at all for information. One of them, Rick, criticized television broadcasting for not taking time to fully explain the issues at hand. "TV reporters are unbelievably superficial in their reporting, and don't appear to have a personal stake," he said. "I think most of the TV reporting is weak at best. Radio – especially with Public Radio – is better. Print media tends to be the best." Zac, a media spokesperson for No More Deaths, was once a reporter for indymedia. He feels these independent sources can take more time to cover the issues in-depth, explaining the circumstances that contribute to current immigration patterns. "Most media tend to sensationalize our work or present it with little or no context to broader economic issues," he said. "I think they are hindering [our efforts] by the lack of connections they draw between everything that affects migration."

Minuteman Civil Defense Corps survey and interview results also showed very distinctive trends and common media preferences among the group's volunteers. Members of this organization overwhelmingly indicated that their primary, preferred sources of news and information – particularly about border issues – were well-known conservative television and radio stations and personalities. Of the 14 interviews and questionnaires analyzed, all but two of the MCDC respondents listed FOX News as a primary news source. Five specifically mentioned that they watch FOX News personality Bill O'Riley, and four specifically named Hannity & Colmes. The general sentiment among these volunteers was that other mainstream network news sources were either inaccurate or incomplete in coverage, and therefore could not be trusted.

Most of the MCDC respondents also listed CNN as a primary trusted source of news, with four making specific mention of Lou Dobbs as a reliable voice for the border, and four listing Glenn Beck as a source on whom they rely. Owen, a volunteer from Ohio, credits these two television news hosts with helping the national public better understand what is happening with immigration. "Lately," he said, "CNN's Lou Dobbs and Glenn Beck have picked up the illegal immigration gauntlet and begun to make their audiences aware of what is going on."

Other comments from MCDC respondents indicated similar support for these personalities and their programs. Max, a media relations director for MCDC, thinks Lou Dobbs portrays the problem on the border very well. He adds, "FOX News does a pretty good job at [border reporting]. They've been out here with us; they've done live feed with us out on the border here...I think CNN, FOX News have educated the public into understanding exactly what we're doing and why we do it, and that we're not a vigilante group."

Not everyone is so optimistic. Duane feels that most media do a poor job of accurately representing what MCDC is all about. "Mainstream media is only interested in sensationalism and portraying the Minutemen Civil Defense Corps as a bunch of gun-toting vigilantes to confirm President Bush's words on national TV." Graham agrees. "Most media report us as vigilantes. We do not have ONE mark against us." He lists FOX and CNN's Lou Dobbs as usually being very fair in their coverage, and CBS, NBC and CNN (other than Dobbs) as being very unfair. Stu is of the same opinion. "Mainstream media puts their own spin on it; FOX seems to be about the only one who tells the truth." Philip concurs that the public must be selective about choosing news sources. "Any of the network news stations don't give you a true picture of what's going on down here. FOX News does. CNN, sometimes. But that's basically the only source of real information of what's going on."

Some volunteers note that there is a difference in coverage between local and national news sources. Kirk, who only trusts FOX because the political views of that station reflect his own, claims he has pretty much boycotted most major radio stations, TV stations, and newspapers. "Most of the mainstream media and their affiliates are sugar-coating everything," he says. "The illegals are not being called illegals. The murders are not being called murders. So I would say that right now, thanks to Chris Simcox and the Minutemen, the national news does a better job of representing the border news than the local news in Arizona."

Marissa, a native of Montana who retired and built a home just a few miles north of the border, says the only thing she watches consistently that she likes is Lou Dobbs. "I trust Dobbs," she says. "He tells it like it is. It's not pretty, but he tells it like it is."

In terms of radio, MCDC volunteers also listed almost exclusively conservative broadcasters, with Rush Limbaugh getting the most nods among listeners, and Laura Ingraham, Michael Savage, and Michael Medved also being mentioned as popular choices for news information.

There were a handful of exceptions to the conservative media choices among MCDC members. A few volunteers said they gather *local* information from *local* newspapers or television stations, one mentioned watching *NBC Nightly News* as a source of information, and various responders said they access a variety of Websites (not necessarily politically oriented) for gathering news. One volunteer also mentioned that he gets his news from Public Broadcasting as well as Glenn Beck.

Chris Simcox, MCDC founder, proved to be an exception to all of the aforementioned general media consumption tendencies. Simcox cited numerous on-line newspaper sources – both liberal and conservative – as his primary founts of news information, as well as all the news and talk programs that he can possibly find. He did list CNN and FOX as two television networks he watches, but added, "FOX is just as bad as any of them. All of them are terrible." Simcox says he thinks it is important to stay informed through all kinds of different sources – not just those that might reflect his own views. "I want to read everything from the crap on salon.com to Town Hall, to human events. I love reading the socialist columns and stuff so I know what the youth of America are thinking on college campuses." Simcox says he takes everything with a grain of salt, because he realizes everyone has an agenda. In order to keep up with border and immigration issues, he has a Google alert with keywords programmed into his phone. "[I'm] always on the run, reading, reading, reading, keeping up on things. I just read everything I can," he says.

Strategic Approaches to Media

In addition to their discontent with federal responses to immigration, Humane Borders, No More Deaths and the Minuteman Civil Defense Corps (MCDC) also share in common an understanding of the importance of media: both for receiving information about border-related issues and for proliferating their own messages and calls for reform. The official websites for all three groups have links to extensive local, regional, national and international media coverage of their activities. Leaders and volunteers of the organizations cite coverage by journalists, authors, broadcasters and media crews from as far away as India, Spain, Turkey and Brazil who came to the southern Arizona desert to see firsthand what civil society is doing there.

Furthermore, the leaders of all three groups have extensive personal experience with media. Chris Simcox, co-founder of MCDC, purchased and ran a local newspaper (the *Tombstone Tumbleweed*) for nearly four years in Tombstone, AZ. Simcox used the paper as a means to publicize and disseminate his views of the border and border policy. After closing the newspaper in 2006, Simcox promoted his cause through other media outlets including radio, television, and print sources. As President of MCDC he made thousands of media appearances and hundreds of public presentations throughout the United States that were also covered by media. In April of 2009 Simcox resigned his position with MCDC to run for the Republican nomination for U.S. Senate, giving him further media exposure as he challenged former presidential candidate John McCain. Simcox dropped out of the race in February, 2010 but continues to serve as a spokesperson for state and national media coverage of border security issues.

Robin Hoover, co-founder of Humane Borders, holds a master's degree in journalism/mass communication and a Ph.D. in political science. Because Humane Borders was among the first groups to form in response to increasing deaths in the desert, Hoover's experience makes him one of the most well-versed and involved activists on the border. He has been a spokesperson for this issue for ten years, giving interviews to media corporations as diverse as CNN and Al Jazeera. Under his leadership, Humane Borders created a media library holding thousands of articles, broadcast reports, documentaries and other coverage of the group and its efforts.

Rick Ufford-Chase and Reverend John Fife, two of the organizers of the No More Deaths movement, are also no strangers to publicity. Ufford-Chase placed the objectives of this movement on a national platform while he served as moderator of the Presbyterian Church, USA from 2004-2006. Prior to his involvement with No More Deaths, Ufford-Chase founded BorderLinks and was deeply involved with the Sanctuary Movement, both of which also garnered media attention for the concerns they raised about immigration policy. Rev. John Fife drew widespread publicity in the 1980s as a co-founder of the national Sanctuary Movement. His role in that movement, and in the establishment of No More Deaths, has been well documented in various mass media outlets. Both Ufford-Chase and Fife have written published articles about the border and the need for immigration policy change.

The three organizations studied all recognize that mass media form a critical link between their immigration and border-related arguments and public support for their causes. Therefore, all three have developed well-designed media strategies to further their messages. No More Deaths has organized a media working group that handles all media relations and develops talking points around issues the group feels are most important, primarily that providing aid to fellow humans should never be considered a crime regardless of legal status. The organization holds press conferences, issues press releases and seeks to generate positive op-eds and letters to the editor supporting their positions. All of the group's press releases are archived on its website, as are links to news articles about the group and its members and a calendar of events detailing No More Deaths activities. The website provides links for readers who wish to contact lawmakers and lobby on behalf of immigration reform. According to the media relations coordinator, the organization has found its greatest success in recruitment through media outreach, particularly news media, but also through the internet as a means of maintaining communication with supporters and former volunteers. Additionally, group members place great importance on face-to-face contact and conversations with community members through presentations at churches, public events, or other outreach opportunities.

For its first ten years, the Humane Borders message predominantly reached the general public through the written word, power of the individual voice, and educational forums. Founder Robin Hoover served as the primary media spokesperson for the group from its creation in 2000 until 2010. Hoover, understanding the important role of the press, blended the moral message of preventing needless deaths with the physical image of water stations in the desert, creating a straightforward but powerful message about the ethical responsibility of fellow citizens to respond to those in need. He also utilized media channels to publicly challenge the actions of elected officials and to defend the work of his organization.[8] The Humane Borders focus on preventing needless loss of life among the migrant population is best summed up in Hoover's well-known mission to "take death out of the immigration equation" (Humane, 2010).

The Humane Borders media strategy has changed over the ten years of the organization's existence. According to co-founder Sue Ann Goodman, Humane Borders did not initially develop a specific media strategy or intentionally invite media to cover the group's activities. That approach later changed as spokesperson Robin Hoover in particular began actively pursuing relationships with media and inviting media to cover the group's efforts. When reflecting on the evolution of the group's media strategy, acting media representative Liana Rowe said Hoover's contact with media was critical to making the public aware of Humane Borders and its efforts. "Somebody had to orchestrate it," she said, "or [media] would not have paid attention."[9] Now, those involved with the organization are eager to help media understand more about not only the primary activity of placing life-saving water in the desert, but also of the circumstances that drive migration and the policy changes the group hopes can be made to prevent future deaths. Although Hoover is no longer the organization's spokesperson, Lowe cites Hoover's consistent contact with media as the reason for the widespread attention Humane Borders has received.

From its inception, the goals of the Minuteman Civil Defense Corps (MCDC) have always included media coverage as a means of disseminating the group's views and ideologies. In fact, attracting media attention was the original intent of Simcox and Gilchrist when they organized the initial border muster in 2005. After the first day of the gathering, Gilchrist claimed victory to the hundreds of journalists who had gathered. "We have already accomplished our goal a hundredfold," he said. "We've got our message out to the American public" (Carroll, 2005).

In addition to holding widely publicized events such as border musters, the media strategy of the national MCDC organization involved the work of a professional media group, hired to handle press releases, seek out interviews with radio and television stations and connect MCDC leadership with the myriad of media inquiries MCDC receives. Great efforts were made to ensure that MCDC's president, vice president, or other representatives were always available to talk with media, and volunteers interviewed by media were given training to learn the group's primary talking points and ensure they understood and communicated the message of the organization. Direct relationships were cultivated with many media professionals who were invited to the border to take part in musters or other organized events. MCDC also provided video footage of the border to media, including FOX News. The organization's focus on its communications outside the membership has in large part created its notoriety. It is somewhat ironic that it was a new, more assertive communication strategy by MCDC leadership, the "locked and loaded and ready" e-mail by President Carmen Mercer calling on MCDC volunteers to come to the border armed and ready to defend their country (Mercer, 2010), that contributed to the national organization's demise in March of 2010.

Media as Friend or Foe? Exploring Issues of Trust

The efforts of civil society organizations along the southern Arizona border would be little known if it were not for media accounts of their activities. Statements of volunteers from across the United States who said they became aware of the organizations through media reports is evidence that these three civil society have in fact reached a wider public and drawn attention to the immigration issue through media. As MCDC member Kirk stated, "If it weren't for that take on FOX News, I might not have found these people."

By employing definitive media strategies and framing the immigration issue in specific ways, these groups also hope their ideologies will be transmitted to an interested public sphere far beyond the immediate border area. They aim to promote public discussion, debate and active reform of immigration policy. However, the implication that there is a Habermasian-type public sphere in today's mediated society depends a great deal on the assumption that there is an informed public willing to engage in debate. After all, "The policy process for immigration is no longer confined to a narrow governmental arena of ministerial and administrative action. Public opinion and public political debate have become part of the space wherein immigration policy is shaped" (Sassen, 2006, p. 5).

In contemporary society, those debates are often played out through media channels: letters to the editor, blogs, chat rooms, on-line forums, magazine articles, books, television and radio programs that invite call-in participation to name a few. Citizens rely on media reports to provide the factual information that serves as a foundation for their own views and ideas about immigration-related issues. Subsequently, they engage in conversation (mediated or otherwise) with a wider public, adding their own experiences and opinions to the debate.

However, in order for media to serve as a foundation for critical public discussion in the ideal Habermasian sense, the public must see media as reliable sources of information or – at the very least – be willing to engage with media even though they do not have confidence that issues will be reported fairly or accurately. This is an idea central to the research, because *media trust* was an issue that elicited strong reactions from all of the civil society groups being studied. While some groups generally had a favorable view of media's representation of the topics being covered, others felt betrayed by inaccurate reporting and incomplete coverage of what they consider a national crisis. As a result, a few have even shunned all forms of mainstream media. Others have determined they must rely on their experiences and their relationships with likeminded individuals, not news sources, for accurate information about the border. The varying views represent differing levels of trust in media to tell the immigration story.

Minuteman Civil Defense Corps (MCDC)

Many of the members of MCDC expressed distrust or distaste for media, even though they acknowledge that it is through media that most of them became aware of the organization and thus became involved. In fact, ten of the fourteen participants of the study (71%) indicated that they had learned about the organization through media channels. This demonstrates media's incredible power to disseminate information and elicit responses from citizens across the country; the 14 MCDC participants with whom I spoke represented seven different states and lived as far away as Maine, Florida, and Washington. Despite the important role that media played in bringing them to the border, however, most were very skeptical of all but the standard conservative sources upon which they rely for information.

> MARISSA: I'll be honest, I think they [media] have less credibility than a used car salesman. That's how I feel about the media anymore, because I've seen what they do to us.

> INTERVIEWER: Radio, TV, print?

MARISSA: It doesn't matter. Especially print. I have less use for print because, for instance, if you want to rebut something in the paper and you write a letter to the editor, they pick and choose what they want out there. You're never going to get in if you've got a conservative point of view if he's a liberal, which most print media is liberal... But I don't trust what they write because they don't want to look at both sides of the picture.

One major reason for volunteers' distrust of media has been negative coverage of the organization. A content analysis of 78 articles about the Minutemen in *The Arizona Republic* and *The Arizona Daily Star* from March 2005 to March 2006 found that while this group was given far more coverage than any other civil society group active on the border, the majority of that coverage was negative in tone. [10] Many stories criticized the group's activities as efforts to take the law into their own hands while others condemned the carrying of weapons by volunteers. Although this research did not include broadcast media coverage of MCDC, similar stories questioning the motives of the organization have appeared in those media channels as well. The breadth of the overall coverage did earn the group widespread recognition, which was part of Simcox's original goal, and not all media coverage was negative in tone. Nonetheless, the MCDC volunteers with whom I visited were angered because they feel media do not try to report them fairly.

Terrence, a retired electrical engineer from Maine, says it was actually his distrust of media reporting about the group that led him to become involved in the organization. He also indicated that, as a volunteer, his own experience with the group far outweighs any negative media coverage of the organization in terms of what he chooses to believe.

TERRENCE: Most news coverage is negatively slanted or outright lies – such as the vigilante accusation. Knowing this, it was a clue that this (MCDC) must be a constructive and patriotic organization. ... I am better informed than the media, and I would never rely on the media as a prime source for something important like this.

MCDC founder Chris Simcox is even more explicit in his distrust of media. He says he gathers information from a variety of media sources, but does not have confidence in any of them. "I wouldn't trust the media as far as I could throw President Bush," he stated during a personal interview.[11] "I don't trust any of them. FOX is just as bad as any of them. All of them are terrible."

This is an interesting point of view, considering that Simcox knows he must maintain a close relationship with media in order to continue to place his objectives on a national platform. It was media coverage that brought him widespread recognition, and it has been continued media coverage that has allowed him to spread his message of stopping illegal immigration across the country. This was particularly true as Simcox stepped down from MCDC leadership and incorporated his border security message into his campaign for John McCain's U.S. Senate seat.[12]

Members of MCDC who saw media as untrustworthy often pointed to the lack of "truth" being portrayed in media accounts of the border.

> MARISSA (MCDC): I don't care what you think about what I do. I care that you report the truth. That's your responsibility. ... You will hear, if you are listening to CNN, what I call the "bimbos" – the morning girls, you know? They talk about a border wall. Well there is no border wall. It's a fence. But if you ever hear it on CNN other than through Lou Dobbs, who is their conservative person, they will call it a wall. Those little words that drop into people's minds are visual. So people anticipate, like the Berlin Wall. It's not that. It goes right by my house. It's mesh. You can see through it. It's really not bad... But that's the thing that really kind of bothers me is the verbage that is used that is negative to turn peoples' opinion. And how dare they. That's not right.

Volunteers from MCDC often indicated distrust of the media or discontent with the nature of reporting, largely because of misrepresentations of their organization. Many were angry that the media widely repeated President Bush's accusations that they are vigilantes on the border. Vigilantes, they say, take the law into their own hands. MCDC volunteers just observe and report what they see to the Border Patrol. Many also felt media do not paint an accurate picture of what is really happening on the border – either by reducing a complex problem to sound bites or by not taking the time to actually come and see for themselves what is happening there.

Terrence was quick to point out that reporters often only tell half the story, or else they mischaracterize what they see. He replied, "Do some serious investigation and tell the whole truth." When Graham, a volunteer from Washington was asked what message he would like to relay to the press about MCDC, he replied, "Report the true facts... Please report us fairly. We are not vigilantes." Wendy had a similar message for the press: "Open your eyes and report accurately...The media doesn't cover completely and *correctly* the work that the Border Patrol and MCDC do."

Humane Borders and No More Deaths

Volunteers for Humane Borders and No More Deaths generally demonstrated a greater trust for media overall, but were quick to point out that there are often discrepancies in both what is reported and how it is reported. No More Deaths volunteer Abby, originally from New Hampshire, says one of the things that has had the greatest impact on her since becoming involved is "seeing how misrepresented migrants are in our media – coming out here and actually seeing for myself who is crossing the border... People do form opinions about 'illegal immigration' based on what they read and hear in the media. It is easy to breed fear of the unknown, especially if you've never seen a Mexican person before because you grew up in New England."

One major issue that many of the volunteers raised for both of these groups was that media tend to want to create a dichotomy between "opposing sides" of the immigration debate. Humane Borders volunteer Mona points out that "media likes to pit people on one side against another – so they present the most inflammatory aspects of our mission." Quinn, a No More Deaths volunteer from Louisiana, is frustrated with these comparisons, too, but acknowledges that they can serve to draw in like-minded individuals. "The media creates false dichotomies like No More Deaths vs. Minutemen," she says. "These help and hurt us." No More Deaths co-founder Rick Ufford-Chase dislikes the discord created by such comparisons. "Reporters think that the way you cover a story nowdays is you have to get a pro and con, and you have to get a conflict going." Volunteer and media spokesperson Zac agrees that this approach is nonproductive.

> ZAC: With a group like No More Deaths ... our media coverage tries to humanize the situation that we are experiencing, and the corporate media folks can only handle so much of that. I have had several interviews where the press has tried to place No More Deaths and the Minutemen on polar sides of the "debate." I usually have to show that we are not comparable in our missions and we don't really contradict each other, at least not in how the media wants it to be. So instead of getting their juicy story that pits supposedly pro-immigrant groups and anti-immigrant groups against each other, they end up getting a thoughtful reflection on U.S. trade and economic policy conflicting with border and immigration policy – not something terribly exciting for the six o'clock news.

This purported tendency of media to create dichotomies between "opposing" sides is problematic in another sense as well. While it is true that Humane Borders and No More Deaths differ from MCDC in their views about how immigration-related problems should be addressed, all three groups share the *same* view that the immigration system is broken and needs to be fixed. Each has made tremendous efforts to help the public understand the various ways in which current policy creates chaos or danger along the border and beyond. Thus, a notion of opposition creates a false impression that these civil society activists disagree on everything. They do not; all three call upon the United States government to use its resources wisely to enact effective solutions.

Robin Hoover of Humane Borders stated he would like to see the nature of reporting change to be more substantive and more reflective of the journalism practices observed in other countries. "Journalism [in the U.S.] is methodologically driven, or driven by an editor," says Hoover. "So they want to do a counterpoint and they don't know how to figure out who's the point and who's the counterpoint - whether or not it's us and the Border Patrol or it's us and the Minutemen...I think the media has tried to show a counterpoint without a substantive analysis. I want Edward R. Murrow's *Harvest of Shame* kind of journalism and we're not seeing that." Hoover goes on to describe the differences he sees between domestic and foreign reporting. "Foreign journalists are unlike U.S. journalists. They'll just get involved, interview the migrants, carry jugs of water, they'll get involved in the issue and take positions and make normative statements. They don't carry the liberal fiction of the U.S. media that they're supposed to be objective. They don't even accept the fact that you can be objective." Hoover also went on to say, "The foreign journalists have done far greater analysis and have done far better homework, preparing themselves, reading more books before they got here. They read books, not just articles. They didn't come over here from Italy, Brazil and Chile, or wherever, just to chit chat about 'What do you think?' They're here to try to shape the public opinion. And U.S. journalists don't do that."

Although the approach of foreign and domestic journalists to immigration issues may differ, it is, in fact, the intentional media efforts to shape public opinion that have created much of the distrust among members of the three groups. Conservative media personalities such as Lou Dobbs or Michelle Malkin are very purposeful about the views they share of the border and immigration, as are liberal personalities such as Bill Maher. Critics of both liberal and conservative media argue that certain domestic media sources do deliberately try to shape public opinion. For example, the fact that FOX News uses video supplied by MCDC (rather than by FOX reporters) for many of its reports on border issues has serious implications. Such a close relationship necessarily defines to a certain degree the nature of the message that is transmitted to the public. The end result of such concerted efforts to influence public sentiments about immigration is a muddle of biased views and misinformation amidst objective reporting that polarizes the public, confuses media consumers, and does little to promote serious dialogue and conversation about the issues at hand.

Many volunteers also expressed concern about the amount of anti-immigrant rhetoric currently being disseminated through national media channels. Co-founders of the No More Deaths movement John Fife and Rick Ufford-Chase warn that biased reporting from conservative media has created an environment of fear among both the public and politicians. "It's Lou Dobbs, it's Rush Limbaugh, and it's the Right Wing radio folks who are dominating the agenda who claim that comprehensive immigration reform is amnesty and these people are law-breakers, they're criminals, and the rhetoric just goes on and on," says Fife. "They have the politicians scared to death." [13] Ufford-Chase agrees, saying media-driven efforts are one of the primary ways civil society is affecting immigration right now, especially through "the hard Right played out most spectacularly by Lou Dobbs and Bill O'Riley. I'd say that the sector of civil society that they - I won't say that they represent, but they foment - I think has had a huge impact on public policy."[14]

Humane Borders volunteer Gary, a retired homicide investigator, is also concerned about this influence. "Lou Dobbs is a major player at CNN. For over a year now he has been obsessed and fixated with the issue of 'illegals.' He is suggesting that illegals are ruining America. I am confident that his hate-mongering is poisoning the well of popular opinion by virtue of his massive exposure combined with his myopic vision regarding the issue." Glenn, a priest from Nebraska thinks such negative attitudes by media professionals must be changed. "I do not see the media as even trying to address the misinformation, racism and promotion of fear. Why this is so is a mystery to me."

Despite these concerns, on the whole both Humane Borders and No More Deaths volunteers see media as a positive force, and are generally pleased with the nature of the coverage their groups have received. Fife appreciates the coverage No More Deaths has been given over the years, particularly after the 2005 arrest and trial of two of the group's volunteers. Reports of the "Humanitarian Aid is Never a Crime" campaign throughout Arizona raised awareness of the volunteers' plight and made the general public more aware of the humanitarian efforts being waged in the desert. "They [media] were very helpful," he said. "We've had very good media coverage, almost exclusively. I can't think of a bad example."

Humane Borders volunteer Rose thinks the media generally "get it" when it comes to what her organization is trying to do. "Generally speaking, the media have been very good to us. They have told our story, promoted our work. There certainly were a few times when they were highly critical of it or questioned our legality, but I would say as a whole I do think media covered us very well." Gary agrees. "Overall I would say that most of the local reports ... emphasize our life-saving mission."

Sue Ann Goodman, wife of Robin Hoover and co-founder of Humane Borders, has a keen understanding of the coverage the organization has received. She helped organize the group's media archives room, filled with over 2100 print articles that address the work of Humane Borders. "Over seven years," she says, "it's been extraordinary, I think extraordinary, how accurately reports about our organization have been printed. Because I think there is lots of room in the media for facts to get a little twisted, or biases to come out and that sort of thing...so Robin and I have always commented on how fairly we've been treated and how accurately we've been treated in the media."[15] Robin adds, "I have only had one unfortunate experience in the media, and that's out of literally thousands of interviews, hundreds of hours of radio, [and] a zillion hours of interviewing."[16]

Current media spokesperson Liana Rowe agrees that in spite of a few instances when Humane Borders has been equated with other, dissimilar organizations, media have been fair overall in their coverage of the group. She feels this is partly a result of certain media professionals coming to Arizona to study the issue of immigration by spending time with Humane Borders volunteers. "It's a partnership, really," she says of the relationship between media and the organization.[17]

Border Patrol

Although not a part of civil society, the U.S. Border Patrol Agency also has important concerns about the way media portray what is happening along the border. Agent Gustavo Soto stated that media have accurately portrayed the nature of the Border Patrol's job, but they have not always called the Border Patrol to confirm facts and have therefore ended up making assumptions based on inaccurate reports.[18] For example, Soto says he was frustrated by media inaccuracies about the role of the National Guard along the border.[19] "I've seen various news entities that have come out and said that the National Guardsmen are not armed while the B-Roll that's playing behind shows an armed National Guardsman." He is also frustrated by false media reports that "They [the National Guard] are not doing anything on the border." That's simply not true, he says. The National Guard has been armed from day one – they are simply not authorized to take enforcement action. If they are threatened, they have weapons to use in their defense. Otherwise, they are there to be "extra eyes and ears for the Border Patrol." And, he adds, their main task is to support the Border Patrol by building roads and maintaining infrastructure – not arresting the people crossing the border illegally.

Soto's comments reflect a desire for media to take the time to come to the border and see up close how complex the situation is. Like volunteers from all three civil society groups being studied, Soto says he sees media professionals who do come to "ground zero" walk away with a completely different conception of the immigration issue, the international boundary, and the difficult task of finding effective solutions.

> SOTO: They [media] simply don't get down to the border. They are making the decisions from the beltway instead of actually coming down to the border itself…They make assumptions based on other assumptions from other reporters. That in a sense is where I believe the media has gone terribly wrong. They haven't come down to the border to ask the experts, ask the boots on the ground what's going on.

> INTERVIEWER: So do you think, then, that because the media don't take the time to actually be on the ground here and talk to the experts, that the average Tucson citizen or the average Phoenix citizen or citizen in South Dakota where I'm from really has an accurate picture of what is happening along the border?

> SOTO: I do believe that a lot of mainstream America doesn't know what's going on because a lot of people think when they come down to the border – they expect to see a fence already there. When I show somebody – before we actually built the border fence, this was the border right here [they say] "Well, I can't believe that! I never pictured it." Again, you've never pictured it because it's never portrayed accurately in the media.

"Borderline" Misinformation

There is one additional aspect of the relationship between media and civil society along the border that deserves mention because of its incredible impact – the content of the reporting that drives national debate. While media messages are primarily controlled by the reporters or networks themselves and not by civil society groups along the border, the mediated messages that are disseminated very much affect the public understanding of the immigration issue and therefore affect the support (or lack of it) for the groups trying to make a difference.

Of particular concern to many is the spread of falsehoods or fear-based rhetoric that has prompted concern among much of the general public in recent years. Misinformation, they contend, contributes greatly to the contentious debate between those who see illegal immigration as a national security issue and threat to American sovereignty, and those who see it as the product of larger global forces that involve trade and labor movement. One particularly disturbing trend has been the use and release of misinformation to justify anti-immigrant sentiment and/or the need for tougher United States immigration policies. These contested "pieces of evidence" have provided the foundation for many of the ideologies held by border watch or anti-immigrant groups involved in the immigration debate.

As discussed earlier, results of this research showed that most MCDC volunteers rely on FOX News (particularly Bill O'Riley and Hannity & Colmes) and CNN (especially Glenn Beck and Lou Dobbs) as their primary sources of news and information. This selection of conservative media sources makes sense; most MCDC members come from conservative political backgrounds and naturally will gravitate toward media sources that reaffirm their prior beliefs. The same is true for members of humanitarian groups who rely principally on more liberal media outlets for their primary sources of information.

The common media choices of members of the three groups being studied are likely influenced by both their group membership and their pre-existing beliefs. While only consuming media that reinforce preexisting beliefs can be limiting, it can also serve as a motivation for further involvement among likeminded individuals. When the source of that reinforcement manipulates opinion based on false or misleading information, however, a breach in trust is created and a disservice done to the audiences subscribing to the accuracy of the source. Worse, the untruths are often further circulated by those very individuals who trust the source's credibility.

This is precisely the situation that has caused great controversy on a national scale, as prominent media personalities have been accused of disseminating false information about unauthorized immigrants that has in turn been spread by members of their media audiences. My own research points to evidence of this taking place. During the interviews I conducted with MCDC volunteers, many cited frightening statistics about crime rates, percentages of "illegals" in prison populations, health epidemics, and other social issues related to immigrants as the reasons for their involvement with MCDC. However, the statistics they cited were not always accurate.

For instance, during a November, 2007 interview volunteer Max stated numerous times that there are between 12 and 37 million illegal aliens currently living in the United States. He had heard this figure on a news report. Indeed, as early as 2005, conservative broadcaster Lou Dobbs cited the number of unauthorized persons at 20 million (Lou, 2005). However, these numbers were highly inflated compared with official reports. A Pew Hispanic Center study of the unauthorized immigrant population in the United States estimated that in 2005 the number was 11.1 million.[20] A subsequent report by the Department of Homeland Security estimated that as of January, 2007 the number was 11.8 million (Hoefer, Rytina & Baker, 2008). Pew Hispanic Center research in March, 2008 similarly placed the estimate at 11.9 million (Passel & Cohn, 2008). No study has indicated any type of huge spike in the unauthorized immigrant population between 2005 and 2008; on the contrary, official reports indicate stabilization after 2006 (ibid).

Other media inaccuracies have been reflected in fears over immigrant-related diseases and crime. MCDC member Marissa listed health epidemics and fear of Methicillin-resistant Staphylococcus aureus (MRSA)[21] and leprosy as major concerns related to illegal immigration. However, neither MRSA nor leprosy has been linked exclusively to unauthorized immigrants, and neither has caused a major health epidemic in the United States. Another volunteer, Stu, made a special point to write on his questionnaire "The news does not tell the truth when it comes to this issue, 30% [of the] prison population is illegal." This 30% figure was widely disseminated by Lou Dobbs until his figures were challenged by other journalists and broadcasters. Eventually, Dobbs admitted his statistics were inaccurate (Dobbs, 2007; Fact-Checking, 2007). Contrary to much of the rhetoric, crime rates seem to be decreasing in border states. According to United States Border Patrol Chief Michael J. Fisher, by 2011 "violent crimes in Southwest border counties have dropped by more than 30 percent and are currently among the lowest in the Nation per capita, even as drug-related violence has significantly increased in Mexico" (Fisher,2011). Nevertheless, erroneous statistics such as those of Dobbs continue to be disseminated by members of border watch groups and individuals who believe them to be true.

Lou Dobbs, perhaps more than any other media professional, has often been the focus of scrutiny over his statements about immigration-related issues. Dobbs, who calls himself an advocacy journalist, is considered a hero by many border watch or anti-immigration activists because he used his nightly television program to boldly confront the issue of illegal immigration before a national audience. Those who liked his approach were thrilled to see a prominent media personality taking on an issue that they felt had too long been swept under the rug. However, not everyone agreed with the approach Dobbs chose to discuss immigration issues. U.S. Representative Luís Gutiérrez of Illinois, Chairman of the Democratic Caucus Immigration Task Force, referred to Dobbs as one of the people "who stoke the fear and trepidation of the American public by fueling this complex debate with inaccuracies and distortions."[22] It is precisely because his facts and figures have often been inaccurate or misleading that Dobbs himself landed in the national spotlight.

During an April 2005 segment of his CNN program, Mr. Dobbs ran a news report addressing the "rising fears that once eradicated diseases are now returning to this country through our open borders." In his introductory remarks, Dobbs stated "Those diseases are threatening the health of nearly every American as well as illegal aliens themselves." Correspondent Christine Romans then went on to state that many contagious diseases, including leprosy, are reportedly linked to illegal immigrants. Romans cited medical lawyer Madeline Cosman as saying the country's incidence of leprosy had risen to 7,000 cases in just the previous three years (Lou, 2005).

Later, in 2007 while being interviewed for a *60 Minutes* program, Dobbs was asked about the statistic and stated that "If we reported it, it's a fact."

The day after the *60 Minutes* interview, May 7, 2007, Dobbs again invited correspondent Christine Romans to repeat the Cosman figure that 7000 cases of leprosy had been reported in the U.S. in the last three years. Dobbs indicated that he believed the number was low, saying "nearly everyone suspects there are far more cases of [leprosy]" (Lou, 2007). However, United States Department of Health and Human Services findings confirm that 7,029 cases of leprosy have been reported in this country – in the past thirty years, not three.[23]

When asked about the inaccurate statistic by *The New York Times* writer David Leonhardt, Dobbs indicated he had rectified the mistake in a subsequent report when he invited two representatives from the Southern Poverty Law Center[24] on the show, and re-stated the number of cases accurately. In reality, however, Dobbs never acknowledged that the information he previously presented on his program – twice – was false. Instead, he denied that he had ever made false claims, and instead attacked the two guests for challenging his reporting of the issue[25] (Leonhardt, 2007).

Dobbs promoted other controversial messages on his show that have been challenged, including statistics regarding the number of non-citizens in federal prisons, effects of immigrants on U.S. wage depression, and the danger of racist conspiracy theory that Hispanic groups are trying to take back the Southwestern United States. He implied that illegal aliens are the source of the problems being experienced by middle-class Americans (Lou, 2006) and that education and health care problems can also be largely attributed to the presence of illegal aliens in this country. Such broad statements combine facts with speculation - and then present them as truth. As Leonhardt of *The New York Times* explains, "The problem with Mr. Dobbs is that he mixes opinion and untruths. He is the heir to the nativist tradition that has long used fiction and conspiracy theories as a weapon against the Irish, the Italians, the Chinese, the Jews and, now, the Mexicans" (2007, p. 1). Supporters disagree, saying Dobbs brought important information to the public that no one else was daring to discuss.

Dobbs garnered a large following with his outspoken style and the impassioned views about immigration he developed over the course of 30 years in the cable news business. President of CNN/U.S. Jonathan Klein said in 2006 that "there is certainly a correlation between Lou's outspokenness and the ratings he has gotten" (Carter & Steinberg, 2006). However, by late 2009 his controversial tone and advocacy journalism no longer fit with the direction of news programming sought by CNN executives. As described by CNN Senior Political Contributor Ed Rollins, "Lou believes in taking a point of view and fighting for it. CNN management and many of the other CNN anchors differ on that philosophy. They believe in presenting the news fully and letting you, the viewer, decide on your own positions" (2009). Although the departure was billed as amicable, it was later reported that CNN executives were so at odds with Dobbs they gave him an $8 million severance package to leave (Shain, 2009). Numerous immigrant and Latino advocacy groups that had mounted a major national "Drop Dobbs" campaign calling for removal of Dobbs from CNN saw his departure as a victory for their efforts. Co-founder of Presente.org Roberto Lovato stated, "We are thrilled that Dobbs no longer has this legitimate platform from which to incite fear and hate" (Stelter & Carter, 2009).

Chris Simcox has also been at the center of controversy for statements related to illegal immigration. In July of 2004, Simcox (then publisher of the *Tombstone Tumbleweed*) reported that two months prior, the Border Patrol had caught 77 Arabic-speaking males and then covered up the arrests. He stated that his Civil Homeland Defense volunteers would therefore treat all undocumented aliens as "enemies of the state" (Wagner, 2004, p. A1). Despite the fact that no other journalist in the country could verify that 77 Arabs had been captured in the desert of Arizona, and despite the fact that a Border Patrol spokesman verified that every one of the 77 individuals caught on the alleged dates were Mexican nationals, Simcox's story spread through various media outlets and was reported as truth as far away as London (ibid).

During a personal interview, Simcox also made statements that, upon further research, proved inaccurate. Simcox stated that "Sheriff Joe Arpaio has got 5,000 people in his tent city and jails in Phoenix, Arizona and Maricopa County. About 4,000 of them are foreign nationals. I mean, we're basically policing Mexico now. And almost all of them are from Mexico who are committing crime after crime after crime."[26] Correspondence with Maricopa County Sheriff Joe Arpaio proved otherwise. According to Arpaio's office, in 2008 foreign nationals made up about 20% of the population of persons incarcerated in the Maricopa County jail system; the actual number was 1900 out of 9100 inmates.[27] Also, in February 2008 a report was issued that indicated illegal immigrants do not hold a disproportionate number of places in Maricopa County jails. In fact, only 10% of people booked into county jails are subject to Immigration and Customs Enforcement (ICE) holds, a step taken during the processing of unauthorized immigrants. Mesa Police Chief George Gascon stated, "The fact continues to remain that undocumented people here in this country do not commit crimes at any greater rate than any other segment of the population" (Kiefer, 2008, p. A1). While this statistic does not address foreign nationals with legal status who are incarcerated, it is not likely that this number is any higher than the number indicated by the study.

I wish to acknowledge the population that is supportive of the type of messages that Lou Dobbs and Chris Simcox promote. These individuals say that people like Dobbs and Simcox are finally bringing issues of utmost importance to a national agenda – issues that had previously been ignored by the majority of media sources. They complain that liberal media in particular have failed to report on the costs of "illegal immigrants" to society, the effect of undocumented populations on schools, and the health risks posed by entrants who may carry disease, to name a few. A valid argument could probably be made that media had not generally touched on those subjects until people like Lou Dobbs and Chris Simcox forced the issues into the public consciousness. However, there is an important difference between negligible coverage of these issues and coverage of those issues that deliberately communicates deceptive information. Media have an ethical responsibility to the public to report truthfully and honestly, without misleading falsifications or exaggerations. When that ethical code is breached, the public rightfully loses its trust.

Reinforcement, Civic Trust, and the Public Sphere

While audiences may not be directly "injected" with propaganda or information as mass media theorists once believed, media can serve an important function in the reinforcement of personal beliefs. An examination of the media consumption habits of volunteers from Humane Borders, MCDC and No More Deaths indicated that these individuals are most likely to gravitate toward media that confirm or reinforce their pre-existing convictions about border enforcement or immigration policy. Such a finding is not particularly surprising, as the members of these organizations already hold impassioned beliefs about immigration-related issues. Furthermore, it is human nature to seek sources of information that reinforce existing ideologies rather than challenge them. However, to the extent that this practice is true within the groups being studied, the finding is significant because of what it implies for the possibility of a healthy public sphere. Citizens actively engaged in a particular issue such as immigration who primarily (or worse, exclusively) seek sources of information that correspond with their own beliefs may not be knowledgeable enough about other perspectives on the issue to engage in meaningful dialogue that may inspire solutions. They do not typify the type of educated public sphere that Habermas envisaged.

Equally important is the somewhat uneasy relationship between civil society and the media. Participants in this study raised obvious issues of trust with media's ability to accurately report on border and immigration-related issues. Additionally, the trust of the media is put into question when "partnerships" lead to biased reporting or when inaccurate reporting is discovered. To members of activist groups that rely on media for information and reinforcement of beliefs, this distrust can produce great fractures. For some activists along the border, the result is that media have been discounted in favor of personal experience. As No More Deaths volunteer Quinn stated, "I know that the media is almost always limited in their coverage and frequently wrong. They hold no sway." Or to reiterate the words of MCDC member Terrence, "I am better informed than the media. And I would never rely on the media as a prime source for something important like this." More troubling is that this distrust is likely to spread beyond the members of these groups when blatant mistruths are exposed, rupturing the connection between those active on the border who are trying to disseminate mediated messages about immigration and those living far from the border who traditionally rely on media to better understand the issues.

Perhaps the greatest danger lies in the combination of an untrusting public that relies on specific sources of media to reinforce existing beliefs AND a style of reporting that dichotomizes issues and the people involved in them. This mixture could lend itself to an equally dichotomized society that is willing to hear what it wants to hear, but not engage in the type of reasoned communication that Habermas envisioned. Considering the many recent technological advances in communication, today's media networks have the potential to enhance public debate by enabling greater participation from a wider range of contributors. However, if members of the public are unwilling to trust those mediated sources or to think outside of the bounds of either personal convictions or a dichotomized debate, the hope of progress through Habermasian-inspired dialogue becomes severely debilitated.

The success of immigration reform (or enforcement, as MCDC members would emphasize) depends on a public that remains confident in the ability of media to effectively deliver news and information. It also relies on a citizenry that is not willing to allow polarization of the debate on this or any other issue to impede progress toward the development of viable solutions. After all, the effectiveness of civil society to make a difference regarding immigration concerns depends on its ability to relay a message to a national public about the need for change. It needs media to do so effectively. All three activist groups agree that the current system is ineffective at best and futile at worst. Media need (or at the very least, benefit from) their stories, faces, and actions to help the public better understand why such strong sentiment has arisen. The sometimes rocky relationship between the two defines, in part, which frames resonate the loudest and what it is that the general public will come to know about the border and its challenges.

Notes

[1] See Appendix 1 for copy of questionnaire.

[2] R. Hoover. Humane Borders, Tucson, Arizona. (Personal interview, October 31, 2007).

[3] "The Road to Dystopia," March 13, 2008.

[4] "Border Insecurity, " March 4, 2008.

[5] "Looking Over the Wall," October 9, 2006.

[6] September 20, 2007. The DREAM Act is the Development, Relief and Education for Alien Minors Act, federal legislation that has been introduced many times in Congress. Under the proposed legislation, unauthorized minors who were brought here at a young age and who wish to attend college or enlist in the military would be granted an opportunity to achieve legal status.

[7] February 18, 2007.

[8] One prominent examples of this is: Hoover, R. (2007, March 26). Talk Christian (and Jew and Muslim) to our elected officials. *Tucson Citizen,* Guest opinion.

[9] L. Rowe. Humane Borders Media Representative, Phoenix, AZ (Telephone interview, April 3, 2010).

[10] Paper presented at the Association for Education in Journalism and Mass Communication (AEJMC) conference in August, 2006 in San Francisco. Eastman, C.L.S. (2006). Walking the (border) line: Press coverage of activist groups on the Arizona/Mexico border.

[11] C. Simcox, Minuteman Civil Defense Corps, MCDC muster site (Personal interview, October 22, 2007).

[12] See http://www.simcoxforsenate.com.

[13] J. Fife. No More Deaths. Tucson, Arizona. (Personal interview, November 12, 2007).

[14] R. Ufford-Chase. No More Deaths. (Telephone interview, January 28, 2008).

[15] S.A. Goodman, Humane Borders, Tucson, Arizona. (Personal interview, November 7, 2007).

[16] R. Hoover. Humane Borders, Tucson, Arizona. (Personal interview, October 31, 2007).

[17] L. Rowe. Humane Borders Media Representative, Phoenix, AZ (Telephone interview, April 3, 2010).

[18] G. Soto, U.S. Border Patrol: Tucson Sector Public Affairs Office (Personal interview, May 23, 2007).

[19] National Guard troops were stationed along the AZ/Sonora border in 2006 and 2007 to boost security efforts. By June of 2008, only a few hundred guard soldiers remained stationed there. In 2010 National Guard troops were once again sent to the border under the Obama Administration.

[20] Data taken from the Pew Hispanic Center, a nonpartisan research organization dedicated to improving understanding of the U.S. Hispanic population and chronicling Latinos' growing impact on the nation. It is a project of the Pew Research Center, considered a leading source of research

data for a variety of topics. The Pew Hispanic Center does not take positions on policy issues. Figures come from a March, 2006 report by Jeffrey Passel.

Passel, J.S. (2006, March 7). Size and characteristics of the unauthorized migrant population in the U.S. Washington, D.C.: Pew Hispanic Center.

For more, see http://pewhispanic.org/reports/report.php?ReportID=61.

[21] Methicillin-resistant Staphylococcus aureus, an infection that is highly resistant to antibiotics.

[22] Comments written in a letter composed by *60 Minutes* correspondent Lesley Stahl after the airing of a segment featuring Lou Dobbs. The letter was posted on the news agency's website as a rebuttal to comments made by Dobbs during the interview. For the complete letter, see http://www.cbsnews.com/htdocs/pdf/Gutiérrez.pdf.

[23] See http://hrsa.gov/hansens/30yeartrend.htm and http://www.hrsa.gov/hansens.

[24] The Southern Poverty Law Center is a nonprofit organization dedicated to combating racism and promoting civil rights in the United States. The Center is well-known for its efforts to monitor hate groups and extremist activity.

[25] For a full transcript of the report, see http://transcripts.cnn.com/TRANSCRIPTS/0705/16/ldt.01.html.

[26] C. Simcox, Minuteman Civil Defense Corps, MCDC muster site (Personal interview, October 22, 2007).

[27] Captain Chagolla, Paul, Media Relations Commander – Maricopa County Sheriff's Office (Personal correspondence, March 11, 2008).

7

Nationalist Sentiment and Mediated Messages

"In a time of turbulence and change, it is more true than ever that knowledge is power."

John F. Kennedy, Address at the University of California, Berkeley (March 23, 1962)

Defining a National Identity:
Negative Sentiment – Past and Present

In February of 2008, I received an e-mail message from a Minuteman Civil Defense Corps (MCDC) member who writes a regular column about the border and distributes it to a list serve. The main body of the e-mail showed various pictures of stacks of U.S. currency and automatic weapons found in the house of a Mexican drug dealer. The message that followed the pictures read:

> And we want to give ILLEGAL ALIENS amnesty and not build the border fence because of funding!?!?!? SEND THIS TO EVERYONE, INCLUDING YOUR LOCAL CONGRESS REPRESENTATIVE. Our country is bleeding from the outside in!!! Don't you think it's time we take back what WE have sacrificed for over 140 years for??? I do. Build the fence higher and deeper, tighten border control, and send EVERY illegal alien home!!!

This e-mail is obviously an expression of frustration over the presence of "illegal aliens" in the United States. However, there are a number of additional implications expressed in this message. They are: 1) all illegal aliens are involved in the drug trade or other threatening activities, 2) illegal aliens are like a bleeding wound to our country 3) U.S. citizens have made sacrifices to maintain a safe, drug and/or violence-free country, 4) A fence and prevention of any kind of amnesty will keep illegal aliens out, and 5) public pressure on Congress to do something will make a difference.

There are partial truths in all of the above assumptions, but only the last is potentially accurate without further explanation and examination. The remaining messages about unauthorized migrants and their effect on U.S. society make false assumptions about a wide and varied population. These views intentionally identify the unauthorized migrants as members of a criminal element who need to be kept out, and identify U.S. citizens as part of a homogeneously law-abiding, sacrificial community that needs to be preserved. Such wide generalizations are not only inaccurate, but they are dangerous in their tendency to elicit responses based on human fear and emotion. Certainly there is a criminal element among those attempting to cross our borders illegally, but in all fairness, drug traffickers would be out of business if it were not for the U.S. citizenry creating a demand for the illegal goods. And how does such a comment explain the fact that in the most populous state of our country, California, U.S. born adult men are incarcerated at a rate more than 2 ½ times greater than that of foreign born men?[1] Those who know little about the realities of U.S. immigration or who have pre-existing fears or dislikes of foreigners use such statements as justification for reactive measures that fail to consider the complexity of the issue or diversity of the people involved.

The frames used today by some activist groups along the Arizona/Sonora border to present their mediated messages about immigration to a general public are not altogether different in tone from the frames used in historical arguments against foreigners. These frames use nativist sentiment to present unauthorized persons as a danger or threat, and to create an image of dislike, distrust, or outright fear of the foreigner. This chapter explores the use of such frames in earlier historical contexts and their continued presence today in the language used by certain activist groups to describe the current state of immigration.

Consider the following excerpt from an article published in a popular U.S. magazine:

> If we believe, as we do, in our political theory that the people are the guardians of government, we should not subject our government to the bitterness and hatred of those who have not been born of our tradition and are not willing to yield an increase to the strength inherent in our institutions. American liberty is dependent on quality in citizenship. Our obligation is to maintain that citizenship at its best. We must have nothing to do with those who would undermine it. The retroactive immigrant is a danger in our midst. His discontent gives him no time

to seize a healthy opportunity to improve himself. His purpose is to tear down. There is no room for him here. He needs to be deported, not as a substitute for, but as a part of his punishment.

We might avoid this danger were we insistent that the immigrant, before he leaves foreign soil, is temperamentally keyed for our national background. There are racial considerations too grave to be brushed aside for any sentimental reasons. Biological laws tell us that certain divergent people will not mix or blend. The Nordics propagate themselves successfully. With other races, the outcome shows deterioration on both sides. Quality of mind and body suggests that observance of ethnic law is as great a necessity to a nation as immigration law.

We must remember that we have not only the present but the future to safeguard; our obligations extend even to generations yet unborn. The unassimilated alien child menaces our children, as the alien industrial worker, who has destruction rather than production in mind, menaces our industry. It is only when the alien adds vigor to our stock that he is wanted. The dead weight of an alien accretion stifles national progress. But we have a hope that can not be crushed; we have a background that we will not allow to be obliterated. The only acceptable immigrant is the one who can justify our faith in man by a constant revelation of the divine purpose of the Creator.

This article, while strikingly similar in tone to the e-mail previously indicated, was written by then vice-president Calvin Coolidge and published in the February, 1921 edition of *Good Housekeeping* magazine.[2] Other sections of the article outline the dangers of immigrants on the labor and market practices of the United States. Coolidge's article advocates for restrictions on the type and number of immigrants allowed into this country. Later, as President, he signed a bill into law accomplishing that aim.

This was not the first instance, however, of public animosity toward foreigners. Anti-immigrant sentiment in the United States was being perpetuated through mass media even before the official establishment of our country. In 1751 Benjamin Franklin published a tract titled *Observations Concerning the Increase of Mankind* filled with apprehension about the ability of "outsiders" to assimilate, and displaying racist sentiment toward Germans and Africans in particular:

Why should the *Palatine Boors* be suffered to swarm into our Settlements, and by herding together establish their Language and Manners to the Exclusion of ours? Why should *Pennsylvania*, founded by the *English*, become a Colony of *Aliens*, who will shortly be so numerous as to Germanize us instead of us Anglifying them, and will never adopt our Language or Customs, any more than they can acquire our Complexion (section 23).

And while we are, as I may call it, *Scouring* our Planet, by clearing *America* of Woods, and so making this Side of our Globe reflect a brighter Light to the Eyes of Inhabitants in *Mars* or *Venus*, why should we in the Sight of Superior Beings, darken its People? Why increase the Sons of *Africa*, by Planting them in *America*, where we have so fair an Opportunity, by excluding all Blacks and Tawneys, of increasing the lovely White and Red? (section 24)

Franklin's celebration of the White race and proposed exclusion of unwanted, "inferior" races is, unfortunately, representative of many similar sentiments that paralleled the growth and settlement of the United States. In 1870, San Francisco lawyer and Republican politician Frank Pixley wrote the following about Chinese immigration:

This is a question of bringing a new people here, and are we not planting the seeds of an evil which may develop to our great and permanent injury? (Daniels, 2004, p.14).

Others have used like arguments to warn about negative foreign influence – be it the result of national or ethnic origin (similar attacks were launched against Irish, Italians, and Jews, for example) or religion (anti-Catholic fervor reached its height during the depression-ridden 1890s) (ibid).

Most remarkable about these arguments is their endurance throughout our nation's history. In many cases, the adjectives describing nationality or religion could simply be replaced with the words "Mexican," "immigrant," "foreign worker" or "illegal alien" to be reflective of anti-immigrant dialogue today. For example, consider a 2004 advertisement paid for by the Coalition for the Future American Worker. As pictures flashed across the screen of an inflatable dummy being repeatedly punched, a voice read:

How much longer can Iowa workers be the punching bags for greedy corporations and politicians? First, meatpackers replaced Iowans with thousands of foreign workers. Next, wages were cut almost in half. Now, politicians want new laws to import millions more foreign workers and give amnesty to illegal aliens. Tell the candidates no more foreign workers and no amnesty for millions here illegally.[3]

This image of foreigners as a danger or threat has been perpetuated through other media channels as well. Nevins attributes heightened public concern about the border in San Diego in 1980 to extensive media coverage of unauthorized immigration (2002, p. 73). Leo Chávez examines how media contributed to the atmosphere of apprehension in his book *Covering Immigration: Popular Images and the Politics of the Nation* (2001). The images and messages gracing the front of national magazines between 1980 and the mid-1990s (when militarization of the Southwestern border began) did their part to heighten civic anxiety. Magazine covers reading: "The World's Poor Flood the U.S.,"[4] "Invasion from Mexico,"[5] "The Disappearing Border"[6] and "Go Back Where You Came From"[7] offer a sampling of the often racially-tinged articles published during this period.

Otto Santa Ana in *Brown Tide Rising* (2002) describes the many metaphorical descriptions of Latinos that have infused mainstream media reporting in the past 15 years. His analysis points to numerous examples of Latinos being portrayed in news reports as outsiders, parasites, animals, weeds, diseases and burdens. The study also found that metaphors of "immigrants as dangerous waters "or "immigration as invasion" made up 80% of all metaphors expressed in public immigration discourse (p. 78). For instance, numerous articles in the *Los Angeles Times* described the country as "awash under a brown tide,"[8] spoke of Latinos marching through the streets as a "sea of brown faces,"[9] and commented on "the relentless flow of immigrants"[10] coming into the country. Broadcast media have been guilty of using defamatory language as well. FOX network announcer Bill O'Riley has used the term "wetback" both on his television program and in public forums to describe Mexicans crossing the border into the United States (Laufer, 2004, p. 151).

Politicians also use anti-immigrant rhetoric to create a feeling of crisis or invasion – for which they have the answer. While this approach is not new, it is significant because of its influence on public opinion and understanding of the immigration issue. In his book *Whatever It Takes: Illegal Immigration, Border Security, and the War on Terror* (2006), former Arizona Congressman and U.S. Senate candidate J.D. Hayworth warns that the United States must restrict immigration from our southern neighbor because Mexicans will never be able to become true "Americans:"

> Unlike those earlier periods of immigration, the current influx is comprised overwhelmingly of just one group – Mexicans...Allowing one nationality to dominate immigration this way not only violates one

of the bedrock principles of our immigration policy – diversity of admission – but also makes assimilation nearly impossible. Out of one, many. But out of two, what? (p. 52)

Hayworth[11] goes on to say later in the same chapter:

Hispanic immigrants have a harder time assimilating than other immigrant groups ... Assimilation – and by that I mean Americaniza- tion in the early twentieth-century sense of immersing immigrants in English, American patriotism, and traditional American values – was good for immigrants and good for America. It cannot be replaced by the multicultural whim of the day (p. 59).

Samuel Huntington also uses an anti-assimilation argument in his writings that sounds very much like the sentiment expressed by Benjamin Franklin and likeminded individuals of the 18th century:

The criteria that can be used to gauge assimilation of an individual, a group, or a generation include language, education, occupation and income, citizenship, intermarriage, and identity. With respect to almost all of these indices, Mexican assimilation lags behind that of contemporary non-Mexican immigrants and that of immigrants in the previous waves (2004).

These statements completely discredit the fact that Mexicans (and Hispanics in general) have not only successfully assimilated and established themselves in all aspects of contemporary U.S. society – including business, educational, and cultural institutions – but also that their contributions *to* this society have in part shaped our national identity. The Southwestern United States in particular, once part of Mexico, reflects a rich tradition of Hispanic-American heritage that is celebrated by citizens of all backgrounds. And for more than a century the music, foods, art, literature, sport, architecture and hundreds of other aspects of Hispanic-American culture have been regarded as a unique part of this country's national heritage.

Additionally, research findings conflict with Hayworth and Huntington's statements and the studies from which they arise. The reports concluding that Hispanics are not assimilating into U.S. culture lump *all* generations of immigrants together rather than distinguishing the unique challenges faced by first, second and third generations (Smith, 2003). In actuality, Latinos have experienced substantial progress across generations. For instance, a 2002 Pew Hispanic Center and Kaiser Family Foundation study shows that while 4% of first-generation adult Latinos speak English as their primary language, the figure increases to 46% among second generation Latinos and 78% among Latinos who are a third generation or higher. The same study found that children of Latino immigrant parents predominantly use English as their primary language when speaking to their friends; only 18% were reported to use Spanish instead (Pew, 2002). Finally, an economic study concludes that second and third generation Hispanic men have made great progress in closing their economic gaps compared with native whites, because each successive generation has achieved higher levels of education. More education has then translated into generationally progressive higher incomes (Smith, 2003).

The cultural and racial "othering" that results from perpetuating the image of an American culture vs. a threatening foreign entity is all too reminiscent of the Orientalism described by Edward Said (2003). This attitude that foreign cultures are somehow inferior hinges on an invented notion of national identity that fits the ideals of the dominant culture. Furthermore, it undermines decades of shared cultural experience between Mexicans and Americans that has helped to shape a new form of "American" identity. The development and popularity of Tejano music, nationwide observances of Cinco de Mayo celebrations, Mexican and U.S. citizens' solidarity for Chávez's labor rights movement – these are just a few of the many additional rich contributions to U.S. history and cultural sharing that are eroded when people choose to understand each other only in terms of divisions, or in terms of an "us vs. them" mentality. Furthermore, such a mentality usually assumes the superiority of "us" and the inferiority of "them" which lends itself to struggles in terms of rights and power. In a later explanation of his famous work, Said says, "There is, after all, a profound difference between the will to understand for purposes of co-existence and enlargement of horizons, and the will to dominate for the purposes of control" (Said, 2003, p. 2).

Borderline Language and its Implications

A brief glance at on-line reader responses to immigration-related news articles or a few moments listening to talk radio when immigration is being discussed make it clear that much anti-immigrant sentiment can be found among members of the U.S. citizenry. What implication does this have for the three civil society groups most active along the border? Are these groups ever the source of anti-immigrant language or attitudes, or are they ever recipients of such hate speech? The answer to these questions is more than a simple yes or no. All three groups have been the target of hate speech or actions; some have also been accused of perpetuating it.

Many Humane Borders and No More Deaths volunteers with whom I spoke expressed concern over caustic attitudes aimed at their organizations. Both groups have been the target of verbal attacks and have received hate mail from racist or supremacist groups who disagree with their humanitarian efforts. Volunteers like Clara cite instances of anti-immigration crowds showing up at their events: "At one meeting racists purposely disrupted the presentation and we had to call security." Gina, a Humane Borders volunteer from Colorado, says she is sometimes frightened to be in the office alone because of the graphic hate-mails received. Sometimes Humane Borders doesn't even promote its own activities like the annual March for Migrants, a memorial for migrants who have died, because organizers don't want hecklers showing up at these sacred events.

John Fife feels the biggest challenge of the No More Deaths movement is "the lack of understanding of people across the country about this issue." He goes on to say one of the toughest things to face is "the racism and bigotry. It's always present whenever you're talking about migration issues. It's been true throughout history and we're just at the latest phase. So the church's role is critically important because we provide the moral framework, hopefully, for that conversation to take place."

Robin Hoover agrees that hateful attitudes of antagonists are one of the greatest challenges of being involved, and that the church has a special role to play:

> HOOVER: It's difficult to proceed on in the face of hate mail and horrible phone calls and that sort of stuff. I've had death threats, physical plant facilities here have had bomb threats issued, we've had damage done to our water stations, we get hate mail, I've been yelled at by people who burn Mexican flags, and cursed, we've had members spat upon, people on websites calling for my death and passing out my home address and phone number. I've had members of the clergy join in the hate mail. "In the name of God, I order you to quit giving water to those God damned coco bang beaners!" I said, "Have you ever read Matthew 25? Nations are judged by whether or not they give food and water."

MCDC members also cite examples of being the object of negative or hateful speech. Duane, a volunteer from Arizona, says one of the risks involved in being a member of the organization is "being a target of Hispanic hate groups." Kirk adds the thing that has made the greatest impact on him is "how much hatred is out there for people who want to do something to save their country." Chris Simcox travels with a bodyguard to ensure his personal safety. He, too, has received death threats from people who oppose his efforts.

Sometimes the intolerant attitudes encountered by these members of civil society are the result of media coverage. MCDC member Owen from Ohio says, "My wife and I are concerned considering what we have seen and experienced at rallies and counter-protests we have attended. The media definitely contributes to this concern when they label us as racists, bigots and vigilantes."

At times, however, it is the actions or words of civil society volunteers themselves that lead to the allegations of racism. While organizations such as MCDC have often been accused of hateful attitudes or racist speech, members and leaders contest that such characterizations are the result of biased media reports or attacks by racist Hispanic organizations. They also claim that splinter groups – also calling themselves Minutemen – are often behind the hateful attacks on those with differing opinions. While this study does not propose to investigate such accusations, my research did uncover that there are numerous anti-immigrant organizations that have broken off from the original Minuteman Project and formed more radically-oriented membership bases. According to longtime volunteer Marissa, some of the groups splintered off precisely because they did not agree with the rules and standard operating procedures of MCDC.

Establishing a distinction between MCDC members and members of other Minuteman groups is a serious, but often overlooked issue. Reporters often use the designation "Minuteman" in their stories without clarifying which Minuteman organization is being described. Consider the following excerpt from a story about a protest against day laborers in Phoenix, Arizona:

"Pastor Geiger leaves the neighborhood on Saturdays, because it gets deafening. When I was there, a trio singing Mexican ballads strolled through the crush. A Minuteman with a bullhorn followed them. 'Monkeys coming through!' he shouted. His side rushed up to drown the music out: 'Born in the U.S.A.! Born in the U.S.A.! K.K.K.! Viva la Migra! January First!'" [12] (Downes, 2007).

This report paints a grim picture of the Minuteman shouting the racial slurs, but fails to distinguish whether the speakers were members of the Minuteman Civil Defense Corps, Minuteman Project (headed by Simcox's former partner Jim Gilchrist), the Minuteman Project of One (a much more radical anti-immigration organization) or another Minuteman group. Many times, the reporters themselves may not realize there is more than one Minuteman organization. Daniel González, reporter for *The Arizona Republic*, thinks this is often the case. "No, I don't think [reporters] are aware of the splits and I don't think they do a very good job of explaining the differences. One group might not be the same as another. They lump them all together."[13] *The Arizona Daily Star* immigration reporter Brady McCombs agrees that splinter groups make correct identification tough. "They're separate groups, but they can speak to each other's issues and a lot of times they know each other. The Minuteman one has been most confusing. I mean, that one especially because one guy leaves and they start a new group."[14]

MCDC organization leaders, who base participation on adherence to a strict standard operating procedure, makes it a point to insist that members do not engage in racial slurs or any type of racist activity. All members are vetted and run through a background check to ensure they do not have anything in their history that would point to advocacy of racist activity. During my six days with the group, I did not hear racist comments or racial slurs from any MCDC members.

However, there are instances when MCDC members and leaders alike purposely use inflammatory, derogatory, or fear-based language. During my time with MCDC volunteers, I frequently heard the terms war and battle used to describe the situation along the border – an honest reflection of how they perceive the immigration issue at hand. I also witnessed volunteers making comments about "hunting migrants" (in one instance, an MCDC volunteer joked that they should "get some German Shepherds out there to hunt them with"), waiting for the illegals to "come out and play" (waiting to spot and "catch" illegals while on the line watch duty), and "going out to have some fun," (going out to try to find illegals). Kirk told me during an interview that "this [southern Arizona] is ground zero. This is where the fun is." In written communication, Arizona MCDC volunteer Duane told me, "I am glad you got to see how effective the Eye-in–the-Sky[15] was and felt that exhilaration from actually seeing the IAs getting captured by Border Patrol." Mel related similar comments about enjoying the border watch efforts, saying "There's a certain element of thrill and danger to this." During a night out on the line, another volunteer laughed as he described how one Border Patrol agent, instead of identifying himself to a group of migrants, routinely covers up his badge with his hand, sneaks into the line of walkers, and then proceeds to throw them down on the ground one by one while the others scatter in fear, wondering what is going on.[16] Considering the frightening, often life-threatening situations faced by border crossers as they make their way through the desert, such comments are at the very least, insensitive and at the most, inhumane.

This attitude toward the border-crossers was the exception, not the rule, during my participation with the MCDC volunteers. Based on my conversations with other muster participants, I do not believe these comments reflect the views of the average MCDC volunteers – at least those who participated during the six days I observed. I met many kind individuals at the MCDC camp who expressed true concern for the "IAs" and who would have likely been appalled to hear such statements being made by their fellow volunteers. MCDC leadership repeatedly stressed that such attitudes were unacceptable, and during an interview, Chris Simcox even made the comment that nobody should view catching IAs as "having fun." However, it is easy to see how such attitudes or comments would provoke protest or outrage from people who find them cruel. And members of MCDC as well as other splinter groups have been known to change their language depending on the circumstances or situation. A documentary by Nikolaj Vijborg showing Chris Simcox in his earlier Minuteman days exemplifies this. In the video, Simcox states, "I feel that the people that are coming across, invading this country, I think that they should be treated as enemies of the state. We need to be putting them in work camps. Anyone could walk through these borders of this country bringing bombs, chemicals, weapons of mass destruction. I think they should be shot on sight, personally."[17]

In cases like this, members must take responsibility for the images they create for themselves through their words and actions.

MCDC leaders have also been accused of using language that inspires fear or provokes anti-immigrant sentiment. For example, a Chris Simcox article posted to the MCDC website donned the title "Minuteman Civil Defense Corps February 2008 muster: The Invasion Continues."[18] The MCDC Political Action Committee website includes a message from Simcox stating "You've received this because you understand the rising tide of illegal immigrants pouring across our borders poses a **clear-and-present danger** to the United States of America."[19] And a slate of messages written by MCDC Vice President Carmen Mercer to supporters of tougher immigration policies states, "Within the next year, millions of underground workers, criminals, thugs, terrorists and international drug cartel soldiers will harm our economy, citizens and undermanned lawmen unless we SECURE THE BORDER WITH FENCE, ENFORCE THE RULE OF LAW, and put the National Guard back on our Southern frontier IMMEDIATELY."[20] While this language is not directly racist, it certainly furthers the message that the presence of unauthorized migrants is a threat to the well-being of the United States and its citizens.

Identifying "Americans"

Much of the anti-immigrant sentiment examined so far is based firmly on a view that all true Americans share a strong, well-defined common identity. Samuel Huntington specifically argues that national identity is established as a result of a people's culture (in the case of the United States: English language, Protestant religion, political beliefs based on constitutional doctrine, and racial origins) and Creed (in the U.S. this refers largely to political principles based on natural rights and loyalty to country). Other commonly promoted "requirements" for true Americanism include placing high value on education and family, respecting authority, prioritizing security, and celebrating national pride (Huntington, 2004; Hayworth, 2006). Russell Dalton, pointing to examples of international sporting events and support for athletes, concludes in a study that Americans "are the world's most patriotic people" (Huntington, p. 276).

Promoters of the idea of "Americanization" are particularly disapproving of citizens who self-identify not just as Americans, but as Americans with connections to other countries or ethnic backgrounds. American Values president Gary Bauer blamed Latino immigrants for not integrating into American society. "Hyphenated Americans," he claimed, "put other countries and affiliations first, and they drive a wedge into the heart of 'One Nation'" (Dahler, 2007,p. 9A).

Kirk, an MCDC volunteer, invites all the "Native Americans, African Americans, European Americans and Hispanic Americans" to come down to the border, join the Minutemen, and "do something." He adds, "We are true Americans who believe in the American way. We're here simply to maintain the sovereignty of the United States, which give them the freedoms as a little beacon, an island, in a very hostile world."

Hyphenated or not, critics argue that there is no singular "American" identity that unites U.S. citizens into a common, definitive culture. U.S. citizens may celebrate holidays particular to this country like the Fourth of July and Thanksgiving, and they may share rituals that contribute to a collective identity through culture and sport, such as a love of fast food or parties with friends on Super Bowl Sunday. But there is no basic recipe for "being American" and living in the "American way." Scott London described the United States at the end of the century this way: "Never before in history has a society been as diverse as the U.S. is today. And never before have so many different traditions, beliefs and values been integrated into a single culture" (London, 1999, p.n/a). This idea of a culture based on multiculturalism may not fit the ideal of those who seek a preservation of early Anglo-

Protestant cultural ties, but it reflects the reality of a changing cultural landscape that shapes the collective identity of U.S. citizens.

Furthermore, as global forces have created movement and interdependency among nations, they have also blurred identities based on nationality or race. In a critique of Habermas's constitutionalism, Luke Goode (2005) says that globalization has brought about a de-centralization and fragmentation of cultural identities, partially through migration. His comments reinforce the fact that we are a nation of diversity, made up of immigrants from the very start of the republic. And, immigrant advocates add, that diversity is what has always made America strong.

Setting Agendas for Imagined Communities

Not only is a sense of common American identity difficult to define, but in the minds of some scholars, a national community united by common principles is entirely imagined. As Benedict Anderson explains in his well-known work *Imagined Communities* (1991), even those belonging to the smallest nations will likely never meet all of their fellow citizens face-to-face. Yet each of them imagines the nation as a body that holds a certain type of camaraderie or unifying characteristic. Their images of one another and of the nation as a whole are most often formed through the dissemination and reception of like media messages. Media thus play an important role in stimulating a sense of community and homogeneity among audiences, thereby helping to create imagined communities in the minds of the populace.

For civil society groups like Humane Borders, MCDC and No More Deaths, the concept and function of imagined communities is especially important. As the previous chapter indicated, members of these groups are most likely to select media sources that reinforce their beliefs about the border and immigration. Volunteers from each organization share at least one media source in common with fellow members; often they consume media messages from many identical sources. This practice reinforces the idea that these specific civic organizations function as imagined communities. They are comprised of volunteers who, more often than not, live *away* from the border and are not able to physically be in contact with other members except through official communications (newsletters, e-mails, etc.) and mass media. However, their ideologies are largely reinforced through their media selection, which creates a sense of community among them. The comments of an MCDC volunteer illustrate this sense of camaraderie. When asked if he corresponds with other members of the group, Owen responded, "I am in contact with brothers and sisters all over the country and we will return to the border to serve together again this year."

Summary

As examples throughout this chapter demonstrate, the spreading of nativist sentiment is not a new phenomenon. Immigrants – be they European, African, Asian, Hispanic or otherwise - have been treated with suspicion and repugnance throughout the history of this country. The anti-immigrant rhetoric aimed at Mexicans or other Hispanics is nothing new, but neither is it always easy to recognize. Demeaning sentiments toward any group of immigrants are often cleverly wrapped in neat arguments defending the purity, sovereignty and uniformity of American life and culture. Many are also disguised in fear-inducing speech that warns of the dangers immigrants pose to the welfare of this country. The director of the Southern Poverty Law Center's Intelligence Project states that many organizations shape public opinion by "defaming a group of people, like they bring disease, they are terrorist, they are criminals, they are trashing the environment. Anytime you defame a group of people incessantly, you make that group ripe for discrimination" (Uranga, 2006, p. 2).

Such negative perceptions of immigrants are often perpetuated through media, whose imagery and descriptions draw together likeminded citizens as members of imagined communities. Moving beyond the hateful rhetoric that isolates populations based on race, ethnicity or origin requires recognition of the importance of media literacy and critical thinking. It is imperative that audiences learn to analyze the messages they are hearing and evaluate both the sources and motivations for the claims being made. Approaching media content in this way will help to illuminate hateful rhetoric that is often cleverly masked behind security and culture-related "concerns," and will replace hatemongering with the thoughtful dialogue that is critical to a healthy democracy.

Notes

[1] Report issued by Public Policy Institute of California in February, 2008. For more information, see Martell, D. (2008, February 26). Study finds immigrants commit less California crime. *Reuters.*

[2] Coolidge, C. (1921, February). Whose country is this? *Good Housekeeping,* 72(2), 13-14, 109.

[3] For the transcript/description of the advertisement, see http://www. americanworker.org/iowaad1.html.

[4] Business Week, 23. June 1980.

[5] U.S. News and World Report, March 7, 1983.

[6] U.S. News and World Report, August 19, 1985.

[7] American Heritage, March 1994.

[8] October 2, 1994, p. A3.

[9] October 17, 1994, p. A1.

[10] May 30, 1993, p. A5.

[11] Hayworth was publicly supported by Chris Simcox in his failed bid against John McCain for one of Arizona's United States Senate seats. Simcox called him a "champion for border security and a responsible immigration system." See http://www.simcoxforsenate.com.

[12] "La Migra" is a slang word (often considered derogatory) for Border Patrol. "January first" refers to Jan. 1, 2008 – the day Arizona's employer sanctions law went into effect. It was the first state in the country to pass such a law.

[13] D. González. *The Arizona Republic.* Phoenix, AZ. (Telephone Interview, January 18, 2008).

[14] B. McCombs. *The Arizona Daily Star.* Tucson, AZ. (Personal Interview, January 21, 2008).

[15] Eye-in-the-Sky refers to an infrared camera mounted to a tall pole that is used to search the desert for IAs (Illegal Aliens).

[16] The validity of this statement is unknown. Border Patrol policy dictates that agents must identify themselves to those they confront or apprehend. However, incidences in which detainees have sustained injuries or died while in custody of the Border Patrol have raised serious questions about treatment of migrants by Border Patrol officials. A lengthy report of Border Patrol abuses was published in September 2008 by No More Deaths in the report *Crossing the Line: Human Rights Abuses of Migrants in Short-Term custody on the Arizona/Sonora Border.* See http://www.nomoredeaths.org/Border-Patrol-Abuse-Report.

[17] Video retrieved March 30, 2010 from http://crooksandliars.com/david-neiwert/minuteman-chris-simcoxs-past-will-ha.

[18] See MCDC Web page: http://www.borderops.com/index.php.

[19] See MCDC PAC Web page: http://www.mcdcpac.com/pl6.php.

[20] For examples, see GunBroker.com Message forum at http://forums.gunbroker.com/topic.asp?TOPIC_ID=28567 or Yahoo! Group liberty list at http://groups.yahoo.com/group/liberty-list/message/6110.

8

Pulpits, Patriotism, and the Press: How Love of God and Love of Country Motivate Action

"In the field of world policy I would dedicate this nation to the policy of the good neighbor."

Franklin Delano Roosevelt, First Inaugural Address (March 4, 1933)

Using Media to Further Faith-Inspired Action

On a routine volunteer trip into Southern Arizona's Sonoran Desert, retired U.S. Air Force Master Sergeant Brian W. made a startling discovery. Only twelve feet away from the Humane Borders water station he had come to refill lay the body of an unconscious woman. She was an undocumented migrant from Mexico who was being smuggled into the United States with the help of a coyote.[1] When she became sick from dehydration and could not keep up with the group, the coyote abandoned her near the water station and left her for dead. By the time Brian found her, her jaw was locked open, her tongue was swollen, and ants were crawling into her eyes. Brian immediately administered first aid and called for a Border Patrol rescue helicopter. Miraculously, the woman survived. Sadly, many others like her do not.

It is because of experiences like this that Brian makes his weekly trek out into the desert. Brian, like other members of faith-based activist groups, is outraged by what he sees as the disastrous effects of current immigration policy. Some individuals drown while crossing the Río Grande in Texas; others succumb to heat, snakes, or insects of the southern Arizona desert. Thousands more have suffered life-threatening injuries while trying to cross the boundary that stretches all the way from Western California to the Gulf of Mexico.

The response of religiously-based humanitarian groups to the plight of migrants merits discussion here because of the way mediated religious messages have shaped public response to the people whose lives are most directly affected by the debate. While the actions of the Minuteman Civil Defense Corps are reflective of a national movement calling for sovereignty and security that uses ethno-nationalist and oppositional frames to garner support, the actions of Humane Borders and No More Deaths reflect a national faith-based movement framing the issue in terms of rights and injustice, calling for empathy and responsibility to those in need. The participation of faith communities in the debate has challenged leaders to wrestle with issues that pit humanitarian aid practices against mandates of the state. The media coverage they have received in doing so has also offered an aspect of compassion to the national immigration discourse. It has also stimulated the involvement of citizens who, as they learn about faith-based immigration efforts through newspaper articles or other media sources, develop a sense of empowerment that leads to direct action. One example of this is the widely publicized arrest of the two No More Deaths volunteers in 1995. According to the movement's organizers, "Increased awareness of U.S. immigration policy, along with publicity about the arrests of the aid workers, has fueled interest in faith-based organizations that help migrants" (Innes, 2006, p. A1). Based on responses of interested persons from across the country, the number of volunteers interested in helping during the summer of 2006 was nearly double that of the previous summer (ibid).

Furthermore, a strong argument can be made that churches and other faith-centered entities regularly employ their own forms of non-traditional mass media that have a great influence over large numbers of faithful audiences. Preaching is a form of mass communication in its own right, based on the transfer of messages to large numbers of receivers through direct delivery to audiences (in the house of worship itself) or through radio and television broadcasts. In addition to preaching, religious messages are also regularly delivered to large numbers of worshippers through Bible studies, youth groups, church newsletters, and religious magazines, music, and study materials. What's more, it is important to consider that faith-based media messages are not only delivered, they are also intentionally received by those who have placed trust in the source of the message. Individuals make personal choices to read religious materials, watch religious programs or attend religious services. Recent survey data from the Pew Forum on Religion and Public Life (2008) and a study by Baylor University (2006) revealed that between 83 and 90% (respectively) of Americans identify themselves as being affiliated with or involved in some form of organized religion. Therefore, the messages delivered to citizens through their religious leaders are significant not only in terms of the individuals' personal religious beliefs, but also in terms of how those religious beliefs are applied to social or political issues such as immigration. The fact that faith-based groups such as Humane Borders and No More Deaths center their ideologies and actions around common religious mandates to serve those in need or help the stranger reinforces a personalized application of faith-based messages to the immigration debate, and particularly to the situation along Arizona's southern border.

Through participation in groups like Humane Borders and No More Deaths, interfaith activists representing Christian, Jewish and Muslim religious backgrounds have united to protest what they see as unjust, unfair immigration laws. These organizations and others like them have engaged in advocacy, education and direct action – sometimes bordering on illegal – to improve what they see as a desperate situation for migrants. They have also effectively used media to further their ideological stances. In doing so, such faith-based organizations have challenged the dominion of the state, and have disputed the notion that citizenship or sovereignty come before humanitarian aid.

It is important to point out that my research identified some members of Humane Borders and No More Deaths who do not subscribe to religious beliefs, as well as a small number of MCDC members who self-identify as Christians motivated by their faith. It is not my intent to make sweeping generalizations about the religious beliefs of members of all three groups. Nor is it my intent to imply that faith-based groups are not patriotic or that organizations inspired by patriotism have no place for faith. Quite the opposite is true, and my research revealed love of God **and** country within all of the organizations being studied. However, as a general rule, the official formation of Humane Borders and No More Deaths as faith-based organizations has had a great and specific impact on the way their members have responded to the immigration situation at hand. Likewise, members of MCDC generally reported being motivated by a specific set of factors that were non-religious in nature. It is the role of faith and patriotism in border-related activism, and the framing that results from their application to border issues, that I wish to discuss and explore.

This chapter examines ways in which the rights and justice master frames of faith-based civil society groups in Arizona differ from the ethno-nationalist and opposition frames of civil society groups that emphasize securing the border. These distinctive ways of shaping the way people look at immigration issues are a critical element both of the wider immigration debate and of each group's responses to the current situation in the Arizona desert. While all three civil society groups believe the current immigration system is in need of repair, their proposed solutions rest on vastly different views of civil society's responsibility to fellow citizens, and to a country's unofficial guests. Thus, the frames they produce (and that are often reproduced through coverage of their efforts) present very different messages to the public about how immigration should be understood.

Faith Takes a Stand

It was within the context of rising death tolls, increasing nationalist sentiment, and growing public debate about the nature of immigration into the U.S. that citizens concerned about the effects of border policy began to organize and demand a platform of their own. Civil society organizations criticizing the current state of immigration policy and calling for comprehensive reform stepped onto center stage. Among the most prominent and active of these organizations were churches in cities with large Hispanic populations, and faith-based groups (such as Humane Borders and No More Deaths) based in border areas where members saw a need for a direct humanitarian response. Faith-based institutions on local, state and national scales also began to take on active political and educational roles as advocates for policy change and for a humanitarian response to the immigration dilemma. In many instances, the actions they have taken have challenged the delicate relationship between the church and state, and the power of each to address an issue central to the mission and responsibility of both.

The perspective from which church and state entities have addressed undocumented migrants helps to explain the nature of involvement that each has adopted. Professor Olivia Ruiz explains two very different views held by governmental and religious groups. While authorities tend to see immigrants _as_ risk to society through the spread of disease or rise in crime rates for example, religious groups tend to see immigrants _at_ risk, as "victims of dangers created, accepted, and ignored by the countries of origin, transit and destination" (Ruiz, 2003, p. 19). Thus, while the first perspective places the burden of misfortune on the migrants themselves, the second situates such burdens within an international human rights framework (ibid).

Churches and religious organizations and movements have influenced the nature and content of the national immigration debate in the United States by challenging a largely faith-based public to respond by prioritizing the laws of God over the laws of man. In doing so, these groups have tested the boundaries of the church/state divide. Many of their efforts have captured national headlines; others have had a more direct impact on the border areas in which the illegal immigration itself is taking place. Regardless, by drawing attention to what they see as the need for humanitarian, comprehensive reform through acts sometimes bordering on civil disobedience, religious groups have contributed to a vibrant debate about the nature of current U.S. immigration policy in. They have also challenged notions of just law by reminding authorities that official regulations should never prohibit the church from fulfilling its central mission of reaching out to those in need.

Common Mission: The Church's National Involvement

One of the reasons religious civil society has created such a strong and visible presence for itself in the national immigration debate is because participants are bound by a strong sense of common mission. Volunteers come from a wide variety of religious backgrounds and bring varied social perspectives to their work. Nevertheless, these individuals and groups are able to work together effectively because of their shared view of border-related issues. Whether Catholic, Protestant, Jewish or Muslim, faith-based activists hold in common a belief that their God calls them to reach out to the migrant. As theologian Jim Wallis describes in his best-selling book *God's Politics,* "The biblical prophets say that a society's integrity is judged, not by its wealth and power, but by how it treats its most vulnerable members" (Wallis, 2005, p. 236).

Reverend Robin Hoover of Humane Borders points out that it is not theology that unites people of faith on the immigration issue. Rather, it's the social theology that is the critical variable in bringing together such a diverse group of religious perspectives. "The language which is between all of those groups is a 'rights language'- human rights, civil rights, rights of man, constitutional rights. They use the 'rights' rhetoric as their common language more than theology because their theology doesn't speak across all the denominations, but rights does."

That understanding of rights has led to confrontations between houses of worship and law enforcement. Among the most prominent immigration-related headlines in recent years were those describing the controversy of churches offering sanctuary to persons in the United States without official documentation. Religious leaders say that as of June 2007, churches in twenty U.S. cities nationwide had adopted the principle of sanctuary, rooted in the book of Leviticus. The principle states that if justice cannot be achieved, one can run to the temple for shelter until a fair hearing is granted. Churches participating in the New Sanctuary Movement also refer to scores of Biblical passages, including those in Exodus and Leviticus, which instruct believers not to mistreat the stranger in their land.[2] One reverend explains the church's position by stating "We respect the law deeply, but in all of our traditions, there are moments, and they are rare moments, when a law is unjust and in conflict with our faith, and we have to challenge that law" (Religion, 2007, p. n/a).

Although the First Amendment of the U.S. Constitution states in part that "Congress shall make no law respecting an establishment of religion, or prohibiting the free exercise thereof," religious bodies have no formal exemption from federal law that allows protection of undocumented persons. Immigration and Customs Enforcement officials can enter houses of worship at any time and make arrests, but are very unlikely to do so because of the response such actions would evoke from people of faith. Knowing this, a small number of migrants with illegal status have sought a safe haven within churches in recent years. The utilization of churches as a safe haven has its roots in the Sanctuary Movement, initiated in the 1980s by the Reverend John Fife (later co-founder of No More Deaths).

In August of 2007, 31-year-old Elvira Arellano and her seven year old son (an American citizen) sought refuge in a United Methodist Church in Chicago rather than submit to immigration authorities and be deported to Mexico. The two lived in the church for over a year, under constant scrutiny from federal authorities who reiterated that the church had no special protective powers under the law. Although officials could have entered at any time to arrest Elvira, they did not do so. According to Pepperdine University political science professor Joel Fetzer, authorities feared that such a move would look "fascistic" (Babwin, 2007).

Eventually, Elvira left the Chicago church to travel to Los Angeles, where she spoke to media about her situation and about the need for immigration reform. She was arrested in L.A. and promptly deported to Mexico, where she immediately began organizing and speaking to Mexican politicians and organizations about immigration issues (Pastor, 2007).

A similar situation involving sanctuary within a religious institution developed in California. The city of Simi Valley sent a bill for $40,000 to the United Church of Christ for police services rendered when an anti-immigrant activists from an organization called "Save our State" staged a protest outside the house of worship. The protesters were angry over the church's decision to harbor a young mother named Liliana and her infant son (Ventura, 2007). These objectors said the congregation was violating the separation of church and state by protecting an illegal immigrant who, under federal law, should have been deported. The mayor of Simi Valley agreed with protesters and petitioned Homeland Defense Secretary Michael Chertoff, asking for intervention. Chertoff declined involvement (Bakalis, 2007).

Involvement of Specific Faith Groups

Of all the religious denominations in the United States, the Roman Catholic Church has served as leader in the struggle for just and fair comprehensive immigration reform legislation. The official statements, documents, and challenges issued by the church's leadership to government officials have attracted national media attention and have thus helped shape the content and nature of the national immigration debate.

Among the most important of the official documents of the Roman Catholic Church regarding immigration, and the basis for much of the Church's public outcry against current immigration reform proposals, is a pastoral letter (booklet) titled *Strangers No Longer: Together on the Journey of Hope* issued by the Catholic Bishops of Mexico and the United States in January, 2003. This publication examines the impact of immigration on both the United States and Mexico, and outlines five faith-based principles that guide the Church's view on migration issues: 1) persons have the right to find opportunities in their homeland, 2) when opportunities to live in dignity do not exist in their homelands, persons have the right to migrate to support themselves and their families, 3) sovereign nations have the right to control their borders, but nations with greater power and ability to protect and feed their residents have a stronger obligation to accommodate migration flows, 4) refugees and asylum seekers should be afforded protection, and 5) the human dignity and human rights of undocumented migrants should be respected (United States, 2003). One section of the document explicitly states, "We speak to the migrants who are forced to leave their lands to provide for their families or to escape persecution. We stand in solidarity with you. We commit ourselves to your pastoral care and to work toward changes in church and societal structures that impede your exercising your dignity and living as children of God" (United States, 2003, p. 3). Elsewhere, the document speaks to the interdependence of nations caused by globalization, the importance of migration in U.S. history, and the many Biblical references to and teachings about migration and welcoming the stranger.

The "Justice for Immigrants" campaign has been another strong effort by the Catholic Church to speak out on behalf of humanitarian legislation designed to protect the migrant. Comprehensive immigration reform was established as a major public policy priority of the Roman Catholic Church by the United States Conference of Catholic Bishops Committee on Migration and The Catholic Legal Immigration Network, INC. (CLINIC) Board of Directors in June of 2004. One result of that prioritization was the formation of a movement called "Justice for Immigrants," a network of Catholic institutions and individuals and other people of faith working to maximize the Church's influence on comprehensive immigration reform (Justice, 2005). Among the campaign's primary objectives are educating the public about Church teaching on immigration and migration and creating a political will for positive immigration reform (ibid). Although 501(c)(3) status prohibits the church and other tax-exempt entities from actively participating in the political process, their faith-based efforts have garnered support for advocacy work that ensures the church's presence is felt in the halls of Congress.

What has perhaps captured the greatest attention, however, and has challenged the church's obedience to federal law, are the headline-grabbing statements made by Catholic Bishops and leaders during national discussions about immigration reform. When the U.S. House of Representatives passed a border security bill in December, 2005 making assistance to unauthorized migrants a felony, the United States Conference of Catholic Bishops labeled the bill punitive and called on parishioners to oppose it (Swarns, 2006). Cardinal Mahony, leader of the largest Roman Catholic diocese in the country, further sparked national debate by calling his parishioners to civil disobedience if the bill were to be passed. "The church is not in a position of negotiating the spiritual and the corporal works of mercy," he said. "We must be able to minister to people, regardless of how they got here" (NBC 4, 2006). *The New York Times* credits Cardinal Mahony with adding a moral dimension to what was otherwise a political and economic debate. The newspaper's editorial board went on to say that Mahony's stance was "as courageous as it is timely" (Editorial, 2006, p. 22).

Faith and Education

While churches are essentially restricted from direct involvement in politics, certain lobbying and educational efforts are permitted. In the context of the immigration issue, the leadership of nearly all major denominations in the United States have reacted strongly to what they feel are injustices, and have lobbied for changes in current immigration policy. Although space restraints do not permit an examination of the various individual documents and statements that have been produced, all of the major denominations have publically supported and called for comprehensive, humanitarian-based immigration reform.[3] Such statements have repeatedly stressed the moral imperative of remembering the human face of the migrant, often lost in the heated and sometimes volatile political debates. They place care for other human beings above laws that prevent those human beings from being able to live dignified lives.

A number of interfaith efforts have also been launched in response to recent immigration legislation proposals and to the increasing number of migrant deaths. Nearly all of the largest denominational families in the United States have established and publicized official positions on the current border situation and on border policy[4]. Many have made recommendations for reform based on Biblical principles and have utilized the media to inform both the public and policymakers of their positions. In October of 2005, 42 national organizations and over 100 additional local faith-based organizations and individuals from Christian, Jewish and Muslim faiths, came together to sign and support an Interfaith Statement in Support of Comprehensive Immigration Reform. This statement calls for a more humane approach to immigration legislation that looks beyond enforcement-only policies and uphold the human dignity of each person affected. Within the document are examples from the Hebrew Bible, the New Testament, and the Qur'an directing the faithful to welcome the stranger and do good to those in need (Interfaith, 2005).

While this statement explicitly recognizes the right of the U.S. government to enforce the law and protect national security interests, it also states that the complexity of the current system has made achievement of legal status nearly impossible for many immigrants. Reform of this system, the authors argue, would eliminate distractions and allow U.S. law enforcement officials to devote their efforts to the real threats to the country (Interfaith, 2005).

Additionally, say the authors of the statement, reform is needed to help put an end to the suffering endured by many immigrants and their families. This suffering includes losing loved ones to the harsh conditions of the desert, experiencing abuse at the hands of smugglers or unscrupulous individuals along the border, or being exploited in the workplace once they reach the U.S. (Interfaith, 2005).

Faith-Based Groups in Arizona

The establishment of Humane Borders in 2000 and No More Deaths in 2004 was a direct response to migrant deaths and what organizers saw as increasing threats to migrants passing through the Southern Arizona desert. Both groups have made tremendous efforts to create awareness of the problems with the current immigration system while providing aid. Media coverage of their efforts has contributed to public involvement and support for their work.

However, the actions taken by these organizations have not always earned them praise. Both Humane Borders and No More Deaths have been at the center of controversies related to their humanitarian work. As described in earlier chapters, opponents see their efforts to help as aiding and abetting criminals who are illegally entering the United States. Many argue that placing water stations in the desert or offering food to migrants only encourages them to continue on a journey that may very well cost them their lives. "I admire those groups and what they do out here to prevent deaths," says Minuteman Civil Defense Corps founder Chris Simcox. "I think we differ when they say that they're just only going to think about the people that are coming across. They don't think about what happens to the people when they're here...basically what they're saying is that it's just okay to force these people into living in the shadows of America."[5]

Volunteers of the faith-based groups disagree. They argue that people don't make the long trek to the Arizona desert for a drink of water. People were passing through long before aid groups became involved, says Robin Hoover,[6] and they will continue as long as there are jobs in the United States waiting for them. Supplying food and water is simply an effort to prevent more people from dying in the process. John Fife adds that to save lives, it is critical for humanitarian groups to have a neutral presence in the desert. "Because people are going to run from us like they run from Border Patrol or law enforcement out there unless they understand that we're not part of law enforcement and we're not going to turn them in if they need our help. So to maintain that two degrees of separation out there in the desert is a life-saving proposition, literally."[7]

Additionally, the faith-based groups see their mission as involving not only on-the-ground humanitarian response, but also working to change the policies that makes their actions necessary. No More Deaths member Jennifer says, "End deaths in the desert is [our] short term goal. Seeing government pass some laws so no one has to ever take this risky journey would be the ultimate goal." Renee sees these as the primary goals of her organization: "To stop unnecessary deaths in the desert. To put pressure on lawmakers and the public to realize the need for changes in the laws, and in the meantime keep this issue in the public eye." And fellow volunteer Sean challenges politicians who advocate for tougher immigration laws to join him on water runs in the desert. "Which side of Jesus were they raised on?" he asks. "Wasn't Jesus a crusader for the poor? I challenge them to pass Christian-like legislation" (Nix, 2006, p. A1).

As evidenced in the arrest of the two No More Deaths volunteers in 2005 or the hate mail received by both Humane Borders and No More Deaths leaders as the result of publicity of their efforts, participation with these faith-based efforts is not without its risks. But their faith, they say, calls them to reach out to those in need despite the criticisms. As Rose, a Humane Borders volunteer explained, "I think the faith I have is one of the things that gives me energy to do what we do. The energy to stand up and say, 'I am convinced that this is the way to go, and I am convinced that what I am doing is the right way of doing it.' Like giving water...I've personally been accused of aiding and abetting because of giving water. I can't accept that because anyone who is thirsty has a right to drink water." These volunteers believe above all that "The overriding biblical mandate is to care for the stranger or the alien because that stranger or alien might very well be God" (Fears, 2005).

Above all, the struggle between religious groups and government officials in determining how humanitarian response threatens federal law creates new spaces in which dialogue, cooperation, and creative immigration strategies can be explored. Border officials and faith-based civil society both play an important role in ensuring that the needs of migrants as well as United States citizens are considered. In the words of Rabbi Joseph Weizenbaum, "They have their job to do and we have ours. There's room for both of us" (Rozemberg, 2002, p. B7).

Revisiting the Notion of Illegality

People who crossed into the United States without authorization were not always designated as illegals. Joseph Nevins points out that a database search of judicial decisions found that prior to 1950, there were no references to immigrants using the term illegal (Nevins, 2002). According to Nevins, increasing public use of the term has corresponded with federal efforts to institutionalize and enforce the U.S.-Mexico boundary. As the scope of enforcement practices has escalated, says Nevins, "the labeling of unauthorized immigrants – again, as manifested by media coverage – has changed" (p. 111).

This modification of language has also impacted both the activities of civil society along the border and the messages that they have delivered to the U.S. public. One essential difference in the way various civil society groups have chosen to address the immigration issue is rooted in their collective perceptions of the migrants at the center of the dilemma. Distinctive ideas about what it means to be illegal have produced dissimilar responses to the individuals crossing the border without authorization. There are two major ideologies at work on the southern Arizona border: one is based on legal justice while the other is rooted in social justice.

Volunteers with MCDC chose to identify the migrants through the politico-legal labels designated by law enforcement or political authorities: unauthorized, illegal, alien. In the estimation of these groups, the distinction between legal and illegal is of primary importance, and any violation of that legality is a threat to the security and sovereignty of the United States of America. As researcher Roxanne Doty argues, the actions of MCDC and likeminded groups have encouraged "an increasingly bifurcated society that is structured along the lines of the exception" (2009, p. 11). They practice under a politics of exceptionalism that emphasizes the importance of state sovereignty and that creates distinctions between those who belong (citizens) and those who are not authorized to be here (noncitizens, or the exceptions) (ibid). For these activists, status of an individual as legal or "illegal" is of paramount importance as is the illegality of crossing the border itself – not the circumstances that led to the action or the humans themselves who acted.

In much of the mainstream discussion of immigration, "illegal" has become the term of choice used to describe individuals who come to the United States without authorization. What complicates this reaction is the blurring of the political label "illegal" – used to describe an act that is contrary to law – and the use of the term "illegal" to describe the individuals who commit that act. As a point of law, argue religious and humanitarian groups, a human being cannot be illegal. The term simply doesn't function in the law as a noun. The designation as illegal, they say, is placed on the vast majority of individuals for the simple reason that they have crossed the border – not because they have committed any other crime. Currently, they add, crossing the border without authorization is a misdemeanor – the same level of crime as speeding, jaywalking, or walking a dog off-leash in most states. Thus, stepping across a geopolitical border is an illegal act – but the individuals themselves are not illegal individuals any more than a citizen of the United States is an illegal when he or she drives a 66 mph in a 65 mph zone.

Border watch groups disagree, saying the act of stepping across the border makes that individual illegal according to U.S. law. The distinction between person and act is blended so the identity of the person rests only on the result of his or her action to cross without authorization. It is the upholding of the law that matters most.

This perception is well-illustrated in the comments of MCDC volunteer Max as he expressed his frustrations with the number of "illegals" flooding into the United States to take advantage of free education, welfare and health care. "Why," he said, "would the United States, a land of law, why would we want people that are illegal coming into our country?" The notion was also reinforced by Lou Dobbs on his nightly television program. "We are a nation of immigrants, and there is no more diverse and welcoming society than ours," says Dobbs. "But we are first a nation of laws, and upholding those laws and our national values makes this great country of ours possible" (Dobbs, 2005, August 28).

The notion of illegality being a primary distinction of the persons crossing the border was also a concern of Mel, a volunteer with MCDC who first became aware of the organization through TV coverage of public demonstrations at the site of the Mexican consulate in his hometown. When asked why he became involved with MCDC, he replied, "I show up with others with American flags and protest illegal immigration. It's not just Mexico. We have a big problem with all nations coming here illegally. The only thing that interests me is illegal immigration. I don't care what race you are, but if you're not here legally that's my problem."

However, critics say, if committing an act contrary to law makes a person "illegal" and this same standard were held to citizens of the United States, it would not be accurate to say that the U.S. is a land of law because all those who have committed infractions would be illegals as well. The term illegal describes an act, not the person who committed it.

Legal Justice vs. Social Justice

Themes of patriotism run deep in MCDC; many volunteers listed patriotic reasons for their involvement in the organization. Considering that half or more have military or law enforcement backgrounds, this is not surprising.[8] My experience with the group led me to believe that an overwhelming majority of MCDC volunteers are conservative; I did not encounter anyone who claimed to be otherwise, but I did encounter a number of individuals who were angry with liberal media, liberal educational systems, and who felt that socialism is a threat to our country. These individuals see our nation as a nation of laws before all else, and they are angry with the federal government for failing to uphold these laws. Their conservative viewpoints, military backgrounds, and pride in country are reflected in their approach to immigration and how they feel it should be handled.

I asked MCDC volunteers what they saw as some of the greatest benefits of being a member of the organization. The vast majority indicated that the reasons they became involved were either pride in citizenship or concern for their country. Numerous participants responded that their greatest source of pride as MCDC volunteers was serving their country and protecting their families.

> GRAHAM: [Greatest benefits?] Knowing I'm doing the right thing for the salvation of our country as we know it.

> MEL: [The greatest benefit is] pride in being a patriot. I'm proud to be involved in helping my country.

> MARISSA: I'm doing this because it's personal. I don't have any agenda except to protect my family.

> OWEN: The fathers, mothers, husbands, wives and grandparents that you met do not do this for fun, we do this for the future of our children and to protect the sovereignty of our country, the United States of America, which we love.

> BYRON: It's so bad. That's one reason I'm here. It's almost like the country is falling apart. They don't care. And somebody has to care.

> STU: The effort and expense is worth it. It is a way to give something back and secure my children and grandchildren's legacy. We are not racist. We are a group from all walks of life, not a bunch of rednecks with guns. Most are former military who are aware of the risks we take and have done so before in the defense of our nation and for those who don't care or will not take the time to do so.

> CHRIS SIMCOX: Saving my country for the future of my children and my grandchildren. That's all I care about.

A number of MCDC members also indicated sympathy for the illegal aliens they encounter during their border watches. These individuals did not place blame on the border-crossers for wanting to better their lives; rather, they blame the Mexican government for not taking care of its own people.

TERRENCE: My heart literally weeps for the individual IAs[9] I have encountered. They are the direct victims of a craven and corrupt Mexican government. Mexico is full of energetic people and rich in natural resources. Their poverty is a humanitarian disgrace.

KIRK (Describing his role as an MCDC Search and Rescue Volunteer): What really hurts us is what these migrants have to go through...That's truly rewarding, to see somebody's life get saved out there.

Even MCDC founder Chris Simcox expresses sympathy for the plight of the people who come here illegally.

CHRIS SIMCOX: I spend most of my time reminding [MCDC volunteers], "Make sure you keep your anger focused on the right people. Not the people who are here, because you can't blame them. If I lived just on the other side of that line and had a government that I could not petition for a redress of my grievances, and there were not opportunities for me, I would be doing the same damn thing. I would be up here in a minute, and I don't blame those people who are actually coming here to work and to create some sort of life.[10]

I've talked to a lot of [illegal immigrants]...some nice, some not so nice. But I certainly have compassion for them...

For Marissa, one of the original MCDC volunteers, it is the thought of saving her country and protecting the future for her children and grandchildren that motivates her involvement – despite any sympathy she may feel for those who cross illegally. She relates this sentiment in a very emotional story:

MARISSA: I've had experiences that would drive you to tears. I've seen aliens in the desert out here in horrible shape. Probably the most memorable is a guy who was walking, two of them, out there in the desert. Anyway he would walk so far. His sneaker, the bottom, had peeled off. His sock had worn out. He was all cut and he was laying by the road. And my husband and I were on our way from the camp to the line to take some batteries out. And we found them there, two of them. And the one kind of waved, and we pulled over of course. My job is to turn in illegal aliens. That's my job. So I see that they're just hurting and I picked up the radio and I called in and I had two IAs by the side of the road that had just turned themselves in to us. And the one looked at me – they didn't speak English, the one didn't speak any English and one just spoke a tiny bit – and he said, "Immigration" and he started to cry. And his head went down like that and he was a migrant worker. So that just breaks your heart. So I say to my husband, "I've got to go back and get my hard heart back because we're saving our country." And I'm sorry for this – for them – but it's a fact. They've got to stay home.

Despite the sympathies they may feel for the migrants, however, the issue of legality remained paramount in how they viewed the border-crossers. When asked how immigration should be handled, most volunteers remained firm in their convictions that crossing the border without authorization is illegal, and that those who break the law should be apprehended and deported.

OWEN: Hopefully, in the near future, the will of the legal citizens of the United States of America will be heeded by our politicians, our borders secured, and illegal aliens returned to their country of origin. [My message to Congress is] get the fence built, enforce the laws that are on the books and put in motion the deportation of illegal aliens back to their country of origin.... .NO AMNESTY!!!

MARISSA: I have strong feelings about the health and welfare of the migrant people. I always will call them illegal aliens...The minute they come across they're illegal.... .Right now we have to seal the border. Stop it.

KIRK: Well, the very first thing you need to do is untie the hands of the Border Patrol. Let them do their job. If there's criminals running across our border, they need to be able to deal with them as criminals, not as guests. The second thing to do is to secure the border so that the people who want to come and visit our country, and God knows we need them and love them, they knock on the door.

GRAHAM: Secure the borders. Remove illegals. Stop employment. Illegals have no rights.

CHRIS SIMCOX: (After describing how he helped two Europeans crossing illegally who had been robbed and beaten.) I don't care where you come from, what color your skin is, what language you speak, if I catch you breaking into my country in the middle of the night, that's suspicious activity and I'm going to report it.

(During discussion on dangers of the border) Terrorists aren't dumb. I mean, if these people can just walk into the country, they can too. So it's a huge complicated mess that is just mind boggling that our government has got us into. And they want us to just accept it, and we're not. This is where, in the history of the United States, we're at a crossroads where we say, "No. There will be no compromise. We're not going to be suckered into the same thing you did in 1986 where you promised us you would secure the border and we would accept amnesty for two million people. It turned out to be three million. And it took 20 years to process them ... Not this time. And it's a shame we have to take that line – that hard stance on this. You secure the border, you enforce the laws, you send the people back home, and then you replace them with *no* guest workers. I don't want guest workers."

In contrast to activists who identify the border-crossers in terms of their legal status, volunteers with Humane Borders and No More Deaths generally identify the migrants as humans first – engaging in normal human behaviors that are part of the natural desire to live dignified lives. They search for the "whys" in order to better understand what would bring individuals like themselves, or like you and I, to such desperation that they choose to risk their lives crossing through the desert to seek work in the United States. They frequently raise issues of social injustice, noting that many of the individuals crossing the border are not *able* to apply to come legally to this country because they do not qualify for legal visas.[11]

For these volunteers, the term "illegal alien" is a *label* imposed *on* a human being, not an inherent characteristic that defines the human being himself or herself. These volunteers act out of faith, compassion and what they term "the golden rule," a form of the Kantian categorical imperative that seeks to identify the needs of *people* who, like themselves, have worth and value, and then act the way they would hope others might act on their behalf. They call for policy reform that would permit people to be allowed to enter and work in a legal, dignified manner. Above all, the human element remains the most important factor in their decision to stay involved.

MONA (Humane Borders): I was picking up trash for the first time and I found a picture that a migrant had dropped of a little girl getting an award at school. I realized at that moment that migrants are humans doing what they think they have to do to care for their families. I was able to put a face to the "issue," and that has helped me re-think many, many different types of issues. We must remember the human element.

HAZEL (Humane Borders): Yes, I have met people wandering in the desert, and also working on my home and yard as employees of local businesses. Talking to them (as much as possible given the language problems) I feel they are no different than anyone else trying to make a living. They just had to work a lot harder to get to a place with a job... I also know former migrant workers who now live in their home countries; they treat the experience as something that had to be done to survive. I personally have respect for any person who goes through such hardship because I am not sure that I would have the persistence and will to go through the same thing.

ABBY (No More Deaths): It's one thing to study the border and a totally different thing to be here. You actually understand how it impacts people's lives on a local level and that is nothing you can really know just from reading a magazine or listening to a radio station. This is part of my life now in a way that a newspaper article is not. I cry about personal issues which are related to the border. It is very hard to write a newspaper article that is sad enough to make people cry even if you are writing about 200 people dying in the desert.

MURIEL (Both groups): In my experience, many [migrants] have been among the best people I have ever known. The generosity, devotion to family, courage, and willingness to work unbelievably hard are qualities that I have admired in so many of the migrants I have known.

CLARA (Humane Borders): Before making a judgment allow yourselves a first-hand border experience, be informed, and put "faces" on the issue.

These volunteers are not alone in empathizing with migrants and placing humanitarian action at the forefront of their agendas. Researcher David Coffey challenges individuals to examine widespread assumptions about immigrants more closely. "Are they not like the rest of us," he asks, "or is the reality that people of different skin color and a different language fuel our fear and ignorance to invite racism, prejudice, and xenophobia? Do they roam in gangs after innocent women, or is the reality that they roam in gangs because one member can speak, read, or count in English? Are they taking our jobs, or is the reality that their strong backs work hard and long hours at jobs that everyone else is either too lazy to work or that they think are beneath their dignity?" (Laufer, 2004).

Global Interconnectedness vs. Nationalism

The varied views of migrants held by members of civil society organizations also mirror differing approaches to the notion of governance: membership in a global system on one hand or sovereignty and strength through emphasis on national politics and affairs on the other. Both views largely inform their understanding of current policy and the changes that must be made to either reform or enforce it.

Members of civic groups that offer aid to migrants see the United States as part of a much larger global system. They cite the increasing interdependence of nations and the decreasing incidence of isolationist policy as reasons to champion positive relationships with foreign countries. What's more, they feel the actions of the United States require them to take responsibility for the negative impacts those actions have had on other nations. They see their homeland as a nation of people called to treat their neighbors as they would hope to be treated because ultimately, we are part of a greater system. Humane Borders volunteer Mona explains it this way:

MONA: Being involved with Humane Borders has helped me see how complex things can be. When you work in a cause that some people think is wrong, you really have to think about things in a bigger picture. I have learned that our actions as a country and as individuals, our lifestyles and our expectations have huge impacts on other people all over the world. I also have met some of the most wonderful and interesting people – people that I admire and want to model my life after.

HAZEL (Humane Borders): [What made the biggest impression on me was] a group trip to Sasabe (just south of the border) and to Altar (a staging area south of Sasabe). Seeing the people prepare for the journey, seeing them eye-to-eye, not as characters in the news, was very affecting. When I came back, I remarked that, if everyone in the U.S. could make that trip, we would not have the current attitudes…Immigration is a human problem which demands a humane solution.

Other volunteers reiterated the need to recognize our country's role in global practices, and the need for media to report more about the economic and political links to migration.

RICK UFFORD-CHASE (No More Deaths): The most important thing that isn't being addressed by the media is the link between trade and immigration, and the fact that we've created unsustainable trade policies that are the clear foundation for the immigration and border crisis that we're facing today… If you want to solve the immigration crisis you have to work to sustain strong, local economies in peoples' communities of origins. Trickle-down economics will never work!

KIRBY (No More Deaths): [In regard to the reforms that need to be made] De-militarize now! Provide legal paths for migrants to come work and contribute, and leave or stay as they please. Major aid projects [are needed] to pull Mexico and Central America from poverty/corruption cycle.

ANYA (No More Deaths): [We should] reinvest all money spent "protecting the border" into the Mexican economy. Repeal NAFTA.

MURIEL (Both groups): People need to know how serious [the situation] is, how many people are dying, and they need to know, really, more about the personal situations that people are in and why they come...The human tragedies need to be reported. People need to understand that a very large proportion of the people we're seeing out there and that are dying out there – their livelihood has been destroyed by NAFTA and now CAFTA[12]. And the media does not do anything most of the time about getting at those basic causes. It reminds me in some ways of the McCarthy era, which I'm old enough to remember. And those were things that just weren't talked about... And that's the way it feels to me now.

Members of civic groups calling for an end to illegal immigration through tighter border security, however, are part of a citizenry that views the United States as a sovereign national entity. While they acknowledge that U.S. policy has had a negative impact on neighboring countries, they are more likely to place blame on corrupt foreign governments or on ineffective U.S. politicians than on the structure of the capitalist system or neo-liberal policies. Like members of the humanitarian aid organizations, they see NAFTA and similar trade policies as some of the "push" factors that have impelled many from Mexico to seek work in the United States. Unlike the humanitarian aid groups, they think the responsibility for NAFTA's problems lies in the hands of the U.S. and Mexican governments, not the citizenry of the United States. For these volunteers, security and sovereignty are the primary strengths of the nation.

MAX: All these programs, the NAFTA agreements, the Mexican truckers, and all these various elements that are a part of that, it's easy to lump them all together and say, "Let's just pass this one bill and it will solve all the problems on our security issues that are internal problems." Well that's impossible. We know that it's not going to work. Common sense will tell you that if you want to solve problems inside a country, first of all you have to have a sovereign nation. We don't have a sovereign nation. We're being invaded by foreign governments through Mexico, with Mexico not cooperating with law enforcement in the United States to help stop this problem. They're encouraging it. So how can you feasibly secure the borders when your neighbor, your so called "friend to the south" is not willing to do anything about it?

CHRIS SIMCOX: How dare our government ask us as a nation to accept that we have 100,000 violent criminals who've come into this country who have raped, murdered, and pillaged our communities, and the victims are, "Oh, they're just expendable casualties in the global economy to prop up our economy and provide businesses with cheap labor." And what it's going to do when we secure that border, we start saying "no" to the people who are here and they go home. What's going to happen in Mexico? There's going to be reform. They must reform their system and provide for their citizens.

ROY: I am truly sorry for them and wish they could go home and change their country.

And Justice for All

Civil society along the Arizona/Sonora border is divided along the notions of faith and justice. While humanitarian aid groups base their outreach to border-crossers on notions of social justice and moral or faith-based obligations, members of MCDC base their response to border-crossers on principles of legal justice. The views these groups hold of the migrants at the center of the debate are shaped largely by their belief that the current situation necessitates either a legal or a humane response. As media project these opposing views onto a national stage, citizens of the United States are challenged to consider how to apply their own principles of justice and faith to this issue.

Reaching some sort of consensus on how the two views might be combined may be the greatest hope for finding answers to the questions that immigration issues currently pose. The future of the migrant, and of the receiving populace, rests on such an effort to cooperate. In the words of John Rawls, "Although a well-ordered society is divided and pluralistic...public agreement on questions of political and social justice supports ties of civic friendship and secures the bonds of association" (1971, p. 540). Creating policy that recognizes the validity of both social and political justice will not only shape the future of the migrants, but will strengthen the vitality of a democratic system whose greatest asset is its own active and concerned citizenry.

Notes

[1] Human smuggler.

[2] Exodus 22:21 and Leviticus 19:33, *New American Standard Bible.*

[3] The Church of Jesus Christ of Latter Day Saints and Southern Baptist Convention were two mainstream denominations that did not historically support comprehensive immigration reform. In 2010, however, LDS leadership issued a statement publicly supporting principles of the Utah Compact on Immigration (Church, 2010). Similarly, in June of 2011 Southern Baptists approved a resolution advocating a path to legal status for immigrants in the United States without authorization (Associated, 2011, June 17).

[4] The American Religious Identity Survey (ARIS) "Largest denominations/ denominational families in U.S." was used to determine the largest such religious groups in the United States. This survey was conducted by Barry A. Kosmin, Seymour P. Lachman and associates at the Graduate School of the City University of New York, and is based on a sample size of 50,000 Americans. Only adult memberships are considered in this survey. The survey and related information can be accessed at http://www.adherents.com/relUSA.html# religions.

[5] C. Simcox, Minuteman Civil Defense Corps, MCDC muster site (Personal interview, October 22, 2007).

[6] R. Hoover. Humane Borders. Tucson, AZ (Personal interview, October 31, 2007).

[7] J. Fife. No More Deaths. Tucson, AZ (Personal interview, November 12, 2007).

[8] C. Simcox, Minuteman Civil Defense Corps, MCDC muster site (Personal interview, October 22, 2007).

[9] IA is the abbreviation used by Minuteman Civil Defense Corps members to describe illegal aliens.

[10] C. Simcox, Minuteman Civil Defense Corps, MCDC muster site (Personal interview, October 22, 2007).

[11] Most migrants who do not qualify for legal visa application either cannot afford to pay the fees associated with this legal process, cannot prove they have enough savings or assets to meet application requirements, or they cannot produce the legal paperwork (birth certificate, etc.) to apply. (This is common in many poor areas of Mexico where parents cannot afford the paperwork associated with the birth of a child). In addition to these challenges, visa applications may also be denied on health-related grounds, criminal and related grounds, security and related grounds, for those likely to become a "public charge," for certain individuals who do not meet labor certification qualifications, and for aliens who were previously removed or are in violation of immigration laws.

[12] The Central American Free Trade Agreement.

9

Bringing Order to the Border: Capturing Public Attention

"There is an inevitable divergence, attributable to the imperfections of the human mind, between the world as it is and the world as men perceive it."

James William Fulbright, Speech in the Senate (March 27, 1964)

Reaching the Public Through Frames: Whose Message Drives the Debate?

Journalist Charles Bowden calls Chris Simcox, founder of the Minuteman Civil Defense Corps (MCDC) "a natural American genius at publicity" (2006, p. 36). It is a designation that fits him well. Simcox is the leader whose first Minuteman event involved only a few hundred people – mostly retirees – who were outnumbered by media. Nevertheless, he managed to keep both the media and the public's attention focused on the border, not just for the few weeks of the gathering – but for more than five years. "It was a media circus," Simcox describes. "It was political theater at its best."

By many measures, Simcox has been very successful in achieving his original goal of placing the issue of immigration and the problems of the border on a national stage, and he knows it. He acknowledges that doing so required a unique approach. "The best thing that anyone ever did was to bring together a group of people and say, 'You know what? We're going to go out and sit on the border in lawn chairs. And we're going to report suspicious, illegal activity to the proper authorities.' You have to be clever to get the media's attention. So it worked." He goes on to describe how the vision of the organization has evolved, and how media have played a critical role in his success.

SIMCOX: We just became the nation's largest neighborhood watch group. And it (immigration) became the biggest social issue and security issue that we face as a nation now. So, mission accomplished. I mean, if anything we could have already packed up and gone away, I think in a sense. America started to fire. They started the conversation. But we realized that if we were to leave the border then the media wouldn't cover it, and we had to keep driving the issue and then get involved in the reform. Now we have chapters, now we're dealing with legislative issues state by state, community by community, I've testified before Congress, we work with Congress now, we have a political action committee – in fact, two of them – we're now looking to support candidates for office. This is about reforming this government, and hopefully, helping to reform the media a little bit. Because again, the media continues to want to call us vigilantes. Doesn't anyone in journalism school ever read a dictionary? They just use these loaded words to create an emotional response in the public. They want so badly for us to be the bad guys.

INTERVIEWER: But didn't you use loaded words to attract the media?

SIMCOX: Yeah, we did. I sure did. But again, in a way to bring attention to the issue, which worked. So now that's where we are.

In addition to choice of language, another way Simcox has sparked the curiosity of the media is through striking images and statements that made perfect components of front page stories. The camouflage garb and firearms toted by many of his volunteers give the appearance of a military operation rather than a neighborhood watch. The controversy surrounding his political stance on immigration hasn't completely hurt, either. Although members dislike the stories that perpetuate stereotypes or make unfriendly insinuations about their goals, they realize even these reports bring awareness to the issue they are espousing. Member Dylan says, "Even bad coverage brings attention to the problem."

Although he is critical of the way media have covered his organization and the topic of immigration in general, Simcox knows his platform depends on widespread exposure. He understands how to attract media attention, and easily engages in discussion with reporters who come to investigate his efforts. In the process of seeking new channels through which to deliver his message, he has developed relationships with networks and personalities that share his views. According to Simcox, many of the public images of the border come directly from MCDC. "Most of the footage you see on FOX of the illegals, that's our footage. We took almost all that footage that we've given to them." The organization also maintains close ties with professionals in radio who are interested in the group's message. Radio talk show host Darla Jaye of Kansas City says she was invited to come to the border to see for herself what the MCDC organization is like.

> DARLA JAYE: In my opinion, the big news media has not portrayed the Minutemen accurately at all. They have not come out here and done a story, they have not spoken with them personally. I feel that they take their information from groups that don't want people to try to stop what's happening at the border without delving in their sides of the issue. I really don't feel that they've gotten a fair shake.

In addition to drawing attention to what he sees as a flood of unauthorized persons crossing the border, Simcox takes credit for the additional resources allocated for national security, including technology and personnel for Border Patrol. He says the national exposure MCDC has provided about the border has pressured lawmakers into passing legislation that provided more support to law enforcement. When asked about the relationship between his organization and Border Patrol, Simcox answered, "Absolutely stellar. We work hand-in-hand...We are absolute heroes to the Border Patrol. They've got new vehicles, new agents, new technology. We're their advocates. They were out here doing a thankless job with no support from the President or Congress or the American people, and now they have gotten the things that they needed, and they got the respect that they deserve."

Perhaps most importantly, Simcox has done a remarkable job of helping to keep the immigration debate focused on issues of border security, the "threat" of the migrant to U.S. society, and opposition to amnesty rather than comprehensive reform. He has arguably done more than any other single individual to bring such issues to a national public and to sustain the debate about immigration by emphasizing the government's failed role in sealing the border and protecting its people. Daniel González, primary immigration/border reporter for *The Arizona Republic*, thinks Chris Simcox has been one of the most influential voices in shaping the national immigration debate.

> GONZÁLEZ: I think the Minutemen have been extremely influential in bringing national, international attention to what's happening at the border, and I think that groups like Humane Borders and No More Deaths have been very good at focusing attention on migrant deaths. I think what I've seen happen, though, is that in early 2000 'til around 2004 or so, most of the stories that were being written about the border

were the kind of humanitarian stories about desperate people coming across the border and dying. And I think that had a lot to do with the work that Humane Borders is doing, No More Deaths and Border Action Network. And then the Minutemen came along and they have been very effective in shifting the focus to be more of a border security issue. That's where a lot of the stories you see now are about defense, about Border Patrol agents, about drug running, about incursion from the Mexican military. Those are all the stories you're seeing now and much less of the human suffering-type stories.[1]

González credits Simcox's nationwide grassroots organizing with the growth of his organization, and thinks his savvy use of media accounts at least partially for the widespread publicity MCDC has received. The group's website pulled in volunteers from across the country, and continued media interest kept the group's story in the spotlight. González feels the ease of accessibility to MCDC staff or volunteers made it easy for reporters to cover the group.

GONZÁLEZ: In the beginning when they started doing those border patrols, border watches, that brought so much media attention and made people in other parts of the country aware of their work. Then they also created a website. They have a pretty sophisticated website so if people in other parts of the country want to learn more about that organization they can go to their website. So I definitely think the media helped them grow; [they] publicized their activities. They are all frequently interviewed on national television shows, cable network. So if you're interested in being involved, you don't have to go to the border. You can be involved right in your own communities, or wherever you are... .[The Minutemen] have a designated media person, so they know how to put together a press release, they have people who are experienced in writing press releases – the whole format and everything, with the contact name in the upper right hand corner and the phone number and the release date. Someone there has experience doing that. So those kinds of organizations that have people that do that get a lot more media attention. They're also very, very good about making sure that someone is always available to the media.

It was the availability of MCDC staff that eventually brought radio talk show host Darla Jaye of Kansas City to Southern Arizona. During a muster that we were both observing, Jaye indicated that the Minutemen have been an important source of information for her radio show. She regularly visits the organization's web page to stay on top of the latest news, and she receives regular correspondence from MCDC officials. "I get e-mails from the local Minuteman organization every week," she said. "As far as the national organization, I do get e-mails from them less frequently, but probably every other week or something like that."

Volunteers from Humane Borders and No More Deaths agree that to a large extent, opposing voices are "winning" the immigration debate by "winning" the support of the public. They are frustrated with the tone of the national discourse about immigrants that has ensued and the fact that so many efforts to pass comprehensive reform have been defeated.

When asked if he feels the general public has a good idea of what No More Deaths is trying to accomplish, Rick Ufford-Chase was not optimistic.

> RICK UFFORD-CHASE: No, media outlets that are clearly biased and unbelievably powerful (CNN, Lou Dobbs, Anderson 360, O'Riley on FOX) define most of the current public opinion… There are ebbs and flows in terms of anti-immigrant fervor in this country. And we're at a high point right now, and I think that it's going to get worse.

Co-founder John Fife agrees. When asked if he felt civil society has been effective in shaping the national debate, he responded that there is much more work to do.

> JOHN FIFE (No More Deaths): Obviously, we haven't been effective enough. We're losing the immigration debate to a very small minority of virulent racists and anti-immigrant cinema. It's basically because they have an easier rhetoric to engage the American public with. They can use terms like illegals, criminals, terrorists, the threat of terrorism, and all the anxieties around 9/11 now. Our task is much more difficult because immigration policies are very complex and there aren't any 10-second sound bites we can use to get our message across. As I said, I think we have an amazing possibility of coalition building here. Our task is going to be to organize it and organize it effectively.

Humane Borders volunteer Gina also believes that public sentiment has been influenced more by anti-immigrant sentiment than by humanitarian concerns. She explains: "Humane Borders works very hard to influence the media and does a fairly good job with more liberal groups like NPR, news agencies from other countries, and some local newspapers, but we don't have much access to the more popular forms of media – like Internet forums or prime time television. Some of the anti-migrant groups have a strong grip on those forms of media and are, I feel, having a greater influence on the general public."

Zac sums up his feelings about how effectiveness of border watch groups has influenced humanitarian campaigns and the work of No More Deaths:

> ZAC: One of the best media campaigns on the border in recent years was done by the Minuteman Project. The media attention that they received has framed and pushed the national dialogue on immigration for the past three years now. With a group like No More Deaths, we just can't do that. Our media isn't sensationalized or hyped up. If we were to try and sensationalize something to raise our exposure, then we would lose the human side of it. So really, our story is a tough sell. Even though it's vivid and graphic, it's too complex and it doesn't fit into the debate very well.

Interviews in 2008 with the immigration reporters at Arizona's largest newspapers revealed the same feeling that anti-immigrant sentiment pervades the headlines and airwaves. Their desire to give a more in-depth look at the human element of the phenomenon is complicated, they say, by a very vocal audience that is critical of such a perspective. Ernesto Portillo, Jr., whose eight year column for *The Arizona Daily Star* often addressed immigration issues, says he counts himself as somewhat of a lone voice in arguing and discussing immigration.

> PORTILLO, JR: The dominant and *dominating* voices on immigration are the local, regional and national Lou Dobbs, Sean Hannity, Glenn Beck, Michelle Malkin. The truth of the matter is that *they* dominate the public discourse on immigration. The truth is *they* frame the argument. The truth is *they* push the agenda. The truth is *they* have far more readership, viewership and listeners than the supposed and misnamed open border advocates in journalism. How do I know this? You just quantify the listenership of those individuals and those programs, and the readership of say, a column of Ernesto Portillo, Jr. or the editorial pages of the *Los Angeles Times*. The rebirth of a long-existing, sometimes dormant but always present nativist movement in the country has found vigor and has found strength because of the media. How? Because it has been very influential commentators as I mentioned previously who have advanced the agenda of Chris Simcox.[2]

While this study does not propose to quantify the adherents to the various frames being discussed, it does hope to offer explanations for the resonance of certain messages over others. One potential reason that frames based on nationalism, security and closing of the border have seemed to hold such an attraction with media and with the public has to do with the fears faced by United States citizens after the domestic terrorist attacks on September 11, 2001. According to researcher Douglas Kellner, media's role changed significantly after 9/11. Journalism in particular, he says, traded its traditional investigative qualities for a more political approach using "media spectacles" that distract the public from the real issues at hand (Kellner, 2005). One of these spectacles was that of terror or fear, played out on television screens as people watched replays of attacks on the World Trade Center. "In a global media world," says Kellner, "sensationalist terror spectacles have been orchestrated in part to gain worldwide attention, dramatize the issues of the groups involved, and achieve specific political objectives" (p. 27). He argues that media began to pander to President Bush's language of a "war on terror," "good versus evil" or "the free world against the forces of darkness" (p. 31). Media's treatment of the attack as a spectacle furthered ideas of military response being necessary to protect the country.

September 11 changed the way the public viewed its approach to foreigners as well. For the first time since the attack on Pearl Harbor, United States citizens began to fear for their safety and security on their own home soil. Foreigners of Middle Eastern descent suddenly became targets of racial profiling as authorities tried to sort out who was dangerous and who was not. In this ultra-cautious and protective atmosphere, media frames portraying immigrants as a threat also provoked reactions calling for force and militarization to ensure public safety.

While different frames are attractive to different segments of the population, it could be that the more protectionist, "seal the border" type frames generated more public reaction for the very reason that they reminded an already fearful nation of its vulnerabilities through its borders. In spite of the fact that the terrorists had all entered the United States legally with visas, groups like MCDC were able to equate unsecured borders with potential future attacks, thus making anyone crossing those borders without authorization suspect of ill intent. A quote from MCDC member Max supports this assertion.

MAX: (Talking about Hezbollah terrorists using the island of Margarita off the coast of Venezuela for their training ground.) From there they are given documents to get into Mexico where they "learn the language and assimilate as a Mexican just south of the border. Then they can make their move into the United States and come across with other immigrants coming across."

INTERVIEWER: Where does this information come from? I have not heard of that.

MAX: It's AP wire information. I don't remember where I saw it. I think I saw it on FOX news or CNN. But that is from a news source. It's not from one of us talking about it, but it's just a known fact.

What's Missing from the Media?
Bringing Reporting Closer to the Border

When there are discrepancies between how the three civil society organizations frame the immigration issue and how those frames are communicated through media, the conflict usually involves an emotional or physical distancing of reporters from the border. Many volunteers from all three organizations expressed a desire to see more media join them in the desert to see what the situation looks like on the ground. Across the board, volunteers expressed the common sentiment that media professionals who had taken the time to come to the desert walked away from it with a completely different understanding and as a result, they delivered more accurate reports about the harsh realities of the situation. As Rose from Humane Borders stated, "We think it is so important that people see all sides of the situation, not just the government side or any one side. It's important for them to be here and experience it, too. When we talk about migrants or the migrant situation, we are talking about people, about individuals. And I have personally found that once people see migrants as individuals, as real people, their view of the migrants themselves changes. They may not change their ideas on immigration…but it's more their feelings towards the people themselves."

For volunteers with MCDC, the biggest missing piece in media coverage of immigration issues is the accurate portrayal of what their volunteers are doing to improve the situation. MCDC volunteer Owen also sees a difference in the coverage of media professionals who visit the border versus those who do not. "Unless they have been on the border with us, they do not understand. Once they see how closely we work with the Border Patrol and law enforcement, they usually develop an entirely different perspective." Dylan adds that the organization makes it a point to conduct tours and give lectures, because otherwise media generally don't understand the magnitude of the problem.

Media professionals point out that for most news agencies, time and money restrictions make it nearly impossible to send someone to the border, particularly if the agency is located far away. Brady McCombs, primary immigration reporter for *The Arizona Daily Star*, explains it this way: "As with any reporting, the best reporting is done when you talk to "real" people and you're down and you get to where the story is happening. And that doesn't happen enough. Again, this is not at all a sweeping criticism of individuals or individual news agencies. It's hard to do that; it's time consuming to do that. And companies, whether it be TV or radio or newspaper, have to give their employees or reporters and cameramen time to do that. So yeah, I think it would be better if everyone could be on the ground to tell all of these stories instead of just making phone calls or having to do it really quickly, but you could probably find the same problem with environmental reporting, or education reporting in major cities. There's just a crunch."[3]

But Michel Marizco, an independent journalist who formerly reported for *The Arizona Daily Star*, thinks media should make a more concerted effort to cover immigration and to get to the border – *both* sides of it. When he started reporting in Arizona, he said, there were six border reporters for the major publications in the state. As of February 2008, he says, there are only two at each of the three largest newspapers, and one of these is based out of Phoenix, not Tucson. "How in the hell are you going to cover the border from Phoenix?" he asks. "So that goes back to my criticism of the lack of independent, critical reporting *on the border*. There's an entire culture that lives along the border, both sides, and very rarely do you see stories in AZ media where reporters are actually going across the border to get stories. Not to be dramatic, but it's like covering Iraq from the Green Zone."[4]

Searching for the Faces

Overwhelmingly, volunteers with Humane Borders and No More Deaths indicated that what immigration reporting lacks most is the human face of the migrant. They say coverage that emphasizes political or economic effects of immigration to the exclusion of the human story does not paint a complete picture of the human tragedy taking place. For these volunteers, it is imperative for the public to understand that the effects of current policy have resulted in a humanitarian disaster along the border.

> JOHN FIFE (No More Deaths): The basic problem, and the one we've always tried to work on, is [media] do a pretty good job of talking about the "issue" but the human face of the migrants is almost always excluded because it's so hard to get. It's hard for media to put that human face on.

RICK UFFORD-CHASE (No More Deaths): The most important thing that isn't being addressed by the media is the link between trade and immigration, and the fact that we've created unsustainable trade policies that are the clear foundation for the immigration and border crisis that we're facing today.

MURIEL (Both groups): People get off too easily with saying, "Why would anybody bring a child into the desert? Don't they have any sense?" And they [say] something like that, not having a clue about the level of desperation. And the same thing with politicians, not having a clue about the level of desperation. The human tragedies need to be reported.

MONA (Humane Borders): I grew up in northern California. And there were migrants in the fields. They just weren't in my line of vision. I always talked about them and us. Why can't they just come here legally? I didn't understand the real numbers and the real desperation. I didn't think of them as individuals, and I didn't recognize my role as a consumer and U.S. citizen as being part of the reason we see this migration phenomenon. [Message to the public]: Look at the prices you pay in the grocery store. Look at the people who are taking care of your elderly and sick in the nursing homes. Look at who is doing your yard work, building your homes. Look at the prices you pay at Wal-Mart. You live better because there are those who are willing to work for less. And try honestly to think about what you would do if the situation were reversed and you had to try to support your family in a country that can't provide jobs. Be honest about what the situation really is. Treat people as humans.

LIBBY (Humane Borders): The first thing that is happening that needs to **not** be happening is the de-humanization of the migrant. It's a whole sort of vocabulary that sets a very specific tone on the whole issue. Not that I blame the media for doing that because I don't think they created it, but they are certainly continuing the use of damaging language that fails to recognize the very real human nature of the migrants. That's something that shouldn't be lost from the debate.

Media professionals who have covered immigration issues agree that more emphasis needs to be placed on the human stories of those crossing the border. However, this is sometimes hard to do given the prevailing anti-immigrant public sentiment and the negative responses editors receive from audiences who see such a stance as a liberal "skewing" of the issue. Susan Carroll, former immigration reporter for *The Arizona Republic*, explains: "With the mounting anti-illegal immigration backlash, readers have complained more and more about the stories we do about the deaths. They believe that in doing these stories the newspaper is being sympathetic to people who break the law. As the person at the paper who reports on this topic most often, I am grateful that my editors and those at other newspapers – such as the *Los Angeles Times* and *The Washington Post* – remain committed to giving reporters the space and time they need to tell these stories (2006, p. 49).

Ernesto Portillo, Jr. of *The Arizona Daily Star* points out that anti-immigration voices have made themselves very present and available to the media.

> PORTILLO, JR: It is SO easy to find a Minuteman. It is SO easy to find an angry politician. It is SO difficult to find someone who has been chased out of their country because of economic, social, political unrest and dislocation. And they are hiding in this country, they are working, and they are worried *every day* when they go out in public to work or go to their child's school. Is this the day I'm found out and deported? And more and more it's happening today. How many stories are we reading from the undocumented community about their fears? Hardly any. But we sure are reading a lot of stories about the increasing phobia and xenophobia of nativist America.

Daniel González agrees.

> GONZÁLEZ: Even John McCain who was the main proponent of immigration reform two years ago, every day he's talking about, "We've got to secure the border first." I think that's the result of the Minutemen and their efforts. But I would say if anything, despite the coverage and newspapers giving the fuller picture, explaining how immigration is a complex issue; it can't just be solved through enforcement. There's the human element involved. I mean the people coming across have the same values and work ethic as immigrants that we've always valued. [There is a] human rights tragedy taking place at the border. Despite all those stories, the Minutemen have been able to successfully convince the American public that we need to focus on just securing the border first rather than trying to tackle that as a comprehensive issue.

Coming Into Contact: Personal Views of the Migrant

It is obvious that volunteers for Humane Borders and No More Deaths hold vastly different views than volunteers for the Minuteman Civil Defense Corps in regard to the tragedy on the border and how it should be rectified. All of the perspectives held by members of these organizations are based on strong ideologies about the role of the state and responsibility of the citizen to those who are crossing our borders.

But one major difference emerged in this research that helps to explain their dissimilar perspectives on the migrants themselves – personal contact. Over 75% all of the volunteers for Humane Borders and No More Deaths who I interviewed had met or known unauthorized border crossers, and an even greater percentage of the MCDC volunteers I interviewed had not.

It seems that this personal contact, or lack of it, is a strong indicator for how individuals' ideologies are shaped by personal experience. Marissa from MCDC stated that she will not hire undocumented people "because I think that if you're going to talk the talk, you'd better walk the walk. So I've really never interacted because I feel so strongly about it." When asked on the questionnaire if they had ever met or personally known illegal immigrants/undocumented migrants, three of the MCDC volunteers said they had. One of these indicated that he only knows them personally because he *has* to work with them. However, the other two stated that their personal contact went beyond a business relationship, with one saying "Most are hard workers and family oriented. Many are taken advantage of because of their status."

For the vast majority of Humane Borders and No More Deaths volunteers, the face-to-face personal contact with the people for whom they advocate evokes a feeling of empathy and motivates their continued involvement. Consider the following stories:

> RICK UFFORD-CHASE (No More Deaths): My entire attitude about the crisis is formed almost entirely from hearing stories from migrants themselves. I've heard literally thousands of stories over the years, and [they all say basically the same thing]. Most people come because it's their only option. They have no other choice.

> RENEE (Humane Borders): Recently we came across a migrant in the desert on a Humane Borders trip. I was amazed that he was on his way to the East Coast. It was cold that night. I was moved, and gave him the jacket I had worn on the trip.

> GARY (Humane Borders): I have dozens of experiences with migrants in the desert.

> GLENN (No More Deaths): My knowledge of the immigration situation is from 17 years of direct advocacy for victims of our broken immigration system. I worked with street children on the streets of Denver for five years. I spent six years preaching and teaching in churches and communities in 13 states on issues of human dignity and spirituality. I spent five years in southwest Kansas working in rural meat packing communities with large Hispanic communities. Direct

contact with the people shows me how much is lacking in the media presentations of the issues.

MARTIN (Humane Borders): I have met migrants more times than I can recall...These migrants are simply people looking to provide for their families just like you or I would in similar situations. The one story that I like to tell is we took some journalists down [to Altar, Mexico]. They happened to be Canadian journalists. People are always visibly moved by this, but these people were doing their job. They were working, they were filming. We were in Altar and they were just filming, and they're not getting it. And we got to El Tortugo and it was the same thing. They were filming...it was a job and they were doing it. We're leaving El Tortugo and the lead guy, the on-camera guy, was sitting beside me. He was real quiet for a minute, and then he turned and looked at me and he goes, "They're just people" and I said, "Yeah, they're just people." It got through to him.

Sue Ann Goodman says she has met many migrants while out on water trips, and has had contact with others both in her home state of Texas and in the community of Tucson. One of the defining moments for her was a gruesome desert encounter with the body of a migrant who had not survived the journey.

GOODMAN (Humane Borders): We all just kind of stood there in silence for a little while, just a lot of things going through everybody's head. But you know, you start thinking things like, "There for the grace of God go I." I just happened to be born in the United States and have white skin, you know? It's some sort of accident. I could be that person. Then you wonder what her last time was like. We knew she was sick. We knew that she was having extraordinarily heavy menstrual flow, dehydrated I'm sure, and just couldn't go on. She was 18 years old. So you just stand there and hope that it wasn't too painful for too long ... Just standing there and thinking how awful that is, but it's the truth. This is the end product of our border policy. This 18-year-old child who died a horrible death right here, out in the middle of nowhere, in the dirt, under a tree. But that's it; that's the truth in what we've created.

Notes

[1] D. González. *The Arizona Republic.* Phoenix, AZ. (Telephone interview, January 18, 2008).

[2] E. Portillo, Jr. *The Arizona Daily Star*, Tucson, AZ (Personal interview, January 21, 2008).

[3] B. McCombs.   The *Arizona Daily Star.*   Tucson, AZ.   (Personal interview, January 21, 2008).

[4] M. Marizco.   Independent reporter.   Tucson, AZ.   (Telephone interview, February 22, 2008).

10
Reflecting Back, Looking Ahead

"Hope doesn't come from calculating whether the good news is winning out over the bad. It's simply a choice to take action."

Anna Lappe, O Magazine (June 2003)

The evolution of immigration policy in this country has been shaped by many factors, including a long history of pushes and pulls between the U.S. and its southern neighbor. What was at first a fluid border between the two countries soon became a monitored entry point that provided exceptions for laborers, but few others who wished to cross it. By the early part of the twentieth century, the creation of Bracero Programs (guest worker programs) offered legal opportunities for workers from Mexico to find employment in the United States, but these programs were eventually phased out as anti-immigrant sentiment rose alongside economic fears. Eventually, efforts to create partnerships gave way to defense and security-based approaches along the U.S./Mexico border. This shift in policy began in the mid-1990s, but was intensified after the terrorist attacks of September 11, 2001.

As militarization along the southern U.S. border increased, trade restrictions and regulations simultaneously decreased. The passage of NAFTA in 1994 opened doors for trade, but did not include provisions for the movement of human labor. Certain provisions of the agreement had a disastrous effect on Mexico's rural and poor populations, driving thousands of migrants from their homes in search of work (Henriques & Patel, 2004). While there had always been a flow of people crossing the border from Mexico into the United States, these flows had traditionally been centered in urban areas such as San Diego and El Paso. Now, as security along these major crossing areas was reinforced, large numbers of migrants began crossing the border in more dangerous but less patrolled areas such as the desert of southern Arizona (Cornelius, 2001). Also moving through the same desert spaces were drug runners and other criminals who found the creation of routes over this vast, unpopulated terrain favorable for the smuggling of illegal goods (Erfani, 2007).

Southern Arizona's extreme temperatures and rugged landscape can be difficult even for individuals who are well-informed and prepared for these challenges. For those unaware of the dangers, however, the desert often proves fatal. By the late 1990s, the death toll of migrants who did not survive the journey northward had begun to climb. As the statistical figures rose, so did the sense of outrage and alarm among local citizens. In 2000 Humane Borders was established with the purpose of saving lives by placing water in the desert. Soon after, other humanitarian-aid response organizations were formed, and in 2004 a movement called No More Deaths was initiated to unite the efforts of Tucson-area organizations working to save lives in the desert and reform immigration policy.

The increasing number of deaths in the desert was not the only issue that gained attention during this period. During a trip to Organ Pipe Cactus National Monument in 1991, Chris Simcox was appalled by the huge numbers of both migrants and drug runners present in the park. He soon organized a civil militia in southern Arizona called Civil Homeland Defense, which eventually became the Minuteman Project and then the Minuteman Civil Defense Corps (MCDC). Simcox's media savvy and unique approach to bringing attention to the border soon earned his demand for stricter border enforcement a place in the national spotlight.

It was from this point that my research began, looking back at a complex history that led to the present struggle and examining the ways in which the actions of civil society (specifically, Humane Borders, No More Deaths and MCDC), relayed to a national public through media, are defining the present story through the differing ways in which they frame the issues surrounding immigration.

My study of civil society organizations along the Arizona/Sonora border revealed distinctive media consumption trends, reflective of Klapper's reinforcement theory, among volunteers for all three groups. To inform themselves about the border or border-related issues, most individuals, already impassioned members of activist groups, tend to gravitate toward media sources that reinforce their pre-existing beliefs. Those who see immigration as a security issue tend to consult sources championing the idea of tighter borders, more law enforcement, and stricter adherence to laws that require the deportation of persons in this country without authorization. Those who see immigration as a combination of social, political and economic forces tend to select media sources framing immigration stories with considerations of how the present situation impacts not only the individual migrants, but also families, jobs and national security strategies. The exceptions to this trend were the leaders or founders of the three organizations who all indicated that they attempt to access media sources reflecting multiple perspectives of the issue.

The emphasis that civil society volunteers placed on their trust (or distrust) of media was another important finding in this study. Many MCDC members expressed a distrust of media in general, citing "biased reporting" as one reason they rely more on their personal experiences or the leadership of MCDC for information than they do the media. For example, a number of individuals conveyed disgust at the media's constant use of the phrase "vigilante" to describe members of the group. "If media would come to the border and see for themselves what we do," they said, "they would have a much different opinion of who we are." Their feeling was that many media professionals approach their stories about MCDC with preconceived notions that result in "slanted" reporting without having ever visited the border. These individuals also tended to see media (in general) as being driven by liberal forces, thus adding to their distrust.

Members of Humane Borders and No More Deaths, on the other hand, held a generally positive view of media and the coverage of their organizations. Many expressed appreciation for the media coverage that has emphasized their life-saving work and has brought attention to the need for policy reform. While some wished for deeper, more reflective reporting that would not dichotomize the issue into "humanitarians" versus "border watch groups" or Border Patrol, most said the media have generally been fair in what they report. However, these volunteers are quick to point out that when it comes to media coverage of immigration in general, there is often much more to the story that does not get told. They point to the complexity of the issue, and the tendency of media (due to the nature of most reporting) to skim over the surface of the topics being covered rather than devoting adequate space and time to explore them. Many also expressed concern about the strength of anti-immigrant voices perpetuated through conservative media channels that inspire fear, rather than understanding, of the migrant.

The voices of United States Border Patrol agents also add depth to this study. The three agents with whom I visited shared sentiments with all three civil society groups. They appreciated the media coverage they have received, but emphasized the damaging effects of inaccurate reporting. Their jobs are directly affected by a government that responds to the reactions of a public, and the public's primary source of information about the Border Patrol is mass media. Therefore, when media make false assumptions or misinformed statements such as those about the National Guard not being armed, the Border Patrol can be directly affected. The three agents also indicated a desire for more in-depth coverage, and stated that reporters who actually come to the border walk away with a much better understanding of the issues at hand.

Finally, the media professionals themselves provided important insights into the nature of reporting on immigration, the border, and the civil society groups active along Arizona's southern border. Most agreed that coverage is limited and would ideally have greater depth. However, time and money constraints often prevent the type of in-depth coverage they would like to pursue. Furthermore, these same limitations are the primary reason more media professionals do not make it to the border. The cost of sending a reporter and/or crew to the line is simply greater than many media markets can or will absorb. Thus, reporters even as close to the border as Phoenix rely also on contacts with civil society leaders who can provide information from a distance.

The media professionals with whom I spoke also indicated that they intentionally do not always respond to the press releases, press conferences or other sources of information provided by these civil society organizations. Knowing that each group has an agenda, the immigration reporters in particular expressed a strong sentiment of not wanting to be "used" by the organizations to promote any particular cause. Therefore, they said they usually tend to include information from or about the groups not as a story in itself, but as a supplement to a larger story that they have identified as important.

That said, most reporters also admitted that the organizations who are best organized and easiest to reach probably receive more coverage than those who do not place great emphasis on public relations. It only makes sense that a reporter will contact a person he or she knows will be available to answer questions rather than someone who is out of the office or is not able to quickly return calls. This, in part, explains the success of MCDC in presenting its message to a national public. The group has hired media contact professionals (including individuals who write regular press releases), established local chapters all over the country that serve as contacts for local media, and emphasized the importance of timely responses to all media inquiries.

One additional and important insight provided by the media professionals I interviewed is that general public sentiment has turned away from a humanitarian conception of the border and more toward a legalistic, anti-migrant view. Credit for this was partly given to Simcox and the MCDC volunteers whose constant presence in the media has effectively changed the tone of the debate toward security rather than humanitarian efforts. A few of the reporters indicated that it is more difficult now to publish stories that offer a glimpse of the suffering along the border because public backlash is so great. Many of the letters or responses they receive accuse them of siding with the migrants and not caring about the laws of the country. To a degree then, this strong public reaction limits the information they are able to provide to the populace. The larger question that naturally follows is whether that reaction is reflective of the feelings of the general population or just a very active and vociferous few.

Misinformation about immigration and border-related issues was another issue uncovered in this research. The inaccuracies disseminated through voices like that of Lou Dobbs have a great effect on the public's understanding of the issues at hand. To like-minded individuals who wish to see tougher border security measures put into place, Dobbs is a reliable source. Therefore, his statements about the threat of leprosy or the number of illegal aliens in our nation's prisons fuel both the fear and the fire of groups such as MCDC. For members of aid groups like Humane Borders and No More Deaths, statements made by Dobbs (or others who disseminate false statistics) are dangerous not only because they are inaccurate, but also because they distract from the notion that there are grave humanitarian concerns accompanying the issue of immigration that must be addressed.

The survey work and participant observation employed as part of this study also uncovered clear distinctions among the organizations being studied and the way they frame migrants and their efforts to cross the border. Humane Borders and No More Deaths, both faith-based groups, view migrants as fellow human beings above all else. They see labor flows as part of a larger political and economic system that has dictated the migrants' decisions to cross the border without legal authorization. Their actions toward the migrant are most often based on religious principles that emphasize compassion and outreach to those in need. Nearly all of the volunteers from these two groups had met or personally known an unauthorized migrant. Many have known and worked with hundreds over the years. Their understanding of the migrant as a fellow human and their ability to empathize form the basis of their humanitarian approach to the immigration issue. The frames they create are no less powerful than the frames of groups like MCDC, but they are perhaps more difficult to "sell" because they are not as easily personalized as frames that equate immigration to threat. The death of an unknown migrant may not directly affect most United States citizens, but the loss of a job to an unauthorized migrant might, as would the fear of contracting a disease or becoming a victim of identity theft.

Border watch groups such as MCDC, on the other hand, frame the migrant first and foremost in a legalistic sense, using formal, legal terms to describe both the status and the person crossing the border without authorization. Their primary concerns are upholding of the Constitution of the United States, ensuring that the laws of the state and nation are enforced, and preventing terrorists from entering this country through porous borders. For them, the migrant is an illegal person who has chosen to breech a law in order to enter this country. While some express sympathy over the conditions in Mexico that have caused the large "push" of illegal aliens across the border, they still feel the most important consideration is the safety and security of their country and their families. Very few of the volunteers had ever met or personally known an "IA" (illegal alien). To most MCDC members, the legal status of the migrant takes precedence over the human face of the person crossing the border. This view, along with a great concern for national security, guides their border enforcement approach to the immigration issue and defines the frames they create to talk about the issue of immigration.

Finally, and perhaps most importantly, the use of security frames in a post 9/11 context has been extremely successful in shaping the way the public understands and views immigration along the Southwestern U.S. border. One primary reason for the popularity of a protectionist view among certain segments of the population is that citizens of the United States are still dealing with the fear of living in a post 9/11 environment. Prior to September 11, 2001, immigration discourse (which at the time was much more significant in border regions than it was on a national scale) was largely guided by humanitarian frames promoted by groups like Humane Borders and No More Deaths. These frames emphasized the vulnerability of migrants as they attempted unauthorized border crossings, and placed responsibility for increasing death tolls in the desert on official immigration policy. Media delivered stories of human suffering and the need for lifesaving measures to wider audiences without a great deal of controversy. The fear of attack after 9/11, however, resulted in a major shift in public attitudes and immigration dialogue. Greater attention was now given to security and threat frames promoted by the Minuteman Civil Defense Corps and similar groups. These frames, emphasizing the porosity of the border and the criminal nature of those who enter, inspired protectionist rather than humanitarian reactions. They also resonated greatly with media audiences already fearful of what they felt was a weakened national security system and porous borders. Media contributed to the groups' widespread notoriety and success in promoting their messages by providing them with extensive coverage. Media sources generally classified as conservative in nature formed alliances with MCDC and like groups and offered a platform for their messages, while media outlets considered to be more liberal often portrayed MCDC and like groups as extremist. Even though this coverage was largely negative, the fact that it was so extensive heightened public awareness of the groups and their ideologies, and gave organizations like MCDC a certain degree of legitimacy as contributors to the national immigration dialogue.

Hope for the Border, Hope for the Public

The desert of southern Arizona is a far cry from a Habermasian-style coffee house where bourgeoisie citizens once congregated, discussed and debated important issues. Despite that fact, an active and passionate civil society has found a way to inspire such gatherings, discussion and debates both in the desert in places and entirely remote from it. By utilizing the power of various types of media to tell the stories of the migrant, the border, and the need for immigration policy reform, these members of civil society have engaged their fellow U.S. citizens in an active public debate that extends far beyond the state of Arizona. The ensuing discussion, played out through the airwaves, on the Internet, in headlines and across television screens signals an engaged public sphere that, while not perfect, certainly exemplifies the type of expressive civic involvement that Habermas envisioned.

In many respects, this research has reinforced the idea that what happens along the Arizona/Sonora border is less about the individuals who are crossing the boundary and more about the people who await them on the other side. Immigration is an issue that reflects who we are as a country and how we choose to define, protect, and share our place on this earth. It forces us as individuals, and as a nation, to evaluate the way we view ourselves in relation to those around us. In what ways do our efforts to interact with our neighbors reveal our own sense of security, well-being, partnership or compassion? How do the actions of those who live on the other side of the border reflect what *we* do as consumers, humanitarians, patriots, concerned citizens, and in many cases, people of faith?

This study, which offers a glimpse of the immigration issue along the Arizona/Sonora border through the eyes of media and civil society, does not provide the answers. However, it *does* offer a unique view of the issues and the way they are presented to the public that will hopefully prompt those concerned about immigration to wrestle with such important questions. We can no longer "other" the issue of immigration or the people involved in it because we are an indelible part of the system that gives rise to human labor flows. Identifying our own place in that framework and understanding how the stories of the border are framed, reported and received will help us create a more equitable balance that considers both the needs of our own nation and the needs of our neighbors.

The semi-ethnographic nature of this study is limited in its size and scope, and it is not meant to be a comprehensive analysis of *all* media or *all* members of Humane Borders, No More Deaths, MCDC and other key players along the Arizona/Sonora border. However, the findings that emerged from my research do provide important insights as to the nature of civil society's activities in this area as well as the stories that are told about them and about the border in general. Perhaps most importantly, this research offers a sense of hope that the deep convictions of an active citizenry will, through mediated channels, inspire us as a nation to engage in the kind of dialogue that will help us develop a fair and just immigration policy.

Personal Reflections

After more than a year of traveling back and forth to the land that stretches from Tucson south to the Arizona/Sonora line, my perspectives of the border and the people I have encountered there have changed a great deal. In many ways, I feel a deep sense of connection to the vast desert spaces I visited during that time. My thoughts have been shaped by the many hours spent sweating while hiking along worn and winding migrant trails, freezing in lawn chairs during line watches that lasted through the night, scoping for scorpions and snakes as I hauled garbage bags of decaying backpacks and English dictionaries out of migrant "lay-up" areas, and holding my breath as I maneuvered my car through massive dust clouds left by other vehicles on desert back roads. Perhaps even more influential were the hundreds of hours driving back and forth from my home in Queen Valley, AZ, hidden from the chaos of the border region, to the lonesome stretches of dry land along the divide. The four hour round trip offered much valuable time to reflect on my experiences, struggle with my emotions, and watch, watch, watch for the faces of those I knew were moving along beside me, hidden amidst the saguaro and brittle brush.

I never saw those faces on my drives, but I did see them as they were flooded with bright lights in the midst of the dark desert, as they were being loaded into the back of Border Patrol vehicles, and as they waited to be fingerprinted in the processing facility in Nogales and shipped back across the border. I saw in those faces fear, frustration, desperation, resolve, and in many cases, relief. I wondered how my own face would appear to a Minuteman or a No More Deaths volunteer if I had walked a mile, or five, or fifty, in their shoes. Thankful? Afraid? Exhausted?

I also saw the faces of individuals who were so consumed with a sense of calling along the border that they dedicated days, nights, weeks, and months on end to making a difference, hoping that their next efforts would be the ones that would save a life or save a nation. I owe much gratitude to these volunteers for sharing with me their commitment to changing the dire situation that has led to the present circumstances along the Arizona/Sonora border and beyond. These volunteers epitomized the power of passion and compassion that motivates individuals to action, even when that means making sacrifices themselves. I respect them very much for their dedication and determination.

As I began my research, I recognized that my own background and values framework made me more likely to appreciate a humanitarian approach to the dilemma of illegal immigration than a militaristic approach. Based on reports of border security groups I had studied (particularly articles about the Minuteman Civil Defense Corps), I was apprehensive about joining this gun-toting group for musters that would involve field observation, line watches, and possible migrant apprehensions. I fully expected to encounter individuals whose actions were driven by hatred or disdain for migrants, and who would view me as a threat or an "outsider."

What I actually found through my participant observation with MCDC was a dedicated group of individuals who are generally driven by feelings of patriotism and/or fear of foreign threat. The volunteers with whom I spoke were convinced that something has to be done to seal the border and reform the policies that have led to the current state of affairs. My preconceived media-driven notions of gruff, angry men yielded to encounters with a mix of grandparents, college students, and middle aged professionals who were frustrated with the government's response to border security and felt it was up to them to *do something* to call attention to the problem. Not all were compassionate toward migrants, but I did encounter a number of very kind individuals who showed genuine concern for the foreigners trying to cross and who felt it was more humane to keep them from crossing than to allow them to enter the chaotic and dangerous world of living underground in the

United States. Nearly all of the volunteers were driven not by hatred or racism, but by a sense of duty and loyalty to their country and their families.

More than anything, I was surprised by the willingness of MCDC volunteers to tell their stories. I thought I might encounter resistance from individuals who were suspicious of my role as a researcher, but very few had any reservations at all about engaging in conversation and telling me why they had decided to become involved. On the contrary, many were delighted that someone was willing to listen and to form opinions by coming to participate and observe rather than making assumptions from a distance. Although many were distrustful of media in general, they felt that the "truth" would be obvious to anyone (media professionals included) who was willing to take the time to meet them and draw conclusions by spending time with them "on the line." I think to a large degree, they are right.

My experience with the Minuteman Civil Defense Corps was not at all what I had expected. I encountered many thoughtful individuals who were willing to share their insights, personal experiences, and feelings about what they think it will take to "fix" our nation's immigration conundrum. Some of their points are valid, and some are based on rhetoric and false assumptions. However, they deserve to be recognized as a group that is motivated enough about creating change to actively pursue it. I personally do not agree with many of their ideologies or their approaches to "fixing" the broken system, but I do have a deep respect for their commitment to rectifying an imperfect situation and their willingness to act on it. Likewise, I have a tremendous amount of respect for the dedicated volunteers of Humane Borders and No More Deaths who have so passionately sacrificed sweat, tears and countless hours to ensuring that immigration policy does not continue to promote death among vulnerable peoples.

Seeking Solutions

While my research was definitely shaped by a newfound appreciation for the volunteers I encountered and experiences I gained through time with the MCDC organization, my own convictions about what is happening on the border, and what *needs* to happen are still driven by the realization that this issue is much broader in scope and nature than a security-first approach will allow. During interviews, both Chris Simcox and another MCDC volunteer made the analogy of the border being like a boat filled with holes. Rather than just bailing water, they said, the holes need to be plugged to keep the boat from sinking.

I certainly agree that there are holes in the current immigration policy, and that the reality of security concerns do mandate that these holes be filled. However, I also think that plugging holes is futile if no additional thought is given to what it is that is causing the punctures. It makes much more sense to ask questions that will help determine why the holes are being formed in the first place, and how new ones might be prevented. Like many of the Humane Borders and No More Deaths volunteers I interviewed, I feel that immigration policy involves and is shaped by much more than security alone. Economic, political, social and interpersonal forces all play a role in creating the "push" factors that drive large numbers of people across borders in search of opportunity. We would be wise as a country and a citizenry to evaluate the role that such forces have played in the migratory process. Perhaps instead of dedicating so many resources to keeping our neighbors out, we could better secure the borders by enabling those neighbors (through more equitable trade policies, for example) to work and lead dignified lives within their own homelands.

The purpose of my research was not to find a "solution" to the immigration problems our country currently faces. Indeed, there is no singular solution. Reform and change will require concerted efforts from a myriad of actors involved in political, economic and social arenas. However, research such as this can be a critical link in developing the approaches to borders our nation needs to adopt by understanding how differing frames about immigration are produced and dispersed. Some of the "answers" about how our nation should proceed will likely come from other countries dealing with similar border and immigration issues. Much can be learned from the examples of Eastern European countries as well as Spain, Italy and France (Andreas, 2003). Studying the effect of migrant labor originating in regions such as Asia will also help policy makers and citizens of the United States understand the implications of various border strategies (Parrenas, 2001).

But it is the ideas originating in the civil society organizations active along the border that may provide the best hope for the creation of a just and equitable approach to immigration. During the course of my research, I heard many potentially successful ideas about how current policy could and should be reformed. Members of both Humane Borders and No More Deaths were almost in unanimous agreement that deaths could be prevented if more *legal* opportunities existed for migrants to enter the United States. They cite the difficulty (near impossibility for many) of obtaining legal visas under the current system, and maintain that if legal means of entering were offered, circular migration patterns based on earning target amounts of money would largely be re-established among the many migrants who do not wish to stay.

Chris Simcox was adamant that guest worker programs would not work, but that more migrants should be allowed to enter the United States who wished to become full-fledged U.S. citizens. This, he says, will ensure that those who come are willing to contribute to their new country through taxes, etc. and willing to learn the laws and language of the land. While his idea does not address any of the "push" factors previously mentioned that often stimulate illegal immigration, it does support the fact that the identity of the United States has always been shaped by the arrival of potential legal citizens whose pride in their new home contributes to the fabric of U.S. life.

Many other worthy ideas have been developed by those who see the border up close and know intimately the struggles that take place there. Today's media-rich environment offers more opportunities than ever for their voices to be heard. The power of media to tell the immigration story is reflected in the words, sentiments, and experiences of civil society volunteers who participated in this research. Napoleon Bonaparte once said, "History is the version of past events that people have decided to agree upon." It is my hope that one day, the findings of this study will have contributed a small part to helping a public decide how to critically engage with media and analyze the messages they receive to determine which stories should be remembered.

Conclusion

The story of immigration is a story of great consequence for many reasons. To a citizenry concerned about security and sovereignty, it is a story of failed leadership and corporate greed. To a population focused on the struggles of migrants themselves, it is a story that demands recognition of a common humanity and of the need for policies that allow all people to live lives of dignity. For those whose lives are defined by their faith, it is a story that mandates action to help those in need. For those whose lives are defined by a sense of patriotic duty, it is a story that demands action so that justice might be served.

Immigration is an issue that touches on human empathy as well as human fears. For a nation not yet certain how to define the limits of its non-political borders, it is a story that challenges a sense of identity and place. Perhaps more than anything else, immigration is a story conveying a great sense of struggle about how we as a nation choose to identify ourselves in relation to others. It also is an issue that forces us to examine how we, through media, choose to tell others' stories so as to gain credibility and standing in our own imagined communities.

And for those whose lives are most directly affected, the unauthorized migrants themselves, it is a story of a divided society whose response to their presence will dictate their futures. For them, it is a story that, while often tragic, retains a sense of hope for the final chapter. As Bill Wellman, the former superintendent of Organ Pipe Cactus National Monument explained to Robin Hoover of Humane Borders, "When people come here 50 years from now to visit, it won't be to see the cactus. It will be because this was their Ellis Island."

As Minuteman Civil Defense Corps founder Chris Simcox sees it, the story of the border is about protecting the future of the country. To do this, he sees a need to "secure United States borders and coastal boundaries against unlawful and unauthorized entry of all individuals, contraband, and foreign military."

For Humane Borders co-founder Robin Hoover, the story of the border is about more than just water in the desert. "The big question," he says, "is how to teach this hemisphere how to share." Or, as Humane Borders volunteer Libby stated, to help the public realize that "it's a human thing, not a migrant thing."

Many different views. Many different reactions. One divided public. Where do we go from here?

The complexity of the immigration issue itself is reflected in the responses of a vibrant civil society, actively creating change – and discussion – from the desert of southern Arizona. Their efforts to inform the national public offer great insight, controversy and emotion to an issue that in one way or another, affects us all. And in evaluating the responses that each of these groups has offered to the problems caused by current immigration policy, it would be wise to remember that these actions are rooted in deep human convictions and deeply emotional personal experiences. Solutions will not come from opposition, but from cooperation in finding a common ground, common frames, that consider the integrity and safety of citizens on both sides of the line.

Journalist Charles Bowden, in a 2006 article describing the complexities of immigration, describes a guard at a drop house in Phoenix. His description is an accurate summary of the major players in the national immigration debate.

"He is not a bad man. The Border Patrol agents are not bad people. The Minutemen, the polleros, the human rights folks putting water bottles out in the desert, well, I've met them all and they are not bad people.

As for you and me, the jury is still out.

Appendix 1
Questionnaire for Volunteers and Organization Leaders

(Humane Borders version; identical questionnaires were used for No More Deaths and the Minuteman Civil Defense Corps)

Media and Arizona/Sonora Border Issues
Cari Lee Skogberg Eastman – University of CO, Boulder

General Information
Name _____   Male/Female (circle one)
Age category (check one) :
19-29 _____   40-49 _____   30-39_____
50-59 _____   60+ _____
U.S. Citizen ? Yes _____ No _____
Home state (where from) _____
State/community where currently living (if different) _____
Profession_____
Highest educational level obtained (check one):
Grade school _____ High school _____
Trade school _____ Associate's degree_____
Bachelor's degree_____ Master's degree_____
Doctorate or professional degree (M.D., J.D., Ph.D., etc.)__
Other _____
            Military background? Yes _____ No _____

Media Usage Questions
Do you read a daily newspaper? Y / N   If so, which one(s)?
_____

Do you or members of your household subscribe to or have regular access to any magazines? Y / N   If so, which magazine(s)?
_____

Which (if any) news or talk programs do you regularly watch on television?_____

Which (if any) news or talk programs do you regularly listen to on the radio?_____

Which Website(s) (if any) do you regularly visit to gather news or information?_____

Approximately how many hours a day do you spend reading/ watching/ listening to/ surfing for news (through newspapers, radio, television, magazines, Internet, or other forms of media?)

0-1/2 hour _____   ½ hour – 1 hour _____

1-2 hours _____   2-3 hours _____

3-4 hours _____   more than 4 hours _____

8. What are the <u>most</u> important factors you consider when choosing sources from which to get news? (Mark all that apply)

Convenient or easily accessible source _____

The cost of this source is feasible ____

Convenient times / fits with my schedule _____

Personalities / hosts / writers are people I trust _____

The newspaper, network, or company is one that I trust_____

The political beliefs of this source reflect my own views and beliefs _____

The source was recommended to me by someone I trust___

Organization Information and Involvement

How did you first become aware of Humane Borders?

What led you to become involved with Humane Borders?

How long have you been actively involved with the organization?

How many hours would you estimate that you volunteer/ work with Humane Borders:

Per week? _____   Per month? _____

Is your involvement seasonal, or do you take part in activities throughout the year? Explain:

What are the greatest benefits / rewards of being involved?

What are some of the greatest challenges of being involved?

Please describe some of the activities you have been involved in. Do media regularly cover these activities?

Have you ever been contacted by media or interviewed about your work with this organization?

How would you describe the overall goal or mission of Humane Borders?

How is this goal/mission communicated to the members of Humane Borders? Are there regular media channels through which the information is provided?

Did media coverage of Humane Borders have any impact   on your decision to become involved in the organization? (For example, did you ever read a story or hear a report that struck a chord and made you realize you wanted to become involved?)

What media (television, newspapers, radio stations, web sites, etc.) do you regularly consult to keep informed about border issues? How often do you consult them?

What has made the greatest impact on you since becoming involved with this organization?

Have you read, seen or heard any media reports of Humane Borders is your general reaction to these media reports?

Do you feel the media generally have a good idea of what Humane Borders is trying to accomplish? Why or why not?

Do you feel the general public has a good idea of what Humane Borders is trying to accomplish? Why or why not?

When faced with conflicting stances between leaders of Humane Borders and media reports, for example, how do you determine which holds the most sway in your own personal decisions about migration? Why?

Have you personally met the leader of Humane Borders? Contacted him or her? Worked with him or her?

What do you think are the major reforms that need to be made in regard to border policy?

How is current border policy affecting the work or vision of Humane Borders?

Do you feel media are helping or hindering your efforts to educate the public about the border and the need for policy change?

How many total members are there in your organization:

locally? _____

nationwide? _____

Do you ever feel like you are in danger because of your work with Humane Borders? In what way(s)? If so, do media contribute in any way to this atmosphere?

What other risks are involved with being a member/volun-teer of this organization? What are the benefits?

If you could relay one message to the press about Humane Borders, what would it be? To Congress? To the general public?

Do you anticipate that you will continue to be involved with Humane Borders? Why or why not?

Have you personally met or known any undocumented migrants/illegal immigrants? In what context? Please describe your experience.

(If not from AZ) What were your conceptions of the border and what was happening along the border *before* coming here? How did you form those conceptions (from what source?)

Are your conceptions of the border different now that you have been here and seen it up close? If so, in what ways?

Did faith or religious affiliation have any influence in your decision to come here or to be involved with this organization? If so, what is your religious affiliation?

Did religious media influence your decision to become involved with Humane Borders?

(If not from AZ) What are some of the major immigration issues where you are from?

Do you remain in contact with other members of the group? Are they primarily from your community, or do they come from other places? If you do remain in contact, is it through personal correspondence or through media such as blogs, chat rooms, etc.?

Are there any additional comments you would like to make?

Appendix 2
Additional Border and Immigration-Related Activist Groups in Southern Arizona

This list is by no means comprehensive; many additional organizations exist and are too numerous to include here. Additionally, inclusion in the list does not indicate endorsement of any of the following organizations or movements. The groups listed below simply represent additional major players and most recognized activist groups and organizations in southern Arizona speaking out about immigration-related issues.

All quotations in the following descriptions have been taken directly from each organization's website.

Groups Using Humanitarian Immigration Frames

Border Action Network

http://www.borderaction.org/web/index.php
Human rights advocacy network. "Border Action Network formed in 1999 and works with immigrant and border communities in Southern Arizona to ensure that our rights are respected, our human dignity upheld and that our communities are healthy places to live. We are a membership-based organization that combines grassroots community organizing, leadership development, litigation and policy advocacy."

Border Links

http://www.borderlinks.org
Specializes in experiential education to raise awareness and inspire action around global political economics. "Our programs focus on cross-

border relationship building opportunities, issues of immigration, community formation and development, and social justice in the borderlands between Mexico, the U.S., and beyond."

Coalición de Derechos Humanos

http://www.derechoshumanosaz.net
"Coalición de Derechos Humanos ("The Human Rights Coalition") is a grassroots organization which promotes respect for human/civil rights and fights the militarization of the Southern Border region, discrimination, and human rights abuses by federal, state, and local law enforcement officials affecting U.S. and non-U.S. citizens alike."

Samaritans

http://www.samaritanpatrol.org
"Samaritans (formerly Samaritan Patrol) are people of faith and conscience who are responding directly, practically and passionately to the crisis at the US/Mexico border. Prompted by the mounting deaths among border crossers, we came together in July, 2002 to provide emergency medical assistance, food and water to people crossing the Sonoran Desert."

Groups Using Oppositional Immigration Frames

American Border Patrol

http://www.americanborderpatrol.com
"American Border Patrol is the only non-governmental organization (NGO) that monitors the border on a regular basis - mostly by air. It has three aircraft, each designed for a specialized mission. ABP operates from a ranch right on the Mexican border in Southeastern Arizona in the heart of a major smuggling corridor. ABP is a watchdog. We watch what the government is doing and we report to you directly. Glenn Spencer is the president and founder of American Border Patrol."

Author's note: American Border Patrol is a private, non-profit organization not affiliated in any way with the United States Border Patrol.

Border Guardians

http://www.borderguardians.org/index1.html
"We are a group of American citizens who believe that defending America's sovereignty is the most important issue in the illegal immigration problem. For too many decades, American citizens have been subjected to a relentless psy-ops (psychological operations) and propaganda war by the left-wing advocates of illegal immigration."

Author's note: Website includes inflammatory and confrontational language, images and content.

Mothers Against Illegal Amnesty

http://www.mothersagainstillegalamnesty.com
Formerly known as Mothers Against Illegal Aliens (shut down in November 2008) this organization resurfaced in March 2010 as Mothers Against Illegal Amnesty. The MAIA website does not list an official mission statement, but a letter on the site titled "NOT WRONG – JUST FLAWED?" posted March 18, 2011 by president/founder Michelle Dallacroce states, "There can be no doubt that Mothers Against Illegal Amnesty's entire mission has been to see an end put to this practice of giving automatic citizenship to illegal alien BABY's, called Amnesty Babies f/k/a Anchor Babies." MAIA ideology is also apparent in a quote by founder Michelle Dallacroce, made May 18, 2006 on *Your World with Neil Cavuto* (FOX news). Dallacroce complained that there is no reason immigrant women and children need to be in the United States because they have no jobs here "... other than their children's job is to dumb down the American children and overpopulate our schools." A Jan. 2, 2009 entry on the original MAIA website states "our children and our country are at risk of being eliminated!" and a link on the current MAIA site titled "Anchor Baby RESEARCH" includes the following statement, "I recommend that you review the materials below to gain knowledge and insight into how illegal alien anchor babies are taking over the USA! One baby at a time."

Patriots Border Alliance

http://www.patriotsborderalliance.com
"It is the mission of Patriots' Border Alliance to see the borders and ports of the United States secure. We will use all means of constitutionally-protected political demonstration and protest to support that Mission. We will support law enforcement in the active pursuit of the goal of a secure United States, by manning posts at the border and in the interior of the country in order to report suspected illegal border crossers and those who are in the country illegally. We will make all efforts to educate the American public, through those activities, of the porous nature of our borders and the complete failure of the federal government to fulfill its constitutional mandate to Secure Our Borders.
Patriots Border Alliance is a splinter group of the Minuteman Civil Defense Corps. It was formed in 2007 as the result of a dispute with MCDC leader Chris Simcox over leadership decisions and lack of financial transparency. The organization's website states, "PBA aims to recapture to true patriotic spirit of the Minuteman concept."

Ranch Rescue

This group is no longer on-line. The former website (now a dead link) was www.ranchrescue.com

Because there is no online resource, it was not possible to include a description of the group from its own communications.

However, the Southern Poverty Law Center (a nonprofit organization that tracks hate groups) provides this description of the group:

"Ranch Rescue is a group of vigilantes dedicated to patrolling the U.S.-Mexico border region in an effort to deter and repel border crossers and trespassers. They conduct paramilitary operations and equip themselves with high-powered assault rifles, handguns, night-vision devices, two-way radios, observation posts, flares, machetes, all-terrain vehicles, and trained attack dogs."

http://www.splcenter.org/get-informed/case-docket/leiva-v-ranch-rescue

Bibliography

Ackleson, J. (2005). Fencing in failure: Effective border control is not achieved by building more fences. *Immigration Policy in Focus, 4*(2). Retrieved December 9, 2006, from http://www.ailf.org/ipc/policy_reports_2005_ fencinginfailure.asp.

Adams Jr., R. H., & Page, J. (2005). Do international migration and remittances reduce poverty in developing countries? *World Development, 33*(10), 1645–1669.

Alba, F. (2004, March). Mexico: A crucial crossroads. *Migration Policy Institute*. Retrieved February 18, 2008, from www.migrationinformation. org/feature/print.cfm?ID=211.

———. (2010, February). Mexico: A crucial crossroads. *Migration Policy Institute*. Retrieved March 4, 2010, from http://www.migrationinformation. org/Profiles/display.cfm?ID=772.

Almazán, M. (1997). NAFTA and the Mesoamerican states system. *The Annals of the American Academy of Political and Social Science, 550*(1), 42–50.

Alvarado, E. (2008). Poverty and inequality in Mexico after NAFTA: Challenges, setbacks and implications. *Estudios Fronterizos, 9*(17), 73–105.

Anderson, B. (1991). *Imagined Communities*. London: Verso. (Original work published in 1983).

Anderson-Gold, S. (1988). War and resistance: Kant's doctrine of human rights. *Journal of Social Philosophy, 19*(1), 37–50.

Andreas, P. (2003). Redrawing the line: Borders and security in the twenty-first century. *International Security, 28*(2), 78–111.

———. (2006, February). Politics on edge: Managing the US-Mexico border. *Current History, 105*(688), 64–68.

———. (2009). *Border games: Policing the U.S.-Mexico divide*. Ithaca, NY: Cornell University Press.

Annerino, J. (2009). *Dead in their tracks: Crossing America's desert borderlands in the new era*. Tucson, AZ: University of Arizona Press.

Associated Press. (2011, January 14). Obama administration ends high-tech border fence. *National Public Radio*. Retrieved February 9, 2011, from http://www.npr.org/2011/01/14/132940996/obama-administration-ends-high-tech-border-fence.

———. (2011, April 29). Brewer signs bill authorizing Ariz. border fence. *AZCapitolTimes.com*. Retrieved August 7, 2011, from http://azcapitoltimes. com/news/2011/04/29/brewer-signs-bill-authorizing-ariz-border-fence.

———. (2011, June 17). Baptists support immigration fix. *The New York Times*, p. 20.

Babwin, D. (2007, August 16). Immigrant takes refuge in Chicago church. *Associated Press*. Retrieved November 23, 2007, from http://www.breit bart.com/article.php?id=D8JHRKAO2&show_article=1.

Bach, R. (2005, Summer). Transforming border security: Prevention first. *Homeland Security Affairs,* 1(1), 1–14. Retrieved March 26, 2008, from http://www.hsaj.org/pages/volume1/issue1/pdfs/1.1.2.pdf.

Bacon, D. (2004, January 14). NAFTA's legacy—profits and poverty. *Commondreams.org Newscenter*. Retrieved December 9, 2006, from http://www.commondreams.org/views04/0114-04.htm.

————. (2005). Stories from the borderlands. *NACLA Report on the Americas, 39*(1), 25–30.

Bakalis, A. (2007, October 4). Simi asks Chertoff to intervene in illegal immigrant stalemate. *la.indymedia.org*. Retrieved November 23, 2007, from http://la.indymedia.org/news/2007/10/208091.php.

Bane, M.J., & Zenteno, R. (Eds.). (2009). *Poverty and poverty alleviation strategies in North America*. Cambridge, MA: Harvard University, David Rockefeller Center for Latin American Studies.

Baran, S.J., & Davis, D.K. (2006). *Mass communication theory: Foundations, ferment, and future* (4th ed.). Belmont, CA: Thompson Wadsworth Publishing.

Baylor Institute for Studies of Religion. (2006, September). *American piety in the 21st century: New insights to the depth and complexity of religion in the U.S.* Waco, TX: Baylor University. Retrieved March 9, 2008, from http://www.baylor.edu/content/services/document.php/33304.pdf.

Bean, F.D. (1997). *At the crossroads: Mexican migration and U.S. policy*. Lanham, MD: Rowman & Littlefield Publishers.

Benería, L., & Mendoza, B. (1995). Structural adjustment and social emergency funds: The cases of Honduras, Mexico and Nicaragua. *European Journal of Development Research, 7*(1), 53–76.

Benford, R.D., & Snow, D.A. (2000). Framing processes and social movements: An overview and assessment. *Annual Review of Sociology, 26*, 611–639.

Binford, L. (2005). A generation of migrants: Why they leave, where they end up. (REPORT: MEXICAN WORKERS). *NACLA Report on the Americas, 39*(1), 31–39.

Boudreau, A., & Shiffman, K. (2007, November 7). Minuteman's high-tech border barrier called "a cow fence." *CNN*. Retrieved February 15, 2011, from http://articles.cnn.com/2007-11-07/us/border.fence_1_fence-proposal-chris-simcox-minuteman-civil-defense-corps?_s=PM:US.

Bowden, C. (2006, September/October). Exodus: Coyotes, pollos, and the promised van. *Mother Jones*, p. 36.

Brown, D.L., & Fox, J. (Eds.). (1998). *Assessing the impact of NGO advocacy campaigns on World Bank projects and policies: The struggle for accountability: The World Bank, NGOs and grassroots movements*. Boston: MIT Press.

Byrne, D., & Strobl, E. (2004, February). Defining unemployment in developing countries: Evidence from Trinidad and Tobago. *Journal of Development Economics, 73*(1), 465–476.

Calabrese, A. (2004). The promise of civil society: A global movement for communication rights. *Continuum: Journal of Media and Cultural Studies, 18*(3), 317–329.

Calavita, K. (1992). *Inside the state: The Bracero Program, immigration, and the I.N.S.* New York: Routledge.

Calderon, J.M. (2007, March 27). Notes from presentation by the General Mexican Consul in Tucson given at the 2007 International Conference on the Migrant. Tucson, AZ.

Canales, A. (2003). Mexican labour migration to the United States in the age of globalisation. *Journal of Ethnic and Migration Studies, 29*(4), 741–762.

Cannon, L. (1983, June 21). Warns of wave of refugees. *The Washington Post*, p. A1.

Cardoso, L.A. (1980). *Mexican emigration to the United States 1897–1931; Socio-economic patterns.* Tucson, AZ: University of Arizona Press.

Carlsen, L. (2003, June 13). The Mexican experience and lessons for WTO negotiations on the agreement on agriculture. *Americas Program.* Silver City, NM: Interhemispheric Resource Center.

———. (2005). Mexico after 10 years of NAFTA: The price of going to market. *Article based on presentations by the author, Director of the Americas Program of the International Relations Center, at the Asian Regional Workshop on Bilateral Free Trade Agreements held in Kuala Lampur, August 2005.* Retrieved December 7, 2006, from http://www.twnside.org.sg/title2/resurgence/182-183/Cover06.doc.

Carroll, S. (2005, April 2). Border volunteers basking in attention. *The Arizona Republic*, p. A1.

———. (2006, Fall). Reporting on the deaths of those who make the journey north. *Nieman Reports*, 48–50.

Carter, S. (2005, April 19). Minutemen on the move. *Press-Telegram*, p. n/a.

Carter, B., & Steinberg, J. (2006, March 29). Anchor-advocate on immigration wins viewers. *The New York Times*, p. A1.

Castillo, M. (2006, September 12). Tempers flare as Minutemen take to border. *San Antonio Express-News*, p. A1.

Ceasar, S. (2010, January 23). In Arizona, a stream of illegal immigrants from China. *The New York Times*, p. A11.

Chávez, L.R. (1998). *Shadowed lives: Undocumented immigrants in American society.* Fort Worth, TX: Harcourt Brace College Publishers.

———. (2001). *Covering immigration: Popular images and the politics of the nation.* Berkeley: University of California Press.

Church of Jesus Christ of Latter Day Saints. (2010, November 11). Church supports principles of Utah Compact on immigration. *Church of Jesus Christ of Latter Day Saints Newsroom* (online). Retrieved August 8, 2011, from http://newsroom.lds.org/article/church-supports-principles-of-utah-compact-on-immigration

Clark, J. (2007, January 31). Minutemen finish border fence on a Palominas ranch. *Douglas Dispatch*, News section.

Clark, L.S. (2004). Religion and media in a postnational, postmodern world. In P. Horsfield, M. Hess, and A. Medrano (Eds.), *Belief in Media.* London: Ashgate.

——— (2005). The emergence of religious lifestyle branding: Fashion Bibles, Bhangra Parties, and Muslim pop. In P. Horsfield (Ed.), *Papers from the Trans-Tasman Research Symposium, Emerging Research in Media, Religion and Culture* (pp. 22–39). Melbourne: RMIT Publishing.

Clark, M. (2011, April 12). United they stand: Local lawmakers fight illegal immigration with state-by-state strategy. *Columbia Patch*. Retrieved August 6, 2011, from http://columbia.patch.com/articles/united-they-stand-local-lawmakers-fight-illegal-immigration-with-state-by-state-strategy.

Cohen, A. (2007, October 5). Border fence stirs mixed emotions. *National Public Radio*. Transcript from *Day to Day*. Retrieved February 28, 2008, from http://www.npr.org/templates/story/story.php?storyId=15034078#email.

Corbett, J. (1991a). *Goatwalking: A guide to wildland living, a quest for the peaceable kingdom*. New York: Viking Penguin.

————. (1991b). *The sanctuary church, Pendle Hill pamphlet 270*. Wallingford, PA: Pendle Hill Publications.

Cornelius, W. (1978). *Mexican migration to the United States: Causes, consequences, and U.S. responses*. Cambridge, MA: Center for International Studies, Massachusetts Institute of Technology.

————. (2001, December). Death at the border: Efficacy and unintended consequences of US immigration control policy. *Population and Development Review, 27*(4), 661–685.

————. (2003, October 2). Focus: US Southwest border. *Migration Policy Institute Briefing*. Retrieved December 9, 2006, from http://www.migrationpolicy.org/events/100203_sum.php.

————. (2004, May 1). Evaluating enhanced US border enforcement. *Migration Policy Institute*. Retrieved April 9, 2007, from http://www.migrationinformation.org/feature/display.cfm?ID=223.

————. (2005). Controlling "unwanted" immigration: Lessons from the United States, 1993–2004. *Journal of Ethnic and Migration Studies, 31*(4), 775–794.

————. (2006, June 24). The American empire: Will it survive a world without borders? Presentation at Vail Valley Institute, Vail, CO. Retrieved March 13, 2010, from http://www.vailvalleyinstitute.org/empire/cornelius.html.

————. (2006, Sept. 26). Impacts of border enforcement on unauthorized Mexican migration to the United States. In *Border Battles*. Social Science Research Council. Retrieved March 23, 2010, from http://borderbattles.ssrc.org/Cornelius.

Courville, S., & Piper, N. (2004). Harnessing hope through NGO activism. *Annals, AAPSS, 592*, 39–61.

Coy, P.G., & Woehrle, L.M. (1996). Constructing identity and oppositional knowledge: The framing practices of peace movement organizations during the Persian Gulf War. *Sociological Spectrum, 16*, 287–327.

Cunningham, H. (2004). Nations rebound?: Crossing borders in a gated globe. *Identities: Global Studies in Culture and Power, 11*, 329–350.

D'Anjou, L. (1996). Social movements and cultural change: The first abolition campaign revisited. Hawthorne, NY: Aldine de Gruyter.

Dahler, L. (2007, May 1). Freedom to hate? In America, yes. *Daily News Leader*, p. 9A.

Daniels, R. (2004). *Guarding the golden door: American immigration policy and immigrants since 1882*. New York: Hill and Wang.

Davies, S. (1999). From moral duty to cultural rights: A case study of political framing in education. *Sociology of Education, 72*, 1–21.

Davis, D.K., & Baron, S.J. (1981). A history of our understanding of mass communication. In D.K. Davis & S.J. Baron (Eds.), *Mass communication and everyday life: A perspective on theory and effects* (pp. 19–52). Belmont, CA: Wadsworth Publishing.

DeChaine, D.R. (2002). Humanitarian space and the social imaginary: Médecins Sans Frontieres/Doctors Without Borders and the rhetoric of global community. *Journal of Communication Inquiry, 26*(4), 354–369.

Dellios, H. (2003, December 14). 10 years later, NAFTA harvests a stunted crop—rural Mexicans left out of boom. *Chicago Tribune*, p. 1.

Democracy Now! (2007, April 23). Rev. John Fife continues immigrant humanitarian work 25+ years after launching sanctuary movement. *National Public Radio*, 6 pp. transcript.

DePalma, A. (1995, July 16). After the fall: 2 faces of Mexico's economy. *The New York Times*, Section 3, p. 1.

Department of Homeland Security. (2008, May). Immigration enforcement actions: 2006. *Office of Immigration Statistics Annual Report*. Retrieved February 16, 2011, from http://www.dhs.gov/xlibrary/assets/statistics/publications/enforcement_ar_06.pdf.

————. (2010, December 21). Welcome. *Customs and Border Protection Website*. Retrieved August 7, 2011, from http://www.cbp.gov/xp/cgov/border_security/border_patrol/border_patrol_sectors/tucson_sector_az/tucson_index.xml.

————. (2011). United States Border Patrol: Total illegal alien apprehensions by fiscal year. *Customs and Border Protection Website*. Retrieved February 16, 2011, from http://www.cbp.gov/linkhandler/cgov/border_security/border_patrol/apps.ctt/apps.pdf.

Department of State. (1996). Mexico: Economic policy and trade practices report, 1996. *United States Department of State, Washington, D.C.* Retrieved December 7, 2006, from http://www.state.gov/www/issues/economic/trade_reports/latin_america96/mexico96.html.

De Tocqueville, A. (2003). *Democracy in America*. Clark, NJ: Lawbook Exchange.

de Vreese, C.H. (2002). *Framing Europe: Television news and European integration*. Amsterdam: Aksant.

Dillingham Immigration Commission. (1911). *Reports of the immigration commission: Abstracts of the reports of the immigration commission with conclusions and recommendations and views of the minority*. Senate document 747(1), United States Senate 61st Congress, 3rd Session. Washington, D.C., 690–691.

Dobbs, L. (2005, August 28). The new hard line on immigration: U.S. policy on immigration is a tragic joke. *The Arizona Republic*, p. B1.

————. (2006, May 24). Dobbs: Bush, Congress tell working folk to go to hell. *CNN.com*. Retrieved March 11, 2008, from http://www.cnn.com/2006/US/05/23/dobbs.may24/index.html.

————. (2007, May 31). Dobbs: An answer for my critics. *CNN.com*. Transcript retrieved March 28, 2008, from http://www.cnn.com/2007/US/05/29/Dobbs.May30/index.html.

Doty, R.L. (2009). *The law into their own hands: Immigration and the politics of exceptionalism*. Tucson, AZ: University of Arizona Press.

Downes, L. (2007, December 10). Showdown in Arizona, where mariachis and Minutemen collide. *The New York Times*, p. 22.

Duffy, G. (2007, Sept. 12). Pima County Supervisors OK $25K for desert water stops. *The Tucson Citizen*.

Dunn, T. (2010). *Blockading the border and human rights: The El Paso operation that remade immigration enforcement*. Austin, TX: University of Texas Press.

Easterly, W., Fiess, N., Lederman, D., Loayza, N.V., & Meller, P. (2003, Fall). NAFTA and convergence in North America: High expectations, big events, little time. *Economía, 4*(1), 1–53.

Editorial desk. (2006, March 3). The Gospel vs. H.R. 4437. *The New York Times*, p. 22.

Egan, T. (2005, April 1). Wanted: border hoppers. And some excitement, too. *The New York Times*, p. 14.

Egelko, B. (2010, November 2). Court may reverse judge, backs part of Arizona law. *San Francisco Chronicle*, p. A6.

Eisinger, P. (1973). The conditions of protest behavior in American cities. *American Political Science Review, 81*, 11–28.

Erfani, J.A.M. (2007). Whose security? Dilemmas of US border security in the Arizona-Sonora borderlands. In E. Brunet-Jailly (Ed.), *Borderlands: Comparing border security in North America and Europe* (pp. 41–73). Ottawa, Ontario: University of Ottawa Press.

Espinoza, K. (2006, Jan. 18). Humanitarian aid volunteers face possibility of prison. *New America Media*. Retrieved April 18, 2007, from http://news.ncmonline.com/news/view_article.html?article_id=dafd814dfa36ea1699fdc65f0db727b5.

Fact-checking Dobbs: CNN anchor Lou Dobbs challenged on immigration issues. (2007, December 4). *Democracy now! National Public Radio*. Transcript retrieved March 28, 2008, from http://www.democracynow.org/2007/12/4/fact_checking_dobbs_cnn_anchor_lou.

Fears, D. (2005, December 18). Desert Samaritans stand by duty: Move to outlaw aid to immigrants called contrary to Bible. *The Washington Post*, p. A10.

Feds plan 102 suits to build fence on border. (2008, January 10). *The Arizona Republic*, p. n/a.

Fife, J. (2009). Civil initiative. In M.A. De La Torre, *Trails of hope and terror* (pp. 170–174). Maryknoll, NY: Orbis Books.

Fife, J., Taylor, S., Hill, J., Lefebvre, G., Roberts, S., & Tromble, E. (2005). Crisis in the Arizona desert: A faith-based response. *Church & Society, 95*(6), 27–37.

Fischer, H. (2011, April 17). SB 1070's effects felt one year later. *YumaSun.com*. Retrieved August 6, 2011, from http://www.yumasun.com/articles/-69282--.html.

Fisher, M.J. (2011, February 15). Testimony of Michael J. Fisher, Chief, United States Border Patrol, U.S. Customs and Border Protection, Department of Homeland Security before House Committee on Homeland Security, Subcommittee on Borderland Maritime Security on "Securing our Borders—Operational Control and the Path Forward." *Department of Homeland Security Website*. Retrieved February 15, 2011, from http://www.dhs.gov/ynews/testimony/testimony_1297796735363.shtm.

FitzGerald, D. (2009). A nation of emigrants: How Mexico manages its migration. Berkeley & Los Angeles: University of California Press.

Foley, E. (2010, September 3). Making sense of the Arizona SB 1070 lawsuits. *The Washington Independent*.

Franklin, B. (1751). *Observations concerning the increase of mankind*. Published tract.

Frontline World. (2004, June). Interview with Claudine LoMonaco and Mary Spicuzza: A desperate journey. *PBS*. Retrieved February 25, 2008, from http://www.pbs.org/frontlineworld/stories/mexico/interview.html.

Gamson, W.A., Fireman, B., & Rytina, S. (1982). *Encounters with unjust authority*. Homewood, IL: Dorsey.

Gamson, W.A., & Modigliani, A. (1989). Media discourse and public opinion on nuclear power: A constructionist approach. *American Journal of Sociology, 95*(1), 1–37.

Gamson, W.A., & Wolfsfeld, G. (1993). Movements and media as interacting systems. *Annals of the American Academy of Political and Social Science, 526*, 114-127.

Ganster, P. (1995). The United States-Mexico border region and growing transborder interdependence. In S.J. Randall & H.W. Konrad (Eds.), *NAFTA in Transition*. Calgary: University of Calgary Press.

Ganz, J. (2007, July 18). The economic impacts of immigrants in Arizona. *Udall Center for Studies in Public Policy, University of Arizona*. Tucson, AZ.

Garcés-Díaz, D. (2001). Was NAFTA behind the Mexican export boom (1994–2000)? *Social Science Research Network Working Paper, Stanford*.

Garreau, J. (2006, October 27). The walls tumbled time—From China to Berlin, fences have failed to exclude or contain. *The Washington Post*, p. C1.

Gavin, M. (1996). The Mexican oil boom: 1977–1985. *Office of the Chief Economist, Inter-American Development Bank, Working Paper Series 314*. Washington, D.C.

Gaynor, T. (2010, March 16). U.S. puts brakes on "virtual" border fence. *Reuters*. Retrieved March 25, 2010, from NewsBank online database.

Gitlin, T. (1980). *The whole world is watching: Mass media in the making and unmaking of the new left*. Berkeley, CA: University of California Press.

Glaister, D. (2005, May 2). Schwarzenegger backs Minutemen. *The Guardian*, p. 12.

Goffman, E. (1974). *Frame analysis*. Cambridge: Harvard University Press.

González, D., & Carroll, S. (2005, June 19). Siege on border: Costly fortifications fail to deter immigration flow. *The Arizona Republic*, p. A1.

Goode, L. (2005). *Jurgen Habermas: Democracy and the public sphere*. AnnArbor, MI: Pluto Press.

Goodman, A. (2007, April 23). Rev. John Fife continues immigrant humanitarian work 25+ years after launching sanctuary movement. *Democracy now!* Transcript retrieved November 24, 2007, from http://www.democracynow.org/article.pl?sid=07/04/23/1350219.

Gramsci, A. (1971). *Selections from the prison notebooks*. Q. Hoare & G. Nowell Smith (Eds.). New York: International Publishers.

———. (1985). "Journalism" from *Selections from cultural writings*, (p. 413), Cambridge, MA: Harvard University Press.

————. (2000). "Intellectuals and Education" from *Prison Writings 1929–1935*. In D. Forgacs (Ed.), *The Antonio Gramsci Reader*, (pp. 300–322). New York: New York University Press.

————. (2001). The formation of intellectuals. In V. Leitch (Ed.), *Norton Anthology of Theory and Criticism*, (pp. 1135–1143). New York: W.W. Norton & Company.

Greider, W. (2001, December 31). A new giant sucking sound. *The Nation*. Retrieved December 9, 2006, from http://www.thenation.com/doc/2001 1231/greider.

Griggs, G.W. (2007, November 5). Hoping for reprieve from deportation. *The Los Angeles Times*. Grossman, D. (2006, September 5). Entrant rescuers believed acts OK'd. *The Arizona Daily Star*, p. B1.

Gutiérrez, T. (2009, October 9). Tough sheriff's immigration duties face limits after complaints. *CNN, Latino in America*. Retrieved March 13, 2010, from http://www.cnn.com/2009/CRIME/10/08/arizona.sheriff.immigration.

Habermas, J. (1964). The public sphere: An encyclopedia article. (D. Lennox & F. Lennox, Trans.). *New German Critique, 3*, 49–55.

————. (1991). *The structural transformation of the public sphere: An inquiry into a category of bourgeois society* (T. Burger, Trans.). Cambridge, MA: The MIT Press. (Original work published in 1962).

Hall, K. (1999, January 8). WTO official praises international trade pacts for resolving disputes. *Journal of Commerce*, p. 8A.

Hanson, G. (2004). What has happened to wages in Mexico since NAFTA? Implications for hemispheric free trade. In A. Estevadeordal, D. Rodrik, A.M. Taylor, & A. Velasco (Eds.), *Integrating the Americas: FTAA and Beyond* (pp. 505–37). Cambridge: Harvard University David Rockefeller Center for Latin American Studies; distributed by Harvard University Press.

Hayworth, J.D. (2006). *Whatever it takes: Illegal immigration, border security, and the war on terror*. Washington, D.C.: Regnery Publishing, Inc.

Healing the fissures in Mexico. (2006, December 5). *The Boston Globe (Editorial)*, p. 14A.

Hegel, G. (1991). *Elements of the philosophy of right*. (A. Wood and H. Nisbet, Trans.), Cambridge: Cambridge University Press.

Hellman, J. (1997). Structural adjustment in Mexico and the dog that didn't bark. *CERLAC Working Paper Series*, York University: Centre for Research on Latin America and the Caribbean.

Henriques, G., & Patel, R. (2004, February 13). NAFTA, corn, and Mexico's agricultural trade liberalization. *Americas Program of the Interhemispheric Resource Center: IRC Americas Program Special Report*. Retrieved December 9, 2006, from http://www.americaspolicy.org/reports/2004/0402 nafta.html.

Heredia, C., & Purcell, M. (1995). Structural adjustment in Mexico, *Development Group for Alternative Policies, Inc. Paper*. Retrieved December 3, 2006, from http://www.hartford-hwp.com/archives/46/013. html.

Heyman, J.M. (2004). Ports of entry as nodes in the world system. *Global Studies in Culture and Power, 11*, 303–327.

Hobbes, T. *Leviathan*, (C.B. Macpherson, Ed.). New York: Penguin.

Hoefer, M., Rytina, N., & Baker B.C. (2008, September). Estimates of the unauthorized immigrant population residing in the United States: January 2007. Washington, D.C.: Department of Homeland Security Office of Immigration Statistics.

———. (2010, January). Estimates of the unauthorized immigrant population residing in the United States: January 2009. Washington, D.C.: Department of Homeland Security Office of Immigration Statistics.

Hoffman, A. (1974). *Unwanted Mexican Americans in the Great Depression: Repatriation pressures, 1929–1939*. Tucson: University of Arizona Press.

Holstege, S. (2008, February 10). Border fence add-on disputed. *The Arizona Republic*, p. B1.

Holstege, S., & Marrero, D. (2008, February 28). Virtual border fence flawed. *The Arizona Republic*, p. A1.

Hoover, R. (2007, November-December; 2008, January). *Desert fountain.* Tucson, AZ: Humane Borders/Fronteras Compasivas Newsletter.

Hoover, S. (1998). *Religion in the news: Faith and journalism in American public discourse*. London: Sage.

———. (2006). *Religion in the media age*. London: Routledge.

Hoover, S.M., Clark, L.S., & Alters, D.F. (2004). *Media, home, and family.* London: Routledge.

Horsley, S. (2006, December 14). Border fence firm snared for hiring illegal workers. *National Public Radio*. Transcript retrieved February 28, 2008, from http://www.npr.org/templates/story/story.php?storyId=6626823.

House, B., & Kamman, J. (2005, August 21). Franks' communications director is one busy woman. *The Arizona Republic*, p. B6.

Howard, P., & Homer-Dixon, T. (1996). Environmental scarcity and violent conflict: the case of Chiapas, Mexico: Appendix. *Paper for Project on Environment, Population and Security, Washington, D.C.: American Association for the Advancement of Science and the University of Toronto.* Retrieved December 6, 2006, from http://www.library.utoronto.ca/pcs/eps/chiapas/chiapapp.htm.

Hufbauer, G.C., & Schott, J.J. (2005). *NAFTA revisited: Achievements and challenges*. Washington, D.C.: Institute for International Economics.

Humane Borders. (n.d.). Humane Borders Quick Facts [from organization's official website]. Retrieved April 9, 2007, from http://www.humaneborders .org/index.html .

Hunt, J.D. (2005). *An American looks at Gandhi: Essays in satyagraha, civil rights and peace*. New Dehli: Bibliophile South Asia.

Huntington, S. (2004). *Who are we? The challenges to America's national identity*. New York: Simon & Schuster.

Innes, S. (2005, December 1). Feds urged to drop case v. 2 border activists. *The Arizona Daily Star*, p. B5.

———. (2006, May 20). Volunteers to work with Border Patrol. *The Arizona Daily Star*, p. A1.

———. (2008, February 23). Aid volunteer cited in littering. *The Arizona Daily Star*, p. B1.

INS' Southwest border strategy. (2001, August). *United States General Accounting Office Report to Congressional Committees.* Retrieved November 24, 2007, from http://www.gao.gov/new.items/d01842.pdf.

Institute for Economic Research (IIEC) of the Universidad Nacional Autónoma de México. (1995, July). Economía. *IIEC-UNAM Momento Económico Boletín Electrónico, 1*(7). Retrieved December 7, 2006, from http://www. iiec.unam.mx/Boletin_electronico/1995/num07/economia.html.

Interfaith statement in support of comprehensive immigration reform. (2005, October 18). Signed by over 100 faith-based leaders and organizations in the United States. Retrieved April 9, 2007, from http://www.justicefor immigrants.org/ParishKit/InterfaithStatement.pdf.

Jeffrey, T.P. (2010, August 26). Sheriff Babeu: It's "an outrage" Obama stopped building border fence. *CNSNews.com.* Retrieved August 6, 2011, from http://www.cnsnews.com/node/71739.

Johnson, G. (2011, July 18). Arizona launching fundraising website for border fence. *msnbc.com* Retrieved August 7, 2011, from http://www.msnbc.msn. com/id/43796960/ns/us_news-security/t/arizona-launching-fundraising-website-border-fence.

Jones, M.A. (1992). *American immigration (The Chicago history of American immigration).* Chicago: University of Chicago Press.

Jordan, M. (2002, December 10). 3 ex-leaders praise a decade of NAFTA. *The Washington Post*, p. A27.

———. (2007, December 14). Arizona squeeze on immigration angers businesses. *The Wall Street Journal*, p. A1.

Jordan, L., & Van Tuijl, P. (2000). Political responsibility in transnational NGO advocacy. *World Development, 28*(12), 2051–2065.

Jus Semper Global Alliance. (2007, November). Living wages north and south: Wage gap charts for Group of Seven (G7) largest economies and other selected economies, including "emerging" economies with available wage and PPP data (1975–2005). Retrieved February 24, 2008, from http://www.jussemper.org/Resources/Labour%20Resources/WGC/Resourc es/Wage%20gap%20charts.pdf.

Justice for Immigrants. (2005, June 9). Justice for immigrants: A journey of hope. *The Catholic campaign for immigration reform.* Retrieved June 18, 2006, from http://justiceforimmigrants.org/learn_about_justice.html.

Kant, I. (1991). On the common saying: "This may be true in theory, but it does not apply in practice." In H.B. Nisbet, (Ed.), *Political writings* (H. Reiss, Trans.). Cambridge: Cambridge University Press.

———. (1996). The doctrine of right, part I: Public right. In M. Gregor (Trans. and Ed.), *The metaphysics of morals.* Cambridge: Cambridge University Press.

Keane, J. (1988). *Democracy and civil society.* London: Verso.

Kellner, D. (2005). *Media spectacle and the crisis of democracy.* Boulder, CO: Paradigm Publishers.

Kiefer, M. (2008, February 25). Migrant rate of crime even with numbers. *The Arizona Republic*, p. A1.

King, Jr. M.L. (1991). Love, law and civil disobedience. In J.M. Washington (Ed.), *A testament of hope: the essential writings and speeches of Martin Luther King, Jr.* (pp. 43–53). San Francisco: Harper Collins Publishers.

Klapper, J. (1960). *The effects of mass communication.* Glencoe, IL: The Free Press.

Kochhar, R. (2008, June 4). Latino labor report, 2008: Construction reverses job growth for Latinos. Washington, D.C.: *Pew Hispanic Center.*

Kochhar, R. (2005, December 6). Survey of Mexican migrants, part three: The economic transition to America. Washington, D.C.: *Pew Hispanic Center*.

Lacey, M. (2011, July 20). Arizona officials, fed up with U.S. efforts, seek donations to build border fence. *The New York Times*, p. A16.

La Comisión Nacional de los Derechos Humanos México (Mexico's National Commission for Human Rights). (2007, March). *Migration México-United States: Working together for real solutions*. Document presented at 2007 International Conference on the Migrant, Tucson, AZ.

Lakley, J. (2005, March 24). Bush decries border project. *The Washington Times*, p. A01.

Laufer, P. (2004). *Wetback nation: The case for opening the Mexican-American border*. Chicago: Ivan R. Dee.

Leonhardt, D. (2007, May 30). Truth, fiction, and Lou Dobbs. *The New York Times*, Business, p. 1.

Lipsky, M. (1968). Protest as political resource. *American Political Science Review, 62*(4), 1144–1158.

Llana, S.M. (2006, August 9). Politics of corn loom for divided Mexico: The disputed election has heightened tensions over a NAFTA deadline for removal of tariffs. Corn farmers vow to fight it. *The Christian Science Monitor*, p. 6.

LoMonaco, C. (2003, July 30). Many border deaths unlisted. *Tucson Citizen*, p. A1.

———. (2006, August 7). Migrants find care at border. *Tucson Citizen*, p. 4A.

———. (2007, April 17a). Pair from No More Deaths to get award. *Tucson Citizen*, p. 6A.

———. (2007, April 17b). Pair from No More Deaths to get award: Comments on this story. *Tucson Citizen*. Retrieved April 18, 2007, from http://www.tucsoncitizen.com/daily/local/48485.php.

London, S. (1999). The face of tomorrow: Reflections on diversity in America. *At Issue: Interracial Relationships*. Greenhaven Press. Copy of article retrieved March 28, 2008, from http://www.scottlondon.com/articles/newface.html.

Lou Dobbs Tonight. (2005, March 2). Bush vows to fight for social security reform despite flagging support; Middle East changing, but is Bush the reason? *CNN.com*. Transcript retrieved March 27, 2008, from http://transcripts.cnn.com/TRANSCRIPTS/0503/02/ldt.01.html.

———. (2005, April 14). Border insecurity; Criminal illegal aliens; Deadly imports; Illegal alien amnesty. *CNN.com*. Transcript retrieved February 16, 2008, from http://transcripts.cnn.com/TRANSCRIPTS/0504/14/ldt.01.html.

———. (2007, May 7). Tornado levels Kansas town; National Guard stretched too thin?; War on the middle class. *CNN.com*. Transcript retrieved March 11, 2008, from http://transcripts.cnn.com/TRANSCRIPTS/0705/07/ldt.01.html.

Lugo, L. (2003, September 24). Mexicans send home billions. *The Grand Rapids Press*, p. A27.

Madrid, O. (2009, November 7). Neo-Nazis rally against illegal immigration in Phoenix. *The Arizona Republic* (AZcentral online edition). Retrieved March 22, 2010, from http://www.azcentral.com/news/articles/2009/11/07/20091107neonazi.html.

Marizco, M. (2005, November 15). Growing Border Patrol adds buildings in Tucson, S. Ariz. *The Arizona Daily Star*, p. B1.

Martin, M. (Interviewer), & Mercer, C. (Interviewee). (2010, April 1). *Outspoken immigration reform group disbands* [Interview transcript]. Retrieved February 15, 2011, from National Public Radio web site http://www.npr.org/templates/story/story.php?storyId=125457513.

Martin, P. (2003). *Promise unfulfilled: Unions, immigration and farm workers*. Ithaca, NY: Cornell University Press.

Martínez, R. (2001). *Crossing over: A Mexican family on the migrant trail*. New York: Picador.

Massey, D., Durand, J., & Malone, N. (2002). *Beyond smoke and mirrors: Mexican immigration in an era of economic integration*. New York: Russell Sage Foundation.

McCarthy, J.D., & Zald, M.N. (2001). The enduring vitality of the resource mobilization theory of social movements. In J.H. Turner (Ed.), *Handbook of Sociological Theory* (pp. 533–565). New York: Kluwer Academic/Plenum Publishers.

McCombs, B. (2006, September 24). It won't work. *The Arizona Daily Star*, p. A1.

———. (2006, September 25). Barriers have failed before. *The Arizona Daily Star*, p. A4.

———. (2007, August 3). July is deadliest month for illegal-entrant women. *The Arizona Daily Star*, p. A1

———. (2007, August 19). O'odham leader vows no border fence. *The Arizona Daily Star*, p. B1.

———. (2007, September 29). Tally of dead crossers goes up. *The Arizona Daily Star*, p. B1.

———. (2009, April 19). And still, Mexicans come. *The Arizona Daily Star*, p. A1.

———. (2009, May 17). Death count rises with border restrictions. *The Arizona Daily Star*, p. B1.

———. (2010, February 7). Water jugs at heart of dispute; hostility threatens to boil over. *The Arizona Daily Star*, p. A1.

———. (2010, March 25). Border watch group draws to close. *The Arizona Daily Star*, p. A2.

———. (2010, October 5). AZ border saw record 252 deaths in fiscal '10. *The Arizona Daily Star*, p. A1.

———. (2011, February 4). Border Boletín: Finally, fiscal 2010 stats (sort of). *The Arizona Daily Star blog*. Retrieved February 16, 2011, from http://azstarnet.com/news/blogs/border-boletin/article_0065e568-30a3-11e0-ac22-001cc4c002e0.html?print=1.

———. (2011, February 9). Top official notes progress on border. *The Arizona Daily Star*, p. A1.

Medrano, L. (2005, May 22). Kennedy, McCain lead a bipartisan border plan. *The Arizona Daily Star*, p. A10.

———. (2005, August 31). Mexico's poor farmers hurt by NAFTA, economist says. *The Arizona Daily Star*, p. B4.

———. (2006, September 8). No More Deaths migrant-aid group celebrates legal win. *The Arizona Daily Star*, p. B6.

Meissner, D., Meyers, D.W., Papademetriou, D.G., & Fix, M. (2006, September). *Immigration and America's future: A new chapter.* Washington, D.C.: Migration Policy Institute.

Meltzer, E. (2006, September 20). County keeps on funding migrant-water effort. *The Arizona Daily Star*, p. B2.

Mercer, C. (2010, March 23). MCDC president Carmen Mercer's March 16 call to action. *The Arizona Daily Star online (www.azstarnet.com)*. Retrieved February 15, 2011, from http://azstarnet.com/article_5dc9494a-36d8-11df-aff0-001cc4c03286.html.

Mexican Migration Project. (2009, April). MMP124 database selected results: Crossing costs. Retrieved March 4, 2010, from http://mmp.opr.princeton.edu.

Mexico to distribute maps to aid illegal immigrants. (2006, January 25). *The Kansas City Star.*

Meyerson, H. (2006, February 8). NAFTA and nativism. *The Washington Post*, p. A19.

Meza, F. (2008, September 1). Financial crisis, fiscal policy and the 1995 GDP contraction in Mexico. *Journal of Money, Credit and Banking, 40*(6), 1239–1261.

Migration Policy Institute Staff. (2006, June 1). The US-Mexico border. *Migration Information Source*. Retrieved October 21, 2006, from http://www.migrationinformation.org/Feature/display.cfm?ID=407.

Mishkin, F.S. (1998). The Mexican financial crisis of 1994–1995: An asymmetric information analysis. In S. Rehman (Ed.), *Financial crisis management in regional blocs* (pp. 149–182). Norwell, MA: Kluwer Academic Publishers.

Montgomery, D. (2005, November 19). Support builds for full-length barrier along Mexico border. *The Seattle times*, p. A3.

Mowad, M. (2006, October 23). Conference looks at NAFTA 12 years later. *San Diego Business Journal, 27*(43), 1.

Mueren 80 niños diarios a causa de desnutrición. (1995, September 13). *Reforma.com*. Retrieved December 7, 2006, from http://busquedas.grupo reforma.com/reforma/default.asp.

NACLA Report on the Americas. (2005, July/August). Mexican workers since NAFTA. *North American Congress on Latin America*. Retrieved December 4, 2006, from http://www.nacla.org/issue_disp.php?iss=39|1.

NAFTA Secretariat. (2010, March 21). North American Free Trade Agreement: Chapter one: Objectives. Retrieved March 21, 2010, from http://www.nafta-sec-alena.org/en/view.aspx?conID=590&mtpiID=122.

Najam, A. (1999). Citizen organizations as policy entrepreneurs. In D. Lewis (Ed.), *International perspectives on voluntary action: Reshaping the third sector.* London: Earthscan.

NBC 4 TV News. (2006, March 1). Mahony calls on priests to ignore proposed immigration law. *NBC4.TV*. Retrieved June 28, 2006, from http://www.nbc4.tv/news/7589460/detail.html.

Nevins, J. (2002). *Operation Gatekeeper: The rise of the "illegal alien" and the making of the U.S.-Mexico boundary.* New York: Routledge.

———. (2006, July 18). Boundary enforcement and national security in an age of global apartheid. *Dissident Voice*. Retrieved April 9, 2007, from http://dissidentvoice.org/July06/Nevins18.htm.

————. (2008). *Dying to live: A story of U.S. immigration in an age of global apartheid.* San Francisco: City Lights Books.

Ngai, M. (1999). The architecture of race in American immigration law: A reexamination of the Immigration Act of 1924. *Journal of American History, 86,* 67–92.

————. (2004). *Impossible subjects: Illegal aliens and the making of modern America.* Princeton, NJ: Princeton University Press.

Nix, M. (2006, September 3). Taking sides on the border; Humane Borders: It's about saving lives. *The Free-Lance Star,* p. A1.

No More Deaths Official Website. (n.d.). No More Deaths historical summary 2004. Retrieved April 9, 2007, from http://www.nomoredeaths.org/HistoryofNMD.html.

NPR.org. (2007, October 16). Texas mayors oppose plan for border fence. *National Public Radio.* Transcript retrieved February 28, 2008, from http://www.npr.org/templates/story/story.php?storyId=15315131&ft=1&f=1001.

Nuñez-Neto, B., & García, M.J. (2007, May 23). Border security: The San Diego fence. *CRS Report for Congress.* Washington, D.C.: Congressional Research Service.

O'Dell, R. (2010, May 5). City suit will seek to nullify SB 1070. *The Arizona Daily Star,* p. A3.

Oberschall, A. (1996). Opportunity and framing in the Eastern European revolts of 1989. In D. McAdam, J.D. McCarthy, and M.N. Zald, *Comparative perspectives on social movements: political opportunities, mobilizing structures and cultural framings* (pp. 93–121). Cambridge: Cambridge University Press.

Office of the United States Trade Representative. (2003, December 1). NAFTA at 10: A success story. *Washington, D.C.: USTR.* Retrieved December 8, 2006, from http://www.ustr.gov/Document_Library/Fact_Sheets/2003/NAFTA_at_10_A_Success_Story.html.

————. (2008, March). NAFTA—myth vs. facts. *Washington, D.C.: USTR.* Retrieved March 20, 2010, from http://www.ustr.gov/sites/default/files/NAFTA-Myth-versus-Fact.pdf.

Oliver, P.E., & Johnston, H. (2000). What a good idea! Frames and ideologies in social movement research. *Mobilization, 5*(1), 37–54.

Oliver, R.S. (2007). In the twelve years of NAFTA, the treaty gave to me...what, exactly?: An assessment of economic, social and political developments in Mexico since 1994 and their impact on Mexican immigration into the United States. *Harvard Latino Law Review, 10,* 53–133.

Orner, P. (2008). *Underground America: Narratives of undocumented lives.* San Francisco: McSweeney's Publishing.

Orrenius, P.M. (2001). Illegal immigration and enforcement along the U.S.-Mexico border: An overview. *Economic and Financial Review, First Quarter 2001,* 2–11.

Overview of the NAFTA. (2008, March 14). *Foreign Affairs and International Trade Canada Web Site.* Retrieved March 25, 2008, from http://www.international.gc.ca/trade-agreements-accords-commerciaux/agr-acc/nafta-alena/over.aspx?lang=en&menu_id=33&menu=.

Pacheco-López, P. (2005). The effect of trade liberalization on exports, imports, the balance of trade, and growth: The case of Mexico. *Journal of Post Keynesian Economics, 27*(4), 595–619.

Paine, T. (2006). *Rights of man.* Boston: Adamant Media Corporation. (Originally published in 1791–1972).

Papademetriou, D.G. (2003, November). The shifting expectations of free trade and migration. In D. Papademetriou, J. Audley, S. Polaski, & S. Vaughan. *NAFTA's promise and reality: Lessons from Mexico for the hemisphere* (pp. 39–59). Washington, D.C.: Carnegie Endowment for International Peace.

Parrenas, R.S. (2001). *Servants of globalization: Women, migration and domestic work.* Palo Alto: Stanford University Press.

Passel, J. (2006, March 7). Size and characteristics of the unauthorized migrant population in the U.S. Washington, D.C.: Pew Hispanic Center.

Passel, J., & Cohn, D. (2008, October 2). Trends in unauthorized immigration. Washington, D.C.: Pew Hispanic Center.

———. (2011, February 1). Unauthorized immigrant population: National and state trends, 2010. Washington, D.C.: Pew Hispanic Center.

Passel, J.S., & Suro, R. (2005). Rise, peak and decline: Trends in U.S. immigration 1992–2004. Washington, D.C.: Pew Hispanic Center.

Pastor: Illegal immigrant who sought sanctuary in Chicago church deported. (2007, August 20). *FOXnews.com.* Retrieved Nov. 23, 2007, from http://www.foxnews.com/story/0,2933,293757,00.html.

Peach, J. (1996, October 1). Guest analysis: The Mexican economy and the border region since devaluation. *Frontera Norte/Sur*, New Mexico State University. Retrieved December 7, 2006, from http://www.nmsu.edu/~frontera/old_1996/oct96/1096econ.html.

Pew Forum on Religion & Public Life. (2008, February). U.S. religious landscape survey: Religious affiliation: Diverse and dynamic. *Washington, D.C.: Pew Research Center.* Retrieved February 17, 2011, from http://religions.pewforum.org/pdf/report-religious-landscape-study-full.pdf.

Pew Hispanic Center Fact Sheet. (2008, January 23). Arizona: Population and labor force characteristics, 2000–2006. *Washington, D.C.: Pew Hispanic Center.* Retrieved February 23, 2008, from http://pewhispanic.org/files/factsheets/37.pdf.

Pew Hispanic Center and Kaiser Family Foundation. (2002, December). *2002 national survey of Latinos.* Retrieved March 13, 2008, from http://pewhispanic.org/files/reports/15.pdf.

Pomfret, J. (2006, January 27). Tunnel found on Mexican border. *The Washington Post*, p. A3.

———. (2006, October 10). Fence meets wall of skepticism: Critics doubt a 700-mile barrier would stem migrant tide. *The Washington Post*, p. A3.

Powell, S.M. (2011, January 15). The "virtual fence" at border deleted Napolitano: Parts of project will be salvaged; FENCE: Demise of project won't curtail efforts. *Houston Chronicle*, p. A1.

Preston, J. (2008, February 10). In reversal, courts uphold local immigration laws. *The New York Times*, p. A22.

———. (2010, May 2). Fueled by anger over Arizona law, immigration advocates rally for change. *The New York Times*, p. A22.

————. (2010, July 29). A ruling in one state: A warning for others. *The New York Times*, p. A14.

————. (2011, February 2). 11.2 million illegal immigrants in U.S. in 2010, report says: No change from '09. *The New York Times*, p. A15.

Price, V., Tewksbury, D., & Powers, E. (1997). Switching trains of thought: The impact of news frames on readers' cognitive responses. *Communication Research, 24*(5), 481–506.

Ramírez, H. (2005, April 2). Dejan plantados a cazamigrantes—superan reporteros a voluntarios. *Reforma. (Ciudad de México, D.F.)*, p. 3.

Ramírez, M. (2006). Is foreign direct investment beneficial for Mexico? An empirical analysis, 1960–2001. *World Development, 34*(5), 802–817.

Ramos, J. (2005). *Dying to cross: The worst immigrant tragedy in American history*. New York: Harper Collins Publishers.

Randles, J. (2010, February 27). Rally time. *The Signal, Santa Clarita Valley*, News section.

Rawls, J. (1971). *A theory of justice*. Oxford: Oxford University Press.

Regan, M. (2010). *The death of Josseline; Immigration stories from the Arizona-Mexico borderlands*. Boston, MA: Beacon Press.

Religion & Ethics Newsweekly. (2007, June 15). Immigrant sanctuary movement, episode no. 1042. *PBS*. Retrieved November 23, 2007, from http://www.pbs.org/wnet/religionandethics/week1042/feature.html.

Rich, P. (1997). NAFTA and Chiapas. *The Annals of the American Academy of Political and Social Science, 550*(1), 72–84.

Robbins, T. (2006a, April 6). San Diego fence provides lessons in border control. *Morning Edition, National Public Radio*. Transcript retrieved February 26, 2008, from http://www.npr.org/templates/story/story.php?

————. (2006b, April 6). Q&A: Building a barrier along the border with Mexico. *NPR.org*. Retrieved February 25, 2008, from http://www.npr.org/templates/story/story.php?storyId=5326083.

————. (2007, July 31). In deadly desert, border-crossers opt for capture. *All Things Considered, National Public Radio*. Transcript retrieved February 28, 2008, from http://www.npr.org/templates/story/story.php?storyId=12373928.

————. (2010, March 17). Virtual U.S.-Mexico border fence at a virtual end. *National Public Radio*. Retrieved March 25, 2010, from http://www.npr.org/templates/story/story.php?storyId=124758593.

Rodríguez-Scott, E. (2002). *Patterns of Mexican migration from Mexico to the United States*. Paper prepared for delivery at the 82nd annual meeting of the Southwestern Social Science Association, New Orleans, LA, March 27–30, 2002. http://www1.appstate.edu/~stefanov/proceedings/rodriguez.htm.

Rohter, L. (2010, May 28). Performers to stay away from Arizona in protest of law. *The New York Times*, p. A11.

Rollins, E. (2009, November 18). Dobbs and CNN were no longer in sync. *CNN Website, Opinion*. Retrieved February 17, 2011, from http://articles.cnn.com/2009-11-18/opinion/rollins.lou.dobbs.departure. cnn_1_dobbs-departure-lou-dobbs-cnn-management?_s=PM:OPINION.

Romano, L. (2011, January 29). Arizona-inspired immigration bills lose momentum in other states. *The Washington Post*, p. A1.

Rotstein, A.H. (2006, March 11). More border crossers use Sasabe corridor. *The Associated Press*. Retrieved April 9, 2007, from http://www.azstarnet.com/metro/119578.

Rozemberg, H. (2002, July 22). Border patrol keeps tabs on group's migrant aid. *The Arizona Republic*, p. B7.

Rubio-Goldsmith, R., McCormick, M.M., Martínez, D., & Magdalena Duarte, I. (2006, October). The "Funnel Effect" & recovered bodies of unauthorized migrants processed by the Pima County Office of the Medical Examiner, 1990–2005. *Binational Migration Institute Report to the Pima County Board of Supervisors*. Tucson: University of Arizona Mexican American Studies & Research Center.

Ruiz Marrujo, O. (2003). Immigrants at risk, immigrants as risk: Two paradigms of globalization. In G. Campese & P. Ciallella, (Eds.), *Migration, religious experience, and globalization* (pp. 17–28). New York: Center for Migration Studies.

Sabet, D. (2008). *Nonprofits and their networks: Cleaning the waters along Mexico's northern border*. Tucson, AZ: University of Arizona Press.

Sadowski-Smith, C. (2008). *Border fictions: Globalization, empire, and writing at the boundaries of the United States*. Charlottesville: University of Virginia Press.

Said, E. (2003, August 7). *Orientalism* 25 years later. Retrieved March 28, 2008, from http://www.levantinecenter.org/pages/edward_said.html#top

Santa Ana, O. (2002). *Brown tide rising: Metaphors of Latinos in contemporary American public discourse*. Austin: University of Texas Press.

Sapkota et al., (2006). Unauthorized border crossings and migrant deaths: Arizona, New Mexico, and El Paso, Texas, 2002–2003. *American Journal of Public Health, 96*(7). 1–7.

Sassen, S. (1997). Immigration policy in a global economy. *SAIS Review, 17*(2), 1–19.

———. (1999). *Guests and aliens*. New York: The New Press.

———. (2004). Local actors in global politics. *Current Sociology, 52*(4), 649–670.

———. (2005). The repositioning of citizenship and alienage: Emergent subjects and spaces for politics. *Globalizations, 2*(1), 79–94.

———. (2006, July 28). The bits of a new immigration reality: A bad fit with current policy. *Social Science Research Council*. Retrieved March 1, 2008, from http://borderbattles.ssrc.org/Sassen.

Scherer, M. (2005, Jul/Aug). Scrimmage on the border. *Mother Jones, 30*(4), 50–58.

Scheufele, D.A. (1999). Framing as a theory of media effects. *Journal of Communication, 49*(1), 103–122.

Schmidt-Hebbel, K., & Werner, A. (2002). Inflation targeting in Brazil, Chile, and Mexico: Performance, credibility, and the exchange rate. *Economía, 2*(2), 31–79.

Seattle Times News Services. (2010, December 30). Illegal immigration on many states' agendas—close up. *The Seattle Times*, p. A3.

Semetko, H.A., & Valkenburg, P.M. (2000). Framing European politics: A content analysis of press and television news. *Journal of Communication, 50*(2), 93–109.

Seper, J. (2006, January 27). Mexico nixes border map for migrants—says disclosure would tip off watchdog groups. *The Washington Times*, p. A01.

Shain, M. (2009, November 16). Dobbs got $8M to quit—CNN wanted him out. *The New York Post*, p. 003.

Shields, J., & Nieves, E. (2006, October 5). Fencing in immigration reform: Repairs to broken system derailed. *American Friends Service Committee Website*. Retrieved November 27, 2006, from http://www.afsc.org/news/2006/fencing-in-immigration-reform.htm.

Smith, J.P. (2003, May). Assimilation across the Latino generations. *The American Economic Review, 93*(2), 315.

Snow, D.A., & Benford, R.D. (1988). Ideology, frame resonance and participant mobilization. *International Social Movement Research, 1*, 197–219.

Soto, O.R., & Berestein, L. (2006, January 27). 2,400-foot tunnel "beats them all." *San Diego Union-Tribune*, p. A1.

Staudt, K. (2008). *Violence and activism at the border: Gender, fear, and everyday life in Ciudad Juárez*. Austin, TX: University of Texas Press.

———. (2009). Violence against women at the border: Unpacking institutions. In K. Staudt, T. Payan, & Z.A. Kruszewski (Eds.), *Human rights along the U.S.-Mexico border: Gendered violence and insecurity* (pp. 107–124). Tucson, AZ: University of Arizona Press.

Staudt, K., & Coronado, I. (2002). *Fronteras no más: Toward social justice at the U.S.-Mexico border*. New York: Palgrave Macmillan.

Stelter, B., & Carter, B. (2009, November 12). In surprise, Lou Dobbs quits CNN. *The New York Times*, p. B1.

Stern, A.M. (2005). *Eugenics nation: Faults and frontiers of better breeding in modern America*. Berkeley and Los Angeles: University of California Press.

Stiglitz, J.E. (2004, January 6). The broken promise of NAFTA. *The New York Times*, p. 23.

Swarns, R. (2006, March 19). Rift on immigration widens for conservatives and cardinals. *The New York Times*, Week in Review Section, p. 4.

Swart, W.J. (1995). The League of Nations and the Irish question: Master frames, cycles of protest, and "master frame alignment." *Sociology Quarterly, 36*, 465–481.

Swing, J. (1954, September 3). Administrative reforms in the immigration and naturalization service. *Report to the American Section of the Joint Commission on Mexican Migrant Labor*.

Terrazas, A. (2008, July). Indian immigrants in the United States. *Migration Policy Institute*. Retrieved July 3, 2011, from http://www.migration information.org/usfocus/display.cfm?ID=687.

———. (2008, October 8). Immigration enforcement in the United States. *Migration Policy Institute*. Retrieved March 25, 2010, from http://www.migrationinformation.org/Feature/print.cfm?ID=697#14.

The Official Minuteman Civil Defense Corps. (n.d.) About us. *Official Minuteman Web Site*. Retrieved April 9, 2007, from http://www.minuteman hq.com/hq/aboutus.php.

The Oscar Romero Award. (2007). *The Rothko Chapel Website*. Retrieved April 18, 2007, from http://www.rothkochapel.org/Oscar%20Romero%20 Awards%202007.htm.

The White House. (2002, October 26.) President Bush, President Fox discuss migration, trade, world affairs. Washington, D.C.: Office of the Press Secretary, The White House.

Thoreau, H.D. (2009). *Civil disobedience*. Amazon.com:CreateSpace.

Tiebel, D.L. (2007, September 29). Border deaths rise 29% in past year. *Tucson Citizen*, p. 1A.

Timmer, A.S., & Williamson, J.G. (1998). Immigration policy prior to the 1930s: Labor markets, policy interactions, and globalization backlash. *Population and Development Review, 24*(4), 739–767.

Tucson Citizen Editorial Board. (2007, January 11). Bush Iraq plan: Nothing "new," plenty "more"—It was a mistake not to have enough troops in Iraq early. But sending more troops now will not undo that error. [Our opinion: Border info needed.] *Tucson Citizen*, p. 14A.

Ufford-Chase, R. (2005a). 1600 years of border history (in a few pages). *Church and Society, 95*(6), 1–15.

Ufford-Chase, R. (2005b). Wisdom from the desert: Jim Corbett and the principles of civil initiative—A tribute. *Hastings College, Center for Vocation, Faith and Service*. Archive located on website. Retrieved February 13, 2011, from http://www.hastings.edu/igsbase/igstemplate.cfm?SRC=MD006&SRCN=articledetails&GnavID=110&SnavID=136&TnavID=&NewsID=198.

UNDP Human Development Report (2005). *International cooperation at a crossroads: Aid, trade and security in an unequal world*. United Nations Development Programme. New York: United Nations Publication.

———. (2006). *Beyond scarcity: Power, poverty, and the global water crisis*. United Nations Development Programme. Retrieved December 2, 2006, from http://hdr.undp.org/hdr2006.

United Nations. (2005, December). *2004–2005 Economic survey of Latin America and the Caribbean*. New York: United Nations Publication.

United States Conference of Catholic Bishops and the Bishops of Mexico. (2003). Strangers no longer: Together on the journey of hope. Washington, D.C.: United States Conference of Catholic Bishops.

Uranga, R. (2006, August 13). Ranks of anti-illegal immigrant groups swelling. *Inland Valley Daily Bulletin*, News Section.

Urrea, L.A. (2004). *The devil's highway*. New York: Little, Brown, and Company.

U.S. Border Patrol. (1994). *Border patrol strategic plan 1994 and beyond: National strategy*. Washington, D.C.: U.S. Border Patrol.

———. (2008). Northern border, Part 1. Retrieved February 19, 2008, from http://www.usborderpatrol.com/Border_Patrol1920.htm.

U.S. Customs and Border Protection. (2007, February 6). President Bush requests $10.2 billion budget for Customs and Border Protection. *Department of Homeland Security*. Retrieved February 17, 2008, from http://www.cbp.gov/xp/cgov/newsroom/news_releases/archives/2007_news_releases/022007/02062007_4.xml.

———. (2008, February 5). Budget request for CBP totals just under $11 billion. *Department of Homeland Security*. Retrieved February 11, 2011, from http://www.cbp.gov/xp/cgov/newsroom/fact_sheets/cbp_overview/bdget_11bil_factsheet.xml .

————. (2010, January 5). Border patrol history. *Department of Homeland Security*. Retrieved February 11, 2011, from http://www.cbp.gov/xp/cgov/border_security/border_patrol/border_patrol_ohs/history.xml.

U.S. Department of State Visa Statistics. (2000a). Table IV: Summary of visas issued by issuing office. Retrieved December 9, 2006, from http://travel.state.gov/pdf/FY05tableIV.pdf.

————. (2000b). Summary. Retrieved December 9, 2006, from http://travel.state.gov/pdf/FY2000%20summary.pdf.

————. (2005). Table IV: Summary of visas issued by issuing office. Retrieved December 9, 2006, from http://travel.state.gov/pdf/FY05tableIV.pdf.

————. (2010). Report of the visa office 2010 table of contents: Statistical tables. Retrieved August 6, 2011, from http://www.travel.state.gov/visa/statistics/statistics_5240.html.

U.S. GAO. (2001, August). *INS's Southwest Border Strategy: Resource and impact issues remain after seven years*. Washington, D.C.: U.S. Government Accountability Office.

————. (2006, August). *Illegal immigration: Border-crossing deaths have doubled since 1995; Border Patrol's efforts to prevent deaths have not been fully evaluated*. Washington, D.C.: U.S. Government Accountability Office.

USDA. (2008, January). United States Department of Agriculture Foreign Agricultural Service Fact Sheet: North American Free Trade Agreement (NAFTA). Retrieved March 18, 2010, from http://www.fas.usda.gov/info/factsheets/NAFTA.asp.

Vakil, A.C. (1997). Confronting the classification problem: Toward a taxonomy of NGOs. *World Development, 25*(12), 2057–2070.

Valocchi, S. (1996). The emergence of the integrationist ideology in the civil rights movement. *Social Problems, 43*, 116–130.

Ventura County Star Staff. (2007, September 18). City charges sanctuary church for police services. *Ventura County Star*. Retrieved November 23, 2007, from http://www.venturacountystar.com/news/2007/sep/18/no-headline---nxxfcprotest19.

Vergakis, B. (2010, February 26). Hiring illegal immigrants may lead to jail in Utah. *Associated Press Archive*. Retrieved March 13, 2010, from NewsBank on-line database (Access World News).

Villarreal, M.A., & Cid, M. (2008, November 4). NAFTA and the Mexican economy. *Congressional Research Service Report for Congress*. CRS Order Code RL34733.

Wagner, D., & Bazar, E. (2010, January 14). Arizona has become "ground zero" of immigration fight. *USA Today*, p. ARC.

Wagner, D. (2004, August 22). Border no terror corridor—so far. *The Arizona Republic*, p. A1.

Wallace, J. (2010, March 24). Border watch group breaks up. *KOLD News 13*. Retrieved April 1, 2010, from http://www.kold.com/Global/story.asp?S=12200645.

Wallis, J. (2005). *God's politics: Why the Right gets it wrong and the Left doesn't get it*. San Francisco: HarperSanFrancisco Publishers.

Welch, W.M. (2007, July 31). Border-crossing deaths on rise. *USA Today*. Retrieved February 26, 2008, from http://www.usatoday.com/news/nation/2007-07-31-border_N.htm.

Well-meaning. (2006, September 13). Editorial. *Topeka Capital-Journal*, p. 4.

Whitt, J. (1996, January). The Mexican peso crisis. *Economic Review*, 1–20.

Williams, G.I., & Williams, R.H. (1995). "All we want is equality": Rhetorical framing in the fathers' rights movement. In J. Best (Ed.), *Images of issues, 2nd Edition* (pp. 191–212). New York: de Gruyter.

Wise, T.A. (2003, November/December). Fields of free trade: Mexico's small farmers in a global economy. *Dollars and Sense*, (250), p. n/a. Retrieved March 26, 2008, from http://www.dollarsandsense.org/archives/2003/1103wise.html.

Wise, T.A., Salazar, H., & Carlsen, L. (2003). *Confronting globalization; Economic integration and popular resistance in Mexico*. Bloomfield, CT: Kumarian Press.

Wood, D.B. (2008, April 1). Where U.S.-Mexico border fence is tall, it works. *The Christian Science Monitor*, p. A1.

World Bank. (1997, April 8). *Mexico—weekly macroeconomic indicators*. Washington, D.C.: World Bank.

———. (2004, June). Poverty in Mexico: An assessment of conditions, trends and government strategy. Report No.28612-ME.

Zahniser, S., & Coyle, W. (2004, May). U.S.-Mexico corn trade during the NAFTA era: New twists to an old story. *United States Department of Agriculture Electronic Outlook Report from the Economic Research Service*. Retrieved December 7, 2006, from http://www.ers.usda.gov/publications/FDS/may04/fds04D01/fds04D01.pdf.

Zarate-Hoyos, G.A., & Spencer, D. (2003). El movimiento migratorio de México a Estados Unidos en la era del TLCAN. *Comercio Exterior, 53*(12), 1122–1130.

Index